FEDERAL WRITERS' PROJECT
AMERICAN GUIDE SERIES

DUTCHESS COUNTY

AMS PRESS
NEW YORK

AMERICAN GUIDE SERIES

DUTCHESS COUNTY

SPONSORED BY
THE WOMEN'S CITY AND
COUNTY CLUB
OF DUTCHESS COUNTY
NEW YORK

PUBLISHED BY THE WILLIAM PENN
ASSOCIATION OF PHILADELPHIA
MCMXXXVII

Library of Congress Cataloging in Publication Data

Federal Writers' Project, Dutchess Co., N. Y.
Dutchess County.

At head of half-title: Federal Writers' Project.
"Sponsored by the Women's City and Country Club of Dutchess County, New York."
Original ed. issued in series: American guide series.
Bibliography: p.
1. Dutchess Co., N. Y.—Description and travel—Guide-books.
2. Dutchess Co., N. Y.—History.   I. Federal Writers' Project.
II. Title.
F127.D8F4   1975   917.47'33'044   73-3645
ISBN 0-404-57944-2

AMS edition of this book: Trim Size — 5 1/2 x 8 1/2
                           Text Size — 4 3/16 x 7 1/16

Original edition of this book: Trim Size — 5 3/4 x 8 3/4
                                Text Size — 4 7/16 x 7 7/16

Reprinted from the edition of 1937, Philadelphia
First AMS edition published in 1975
Manufactured in the United States of America

AMS PRESS INC.
NEW YORK, N. Y. 10003

PREFACE

The compilation of the DUTCHESS COUNTY GUIDE is based upon such a great wealth of material that the most difficult task has been that of selection. To meet the requirements of a book of useful size much material has reluctantly been omitted. An attempt has been made to include significant historical data and to record for present and future generations the many facts in connection with places, houses, and people which are now known only to older members of the community. Great care has been exercised to secure accuracy, and as a result of this effort with the use of original sources, and much personal consultation, some generally accepted data have been rejected as unreliable. For failures in judgment in selection, and for such errors of fact as may have crept in, the indulgence of the reader is solicited.

The material could not have been assembled without the cordial cooperation of many citizens of the county. Grateful acknowledgment is made to the librarians, to the clerks of the county, town, and city offices, and the Highway Department; to the officials of schools, churches, and other organizations. Acknowledgement is due James Reynolds for the use of his grandfather's diary; to Isaac Platt for access to old documents, newspapers, and maps; to Dr. H. D. House, New York State botanist; Dr. Emmeline Moore, chief aquatic biologist; K. F. Chamberlain, assistant state entomologist; W. J. Schoonmaker, assistant state zoologist; to President MacCracken and Miss Cornelia M. Raymond, of Vassar College, and members of the faculties of Vassar and Bard Colleges. Members of the Dutchess County Historical Society, many old families, and local historians have rendered valuable assistance.

If the guide adds pleasure and profit to travelers driving over Dutchess County roads, the book will have accomplished its major purpose.

THE EDITORS.

Contents

	Page
PREFACE	III
LIST OF ILLUSTRATIONS	VII
LIST OF MAPS	VII
DUTCHESS COUNTY: PAST AND PRESENT	1
POUGHKEEPSIE	24
VASSAR COLLEGE	54
BEACON	62
FISHKILL VILLAGE	79

TOUR 1
Poughkeepsie—Hyde Park—Rhinebeck—Red Hook—Pine Plains—Amenia—Millbrook—Washington Hollow—Pleasant Valley—Poughkeepsie 86

TOUR 1 A
Junction US 9 and Old Post Road—Staatsburg 103

TOUR 1 B
Rhinebeck—Barrytown—Annandale—Tivoli 105

TOUR 1 C
Red Hook—Dutchess-Columbia County Line 109

TOUR 1 D
Pine Plains—Washington Hollow 110

TOUR 2
Poughkeepsie—New Hackensack—Hopewell Junction—Pawling—Dover Plains—Amenia 112

TOUR 2 A
Junction State 55 and 22—Quaker Hill 122

TOUR 3
Poughkeepsie—Wappingers Falls—Beacon—Fishkill—Brinckerhoff—Hopewell Junction—Billings—Poughkeepsie 124

TOUR 3 A
Junction US 9 and New Hamburg Road—New Hamburg 135

TOUR 3 B
Junction State 9 D and Chelsea Road—Chelsea 136

	Page
TOUR 3 C Beacon—Dutchess-Putnam County Line	137
TOUR 3 D Fishkill—Dutchess-Putnam County Line	139
TOUR 3 E Brinckerhoff—Wiccopee—Dutchess-Putnam County Line	142
TOUR 3 F Junction State 55 and 82—Moores Hills—Verbank—Clove Valley	144
TOUR 4 Poughkeepsie—East Park — Pleasant Plains — Wurtemburg—Schultzville—Clinton Hollow—Salt Point—Poughkeepsie	147
TOUR 4 A East Park—Netherwood	152
BIBLIOGRAPHY	154
INDEX	162

Illustrations

	Page
Saw Mill of Henry Livingston	1
Dover Furnace	7
Van Kleeck House, built in 1702	16
Old Brewery at the River Front	19
Dutch House, known as "Old Hundred," New Hackensack	40
Reformed Dutch Church at New Hackensack	40
Poughkeepsie Railroad Bridge from the Waterfront	41
Interior woodwork of the Lewis DuBois House, Gray's Riding Academy	41
Blodgett Hall Arch, Vassar College	56
Students' Building, Vassar College	57
Along Wappinger Creek	69
Reformed Dutch Church at Fishkill	80
Road to old landing near mouth of Wappinger Creek	81
Milestone near entrance to Crum Elbow	88
Entrance Drive to the Roosevelt Estate	88
Crum Elbow, the Roosevelt Estate	89
A Family Burial Ground north of Rhinebeck	104
The Whitefield Oak at Smithfield	104
Churchyard at St. James' Church, Hyde Park	105
St. James' Church, Hyde Park	105
Doorway to the Oblong Meeting House at Quaker Hill	120
Sycamore Tree, with embedded plaque, used as a whipping post during the Revolution, John Kane House, Pawling	121
Oblong Meeting House, Quaker Hill	121
Mount Gulian, the Verplanck House, Fishkill-on-the-Hudson	129
Pasture Lands near Dover Furnace	136
De La Vergne Hill near Amenia	136
Old Mill and Falls near Amenia	137
Storm—Adriance—Brinckerhoff House, Old Hopewell	143
Abraham Fort Homestead, near Poughkeepsie	153
Doorway of the Brett-Teller House, Beacon	Tailpiece

Maps

Poughkeepsie, 1798	End papers
Poughkeepsie	24
Poughkeepsie Foot Tour	35
Vassar College Campus	54
Beacon	62
Fishkill Village	78
Dutchess County Tours	86

DUTCHESS COUNTY

Saw Mill of Henry Livingston, 1792

Geography and Geology

Dutchess County lies between the Hudson River and the State of Connecticut; and is bounded on the north by Columbia County and on the south by Putnam County. It lies between the parallels of 42°5′ and 41°26′30″ N. latitude. The 74th meridian west of Greenwich passes about one mile west of the western boundary. Its area of approximately 800 square miles is divided into 20 townships.

Dutchess County is a region of great interest to the geographer and geologist.* The economic importance of the county is partly due to its varied surface and types of soil. Except along its extreme southern and eastern edges, the section is gently rolling. Altitudes range from sea level in the western section along the Hudson River to 2,300 feet in the northeast. A truly picturesque country, it consists of long ridge-like hills and trough-like valleys trending generally northeast-southwest. In the western part of the county these hills are low with an average elevation of 650 feet. In the central part,

---

* No detailed study of Dutchess County rocks has been made till recently. Since 1935, two groups of geologists, working in this field, have reached different conclusions which have occasioned a controversy. The generalizations here made are still true, however, whichever set of detailed conclusions finally prevails.

1

however, they attain a somewhat greater height. In addition to the smaller valleys between the ridges, there are a number of more conspicuous valleys such as the Clove and Harlem valleys, the valley east of Stissing Mountain, and that of Wappinger Creek. These are long and broad and have very flat bottoms.

This pleasing, rolling country is known technically as the Middle Hudson Valley. The geologist designates it as a portion of what is called the Great Valley, the longest valley in eastern United States, extending all the way from the State of Alabama to the Province of Quebec, a distance of more than 1,000 miles, and includes the well-known Tennessee, Shenandoah, and Cumberland Valleys to the south.

Bordering Dutchess County on the south and east is a mountainous mass which rises above the rolling country. In elevation it reaches well over 1,000 feet and forms a distinct barrier to southward and eastward travel. On the southern edge of the county this mountainous mass includes Storm King, Mount Beacon, and the Fishkill Mountains. On the east it is represented by Schaghticoke Mountain and other mountains immediately east of the Connecticut boundary. This high barrier is known as the Hudson Highlands. As in the case of the Middle Hudson Valley, the Hudson Highlands are a portion of a much larger physiographic province, which crosses the Hudson River below Beacon and extends many miles to the southwest, terminating at Reading, Pennsylvania.

The marked contrast between the Hudson Highlands and the Middle Hudson Valley is accounted for in a study of the bed rocks which underlie the region. The Hudson Highlands are composed of the oldest rocks in Dutchess County. These consist of granites and altered granitic rocks, which, in places, have a noticeable banded character (gneiss). They have been formed by the cooling and crystallizing of molten rock which has risen from deep in the earth. These granitic rocks have been so greatly metamorphosed (altered by heat and pressure), that much of their original character has been obliterated. The greater resistance of these rocks to weathering, causes them to stand higher than the surrounding country.

In contrast to the Hudson Highlands, the Middle Hudson Valley is underlain entirely by sedimentary rocks (rocks which were deposited by water). These rocks are all younger than the granites of the Hudson Highlands, above which they were deposited. The most extensive of these are shales and slates which have been named the Hudson River formation. They were composed originally of mud which was deposited in horizontal layers on the bottom of a great arm of the sea once covering this area. Since their deposition, however, the mud layers have been buried and folded under great heat and pressure which hardened them into shales and slates. The folds in these rocks trend northeast-southwest, and impart a northeast-southwest trend to the ridges and intervening valleys.

The broad flat valleys, such as Clove Valley, are underlain by the Wappinger limestone formation, which is younger than the granites of the Hudson Highlands, but in part older and more easily eroded than the Hudson River formation. This is also a marine deposit, as shown by the marine fossils, or the remains of ancient sea life, it contains. In the western part of the county, near Poughkeepsie, the Wappinger formation is a true limestone composed of small grains of calcium carbonate. It has been used as a building stone, but does not break well for the quarryman. East of Poughquag the limestone has been highly metamorphosed and recrystallized into a marble. At South Dover the marble was formerly quarried extensively for building purposes.

Dutchess County has had an unusually interesting geological history. After the granites of the Hudson Highlands were injected, the whole region endured a long period of erosion during which many thousands of feet of rock were worn away. Then, as the land sank, the sea crept in and the region was covered with sand and mud. As the sea deepened, the limy shells of sea animals and chemically precipitated lime accumulated on the bottom to form the Wappinger limestone. Later, streams brought in mud to be deposited as the Hudson River shale. These rocks were then buried beneath a great thickness of overlying sediments and were intensely folded, crumpled, and metamorphosed. Since that time the land has risen, the sea has retreated, and the region has been severely dissected by the erosion of streams.

The relatively recent geological process of most importance in Dutchess County has been glaciation. Many thousands of years ago, this region was covered with a vast sheet of ice which moved from north to south. Its thickness here was probably 2,000 feet. Such a load of ice exerted a terrific downward pressure on the region which it covered. At Storm King Mountain, the bottom of the rock channel of the Hudson River is more than 800 feet below sea level, indicating that the Hudson Valley sank after it was formed. At the end of the Glacial Period, with the change to warmer climate, the front of the ice sheet melted back toward the north; and as the ice load was removed, the land rose. The Hudson River Valley was partly dammed at its southern end, and a long, narrow, fresh-water lake was formed. Here the fine clays were deposited which are now used in the manufacture of bricks at many points along the Hudson River. The poor drainage in Dutchess County is the result of the haphazard distribution of sand, gravel, and boulders left behind when the ice retreated.

Flora and Fauna

The characteristic native trees of the lower parts of the county are hickory, oak, sycamore, basswood, soft maple, elm, birch, dogwood, azalea, mountain laurel, laburnum, red cedar, pine, hemlock, black walnut, horse chestnut and tulip. At higher altitudes in the Taconic and Highlands sections there is another characteristic assemblage of native trees, which includes some of the first group together with sugar maple, beech, white cedar, spruce, tamarack, ash, cucumber, and others. Some of the older trees are introduced species, from other sections of the country, from Europe, or the Orient, such as some varieties of spruce, European larch *(see Beacon),* Lombardy poplar, old-world willow, mulberry, locust, and catalpa. These expatriates of Europe and the

3

Orient are generally found on large estates or on lands that have been settled for many years. Chestnuts are exceedingly rare, a blight having destroyed most of these fine, large-leaved forest trees. The second-growth chestnuts are said to be immune.

Real forests are scarce in the county outside of the highland regions. Woodlots, however, are numerous; and hedgerows and road plantings are common. Especially in hedgerows are the smaller trees and shrubs found. Unlike many of the New York counties, there is no State forest preserve land in Dutchess. Taconic State Park, in the northeast, has been reforested to some extent with plantations of Scotch pine, European larch, Norway spruce, and white pine, all of which are relatively quick growers with root stock suitable for soil erosion prevention.

Shrubs of all sorts are found, many having been introduced and planted on estates and in hedgerows. Some of the larger estates use shrubs as walls to hide the mansions from the highways. Rhododendron is somewhat outstanding because it will not thrive much farther north, because it will grow in dark places unsuited to lawns, and because it has pleasing leaves and blooms.

Too numerous to list are all the species of wild flowers. Common meadow flowers are daisy, black-eyed Susan, devil's-paintbrush, Queen Anne's lace, buttercup, wild strawberry, blue violet, thistle, butter-and-eggs, and goldenrod. Cattail, blue flag, broadleaved arrowhead, jack-in-the-pulpit, pond lily, and marsh buttercup are characteristic flowering plants of marsh and pond. In the woods are dogtooth violet (spring), wintergreen, trillium, bitter sweet, arbutus *(do not pick)*, and a host of other colorful plants. Just which plants thrive in any one section is determined by soil conditions, amount of light, and altitude.

Like the plants and trees, animals of the county comprise native and introduced species. In a group by themselves are insects and arachnids (spiders). Lowly worms, slugs, ticks, bats, rats, frogs, toads, mice, shrews, and protozoa usually pass unnoticed.

The largest animal is the common (Virginia) deer found in the mountain areas. It occasionally strays to inhabited sections but scuttles away when discovered. Fiercest of the mammals is the wildcat, which keeps out of sight in the mountains. Prowling domestic cats destroy many birds, moles, and mice. The groundhog (woodchuck) is a common burrower in more remote meadows and hillsides. Raccoons and skunks, although relatively numerous, are seldom seen, as they commonly run about at night. Skunks, attracted by automobile lights, are sometimes spattered about State roads. Gray and red squirrels live in forest, estates, woodlot, and city trees, but rarely are seen together because they are incompatible. Chipmunks, with black stripes reaching down their brown backs to their thin tails, frequent stone walls but shun human company. The nocturnal flying squirrel is also found. Meadows and hedgerows are the favorite haunts of burrowing rabbits. Foxes, gray and red, are sometimes seen and often trapped in the mountains. Intermittently, opossums come to the county, only to disappear again in what appears to be a fixed cycle of about seven to nine years. The little weasels, brown in summer and whitish in winter, prey on smaller animals. The otter and mink are not uncommon. The muskrat inhabits streams and lakes.

The outstanding fowl are classified as game birds and song birds; many of each are migratory, and several are year-round residents. Most sought game birds are duck, goose, pheasant, partridge (ruffed grouse), and quail; the duck and goose are migratory, and the pheasant is introduced.

Among the common birds are robin, sparrow (English sparrow, introduced), house wren, swallow, grackle, starling (introduced), oriole, swift, gull, wood thrush, catbird, warblers, yellow throat, redstart, scarlet tanager, vireos, finches, rose-breasted grosbeak, cowbird, red-winged blackbird, pewee, flycatchers, kingfisher, woodpeckers, flicker, owls, hawks, killdeer, snipe, heron, and common tern.

Only two poisonous snakes are found, the rattlesnake and the copperhead. Both keep to the uninhabited hills, are relatively inactive, and are not dangerous unless bothered or surprised. Other and more common snakes are the garter snake, the spreading adder, the water snake, the little green grass snake, and the black snake.

Dutchess County streams are regularly stocked with game fish, mostly trout, by the State or by local game clubs. Hunn's and Whaley Ponds, as well as other lakes, are well supplied with pickerel, yellow perch, sunfish, and largemouthed bass. Smallmouthed bass and rock bass frequent faster moving water, such as Wappinger Creek. In the Hudson, shad and herring (occasionally sturgeon) run each April to fresh-water spawning pools, and large catches are made. White perch are netted in the winter. Slack waters influenced by tides contain suckers. Carp have been introduced into many lakes and ponds.

Insects of special moment are those which are destructive to shade and orchard trees. The worst offenders are the tent caterpillar, the codling moth, and the gypsy moth. Japanese beetles and Dutch elm leaf beetles, common and very destructive farther south, threaten the county's southern border. Reaching New York harbor from foreign lands, they are found in a widening circle, the Japanese beetle eating foliage, the Dutch beetle spreading a destructive fungus.

Butterflies and moths of varied hues are common inhabitants of meadows and woods. The county has its full share of flies, mosquitoes, bees, hornets, and wasps.

Early Exploration and Indians

The history of the early exploration of the middle reaches of the Hudson River is shrouded in legend and uncertainty. The Florentine pilot, Giovanni da Verrazano, sailing under the French flag in 1524, and the Portuguese, Estevan Gomez, exploring for Spain in the next year, were possibly among the first to enter the mouth of the river. The theory that either of these pushed up the Hudson any real distance is untenable. Certainly neither ascended the river as far as what is now known as Dutchess County.

The first authenticated voyage up the Hudson was made by Henry Hudson in 1609. This voyage was recorded in the celebrated log of Robert Juet, English mate of Henry Hudson's *Half Moon*.

On September 29, 1609, on the return voyage down the "great river of the mountains," later named Hudson's, the *Half Moon* dropped anchor off the present city of Beacon. The inhabitants of this part of the valley, as the Europeans had learned on their trip up the river, were of a friendly disposition. Native canoes brought out pumpkins, maize, and tobacco, which were readily exchanged for trinkets and "fire water." The next day the voyage was resumed, and for another three quarters of a century the Indians roamed the woods of Dutchess undisturbed by the whites.

At the time of its organization in 1683 (November 1), Dutchess County was well populated by the Wappinger Indians, a branch of the Lenni Lenape (Algonquin) linguistic family. They called themselves *Wapani (wapan, east)*, dwellers on the east bank of the river. The name Wappingers, however, is believed to have been derived from the Dutch *Wapendragers,* or "weapon-bearers."

An affidavit of King Ninham, a Wappinger sachem, recorded in Albany in 1730, states that a tribe of the River Indians, the "Wappinoes," were "the ancient inhabitants of the eastern shore of Hudson's River from the city of New York to about the middle of Beekman's Patent." Doubtless this refers to Beekman's upper or Rhinebeck Patent, which would place their northern boundary almost on a line with the southern boundary of the town of Red Hook.

Like other Indian tribes, the Wappingers were divided into clans and villages. Concerning the locations of the various villages so much conflicting testimony has been left by the early Dutch historians who were actually on the scene that it is difficult now to speak with any certainty. But however the precise divisions may have been, it seems clear that the Indian population was centered in the extreme southwest of the present county, where the mouths of the two largest streams in the region provided good fishing and good harbors for canoes.

The name Megriesken, except Ninham the only recorded name of a Wappinger sachem, is preserved in an interesting document dated August 8, 1683—an Indian deed conveying land to Francis Rombout and Gulian Verplanck. Covering land in the southwestern part of the present county, this is considered the only perfect transfer title made by the Wappinger Indians. This sale was of more than symbolic significance: it was a cession not merely of territory, but of those lands which the Indians themselves had chosen to occupy. Other sales followed, three of them before 1687.

The peaceable and friendly intentions which Henry Hudson discovered in the Dutchess County Indians appear to have continued throughout the brief history of their relations with the whites. An impressive instance is the settlement of Amenia by Richard Sackett in 1711 and Uldrick Winegar in 1724. Until the coming of the Winegars the Sackett family was the only one between Poughkeepsie and New Milford, and for many years after

1724 the two families lived in complete isolation. Yet they appear to have had no defenses whatever against the Indians, while at the same time in Litchfield, across the Connecticut border, five houses were surrounded by palisades, and soldiers were stationed to guard the workers in the fields.

Confronted by an untouched wilderness and a rigorous climate, the few bold white settlers had to fight tooth and nail to implant their traditional mode of living. It was perhaps inevitable that they should regard the Indians merely as one of the many forces to be overcome. The peaceable disposition of the latter served only to facilitate their exploitation. Their land was bought for small remuneration or acquired by trickery. When a first foothold was gained, both Dutch and English, at odds with each other, encouraged discord among the Indians. The whole story, to the passing of the last fullblood Indian in Dutchess, about 1800, is one of continuous disintegration in the face of superior force and complex motives. White civilization was in-

Dover Furnace

tolerant and destructive of the ancient Indian modes of life; white man's diseases were particularly fatal to him; and he could not long withstand these influences.

Virtually the last stand made by Dutchess Indians was at the remarkable Moravian mission of Shekomeko, about 3 miles west of the present village of that name, said to have been the first Moravian congregation of Protestant Indian converts in America. The Moravians carried on their ministrations from 1740 to 1744; in the latter year they were definitely ordered to leave the country. (See Tour 1.)

The compulsory emigration of the Indians of Shekomeko was but an instance of the many migrations north, south, and west in which the native population of Dutchess melted away during the 18th century. Large numbers wandered into Pennsylvania, Delaware, and Maryland, and many more into Ohio.

In 1774 the entire Indian population on both sides of the Hudson was estimated by Governor Tryon as only 300, and but a small number of these remained in Dutchess County. Although the proportion of women to men was always higher, a balance was struck by the intermarriage of many Indian women with the white settlers. Indian blood flows in many old families of eastern Dutchess.

Territorial Patents

Between 1685 and 1731, by a series of patents, the British Crown granted the territory of the present county to private persons. Although not valid as titles unless confirmed by Crown Patents, preliminary Indian deeds were required under English law. As noted above, a number of deeds were obtained from the Indians. When Crown Patents were required to cover these deeds, a confusion of claims arose which extended over a number of years and led to some uncertainty as to the number of patents. However, historians are in general agreement that there were 11 authentic patents. The first was granted to Van Cortland and Kip, Dutch merchants, and a Francis Rombout, of Flemish origin. Known as the Rombout Patent, it was based on the purchase of Rombout and Verplanck from the Indians in 1683, and comprised the present towns of Fishkill, East Fishkill, Wappinger, and parts of La Grange and Poughkeepsie. The second was the Minisinck grant, patented by Robert Sanders and Myndert Harmense in 1686, including part of the present town and city of Poughkeepsie. The Schuyler Patent of 1688 comprised two tracts of land: one already partly covered by the Minisinck grant, and the other, along the river, including the greater part of the town of Red Hook. (In 1699 Peter Schuyler conveyed to Sanders and Harmense all his land rights in the present town of Poughkeepsie). Also in 1688, on the same day, the Artsen-Rosa-Elton Patent was granted, including 1,200 acres in the southwestern part of the town of Rhinebeck. This land was in 1702 named Kipsbergen, after Hendrik and Jacobus Kip, whose purchases from the Indians in 1686, shortly after the Artsen-Rosa-Elton purchase, were included in the royal patent.

The most desirable land was along the river, the settlers' highway to the outside world. The first four patents occupied most of the 45-mile river frontage of the present county. The remainder was taken up in four succeeding patents covering territory the bulk of which lay inland. These were the Pawling Patent (1696, Staatsburg); Great Nine Partners Patent (1697, about half the territory between Crum Elbow Creek and Fallkill Creek, the bulk of the domain lying inland); Rhinebeck Patent (1703, Rhinebeck and part of Red Hook); and Fauconier Patent (1705, Hyde Park).

Three wholly inland patents covered the rest of Dutchess: the Beekman Patent (1703, Union Vale, Beekman, parts of LaGrange, Dover, and Pawling); Little Nine Partners Patent (1706, Milan, Pine Plains, parts of Stanford and Clinton); and the Oblong or "Equivalent Tract" (1731, eastern Dutchess from North East into Westchester).

The 11 Crown Patents covering 806 square miles of the present county were issued to less than 40 men, about half English and half Dutch. These freeholders held their rights by annual payment to the Crown of a commodity, usually wheat, which they received in turn from their tenants, upon whom the clearance and cultivation of the county depended. Virtually a feudal system, it was to cause much trouble and unrest in the 18th century, and to prove one of the main incitements, in these parts, to the Revolution.

Territorial Boundaries

Dutchess County was one of the 12 original divisions of the Colony of New York, organized by the first Colonial Assembly on November 1, 1683. It was named in honor of the Dutchess of York, wife of the Duke, later King James II, to whom New York had been granted by King Charles II. Duchess in that day was spelled *Dutchess,* and this has continued as the official spelling of the county name to this day. The original boundaries were tne Van Cortland property (the Westchester line) on the south, the Hudson River on the west, and Roeliff Jansen's Kil (the present Livingston's Creek in Columbia County) on the north. From the river the county was to extend 20 miles east into the woods. Of these boundaries only the river remains unchanged. In 1717 Livingston's Manor was taken from north Dutchess, and in 1812 Putman County was organized from south Dutchess.

The boundary line between New York and Connecticut had long been a subject of intercolonial dispute. The Connecticut Charter established the "South Sea" as a western boundary and the royal grant of 1664 to the Duke of York designated the Connecticut River as its eastern boundary. Crown commissioners sent to settle the conflict agreed upon a line north-northwest from a certain point on the Long Island Sound, supposing it would run parallel to, and 20 miles east of, the Hudson. Actually the line struck the river below West Point. As a result, Connecticut agreed in 1731 to cede to New York a territory equivalent in area to the 61,440 acres which comprise the present townships of Greenwich, Stamford, New Canaan, and Darien. The tract ceded by Connecticut to New York extended the whole length of Dutchess County along the Connecticut border and has been known since as

9

the *Oblong*. A slight ambiguity in the surveying remained undecided until 1879, when the present State line was finally established. *(See Oblong, p. 123)*

Settlement

Before 1664 the Dutch had made three successful settlements in the Hudson Valley (New York, Albany, and Kingston), chiefly for the purpose of exploiting the fur trade, and had systematically attempted to colonize the remaining territory under the patroon system. The wilderness of Dutchess, however, had been left untouched. But it was the Dutch, 20 years after their country had surrendered to Britain the territory renamed New York, that finally formed the vanguard of Dutchess County settlers.

By the time the Rombout tract became the legal property of the patentees, settlement in Dutchess had already begun. A Nicholas Emigh was living at the mouth of Fishkill Creek, and a Peter Lasinck near the mouth of Wappinger Creek. Both family names, after many alterations in spelling, survive today. Almost simultaneously, settlements took place in Poughkeepsie and Rhinebeck. In 1687 Governor Dongan reported that none of these deserved the name of a village, but his notice of them at least indicates their existence.

Although the soil of Dutchess was fertile and the river and streams abounded in fish, the conditions under which the first settlers lived were extremely primitive. The earliest habitations, of which there is little record, appear to have been caves dug into the sides of hills, lined with split logs, roofed with spars, and covered with layers of sods. Smoke from the cook fires found egress through a hole in the roof. Though small, these dugouts were doubtless warmer and snugger than the first crude cabins which succeeded them.

The trend of village settlement in the first quarter of the 18th century was back from the river, as is evidenced by the old village centers of Fishkill, Poughkeepsie, and Rhinebeck. The nature of the land, with its river bluffs and adjacent plateaus, was partly the cause, but the opening of the King's Highway from New York to Albany also exerted a marked influence. Authorized by the Colonial Assembly in 1703, this great artery was to extend from the northern end of King's Bridge, which spanned the Harlem (the first Manhattan bridge), to the "ferry at Crawlew over against the city of Albany." A special dispensation required sparsely settled Dutchess County to maintain only a path or highway wide enough for horse and man. But in 1713 this path was widened to conform to the rest of the highway.

In 1728, three years before the New York-Connecticut boundary line adjustment, the first settlers had arrived in the Oblong. *(See Oblong, p. 123.)* These were Nathan Birdsall and Benjamin Ferris, Quakers from Connecticut, who settled on the long-famous Quaker Hill in the present town of Pawling. *(See Tour No. 2, p. 117.)* Later other settlers came from Westchester, Long Island, and Connecticut, and helped form the largest Quaker community in the county.

By 1731 settlements were finally being made in every section. The county was ready for the great influx of second, third, and even fourth generation pioneers from New England, inured to the climate and conditions of the New World and possessing the experience to establish themselves successfully. In the rapid growth of Dutchess during the mid-century, the abundant water power of the many streams, the fertile soil, and the extensive forests all played a part. Grist and sawmills were erected on many streams in the more thickly settled parts of the county; and as settlements reached farther inland, more mills were built until every hamlet with any potential power at all was self-sufficient in the essential staples of flour and lumber.

County Government

Legislation for a system of county government was passed by the Colonial Assembly in 1691. This was the supervisor system, which, except for its temporary suspension in 1701-3, has continued in effect to the present without material modification. It is said to have been the model of the system now generally prevalent throughout the West.

In 1701 freeholders in Dutchess County were authorized to vote in Ulster County across the river as though residing there. Freeholders, or free property-owners, alone held the right of suffrage. In 1720 their number had risen to 148, but remained a small minority of the total population. The provisional attachment to Ulster County continued until 1713; then Dutchess, with a total of 445 souls, including 29 slaves, was allowed its representatives in the Colonial Assembly. The first county officials, elected in 1714, appear to have divided the county into three wards, the first civil divisions (followed later by precincts and towns), which were established in 1719 by the Assembly as the South (Westchester line to Wappinger Creek); Middle (thence north to Esopus Island off the center of Hyde Park); and North (remainder of the county, north to Roeliff Jansen's Kil).

In 1717 Poughkeepsie was named the county seat. A courthouse, first authorized in 1715 for erection in the most convenient place in the county, was again authorized for erection in Poughkeepsie within three years, and appears to have been completed within the time set. *(See Poughkeepsie, p. 31.)*

The first completely recorded election of county officers was held at Poughkeepsie in 1720. Supervisors of the three wards were chosen, together with constables, collectors, assessors, "overseers of the King's Highway," and in the North Ward, a "ponner for ofending beasts."

Land Tenure

Despite the growth and increasing affluence of Dutchess, there was much economic unrest. The source of all property rights was the Crown, to which patentees expressed allegiance in the form of annual quit-rents of money or produce. These tributes, together with frequently excessive rents, were exacted from the actual cultivators of the land, the tenant-settlers. The man of Dutchess, therefore, could clear his land, build his home, and till his crops, but never could he become independent. Nor could he vote, for the suffrage was extended only to the freeholders, absentee landlords for the most part. It was the feudal system in a form modified to meet American conditions.

Numerous small rebellions against this state of affairs occurred in the Hudson Valley, and culminated in the celebrated "Anti-Rent War" of 1766. Armed resistance by the tenant-settlers to the collection of taxes broke out suddenly in Columbia County and spread rapidly to Dutchess. Here, led by William Prendergrast, a farmer, a formidable band of insurgents assembled on Quaker Hill in the town of Pawling. The grenadiers in Poughkeepsie were ordered to advance against the rioters, but refused until reinforced by 200 troopers and two field pieces from New York. Successful resistance against such a force was evidently impossible, and Prendergrast surrendered. Tried in Poughkeepsie and sentenced to be hanged, he received a royal pardon won by the extraordinary efforts of his wife at the very moment when a company of 50 armed farmers arrived at the jail determined to set him free. The temper of the populace is obliquely illustrated in an advertisement which appeared soon after the sentence of Prendergrast offering a large reward "to any one willing to assist as the executioner, and promising disguise against recognition and protection against insults." Although this brief struggle against the landlords ended in failure, its reverberations did much to loosen the soil for the readjustments that followed the Revolution.

Dutchess in the Revolution

The landlord-tenant situation gives a key to the two distinct attitudes taken in Dutchess towards the Revolution. An English writer at the time of the war estimated that two-thirds of the wealth of the Province of New York was owned by the Tories, or Royalists. Dutchess, with its 964 non-signers of the Revolutionary pledge, as against 1,820 signers, was well represented in this faction. But the thousands of struggling tenants, who had actually cleared and cultivated the now wealthy county, were eager for the political and economic freedom which revolution promised. While the Tory landlords opposed by every means in their power the soon irresistible movement, the common people of Dutchess swelled the ranks of the militia and the Continental Army, fighting not only for the abolition of unjust taxes and the right to representation, but for a freeholder's title to the soil. Thus actuated, they poured out in large numbers, estimated by Governor Clinton at 10,000, to stem the British invasion in 1777.

The first expression of Dutchess in Revolutionary affairs was the passing of mollifying resolutions at a meeting in Poughkeepsie in 1774, in which it was declared that "they (the people of Dutchess) ought, and were willing, to bear and pay such part and proportion of the national expenses as their circumstances would admit of." The following year Poughkeepsie was opposed to the sending of delegates to the Provincial Convention and the Continental Congress, but was outvoted by the county as a whole.

At the first session of the Provincial Congress of New York in May, 1775, county and precinct Committees of Safety were provided for. Circulation of the Articles of Association, or "Pledge," as it was popularly called, to obtain signatures, effectually brought into the open the trend of feeling. Weapons were confiscated from the non-signers.

The Provincial authorities had determined upon the formation of four New York regiments, one of which was to be provided by Dutchess County. This, the 4th Regiment, was completed June 30, 1775.

The year 1777 was critical in the Revolution and was the year in which Dutchess played its most important part. The paramount question was control of the Hudson Valley, by which the British could divide the states and isolate New England. Fishkill, in its strategic location at the head of the Highlands and on a direct line of communication with New England, was the military center of the county. Here troops were quartered, army supplies stored, and prisoners interned. The newly formed Convention of Representatives of the State of New York met here from August, 1776, to February, 1777; and the village was the hospital center for the wounded from the battle of White Plains.

At Fox's Point, Poughkeepsie *(see p. 45)*, the American frigates *Montgomery* and *Congress* were built, as well as fire rafts and other small vessels. At Theophilus Anthony's (in Rudco, 2 miles south of Poughkeepsie) were forged parts of the famous chain strung across the Hudson at Fort Montgomery to prevent enemy craft from ascending the river. The "Steel Works" near Amenia were busy manufacturing steel for the use of the army. Gristmills on every stream were grinding day and night to produce flour for the troops.

In the crucial British advance up the Hudson, which commenced October 4, 1777, little of note occurred in Dutchess County, though much alarm was felt and active steps for resistance were taken. On October 8, Governor Clinton reported that "the eastern militia were coming in very fast," and that General Putnam, who was in command of the forces east of the river and had stationed himself at Fishkill, would have "10,000 to head the enemy should they push up the river." As Putnam is said to have had at this time only 600 regulars, this figure represents almost entirely the militiamen recruited from Dutchess.

On October 12, after breaking the famous river chain at Fort Montgomery (whereupon the two Poughkeepsie-built frigates stationed there for additional defense were fired to prevent their falling into the enemy's hands), a few vessels under Sir James Wallace proceeded up the river to Theophilus Anthony's *(see above)*, where much of the chain had been forged. Here they burned a number of shops and mills.

On October 15 a formidable force under General Vaughn was sent farther up the river. The fleet anchored that night above Hyde Park. On the 22d, General Putnam, who had followed from Fishkill as rapidly as possible, was in Red Hook, where a few buildings had been burned by the British before retiring to their vessels at the approach of the Dutchess militia. On the 24th, upon being apprised of the surrender of Burgoyne at Saratoga, the British fleet turned back towards Peekskill, where the British commander-in-chief, Sir Henry Clinton, had made his headquarters. This drive, the failure of which was decisive in the war, was the

13

nearest approach towards British control of the Hudson. In the remaining four years of the war fighting did not again come near Dutchess County.

Ratification of the Federal Constitution

Doubtless the most important and most dramatic event in Dutchess County history was the ratification of the Constitution of the United States by the State of New York in Poughkeepsie in 1788. The events leading up to the climax of the last ballot were many and varied. From June 17 to the end of July the village was the temporary home of the "best minds" of one of the foremost States of the confederated Nation. Governor George Clinton, Alexander Hamilton, John Jay, Robert R. Livingston, Melancthon Smith, Robert Yates, and John Lansing figured prominently in the proceedings. Sixty of the 65 elected delegates were in attendance. Governor Clinton, the chief opponent of ratification, was unanimously chosen chairman and was thus handicapped in debate, in which he was talented and brilliant. Chancellor Livingston of Dutchess and Alexander Hamilton, who had been largely instrumental in drafting the Constitution, led the ranks of its supporters.

The village throbbed to the debates. Tears flowed freely during some of the passionate pleadings of the talented Hamilton, who, as was proved by the final ballot, did not plead in vain. Nor was the opposition of Governor Clinton without benefit, for it resulted in the adoption of the Bill of Rights amendments, which in later years proved to be the backbone of the Constitution.

Aside from the demand for a guarantee of liberty, opposition to ratification was based on the importance of the Hudson River and the prosperity of shipping in the port of New York. Dutchess delegates subscribed to Clinton's opinion that by a tax on this shipping New York would be called upon to defray a disproportionate share of the Federal expense, while as an independent state it would easily be self-supporting. As debate progressed, the Dutchess delegates yielded this contention, but remained firm in their demand that the proposed Constitution be amended to include the New York Bill of Rights as a condition of ratification.

On June 24 word was received that New Hampshire, the ninth state, had accepted the Constitution. Virginia was still unaccounted for, and without her and New York the success of the Union was doubtful. On the afternoon of the second of July, Col. Henry Livingston, riding a foam-covered horse, galloped into Poughkeepsie to announce to the assembly that Virginia had unconditionally ratified the Constitution. He had ridden from New York in 10 hours, record time for those days. The news he carried was a blow to Clinton and his followers; to Hamilton, Jay, and Livingston it brought fresh hope and strengthened argument. On July 15, Melancthon Smith of Dutchess, one of the strongest opponents of ratification, moved for acceptance "on condition" that the Constitution be amended to include the Bill of Rights. Since the word *condition* would render ineffective a vote of ratification, the proposal was not acceptable to Hamilton and his followers. Finally a motion was made to substitute the words "in full confidence" for "on condition," and to this Smith acquiesced. This proved to be the climax of the assembly. On July 26 a final ballot was taken, and the Constitution was ratified, "in full confidence," by a majority of 30 to 27. Melancthon Smith, Zephaniah Platt, and Gilbert Livingston, three Dutchess County delegates, had changed their votes from nay to aye. Without these affirmative Dutchess votes New York would have remained, for the time being at least, a separate sovereignty, endangering the Union at its very inception.

Commercial and Industrial Development

After the Revolution river traffic increased rapidly. Poughkeepsie, midway on the river shore, soon pushed to the front as a commercial center. *(See Poughkeepsie, pp. 25-26.)* Other river villages, Fishkill Landing, New Hamburg, Rhinebeck, Red Hook also flourished. In all these places power was supplied by the all-important streams. On Landsman's Kil, in Rhinebeck, grist and sawmills stood so close together that the water from one mill pond occasionally backed up and interfered with the operation of the water wheel of the mill above. An ample supply of raw materials encouraged these early industries. The hills of the county were covered with virgin timber, and the cleared fields produced crops unexcelled in the State for quality and abundance. Transportation facilities and the proximity of the growing New York market combined to bring Dutchess to a temporary leadership among the agricultural counties of the State.

Next to the river, highways were most important in determining the early development of the county. The King's Highway (Albany Post Road), the first officially authorized road through the county, exerted a marked influence upon the development of village centers, as in the case of Poughkeepsie, which grew around the intersection of this road with the road from the east, rather than on the riverbank. The cattle drovers' route from Vermont and New Hampshire to New York had an important effect on the growth of the Harlem Valley villages of Amenia, Dover, and Pawling.

Stagecoaches began running regularly over the Post Road from New York to Albany in 1786. The necessity of changing horses every 10 or 20 miles led to the establishment of the stage houses. In the hamlets these taverns were the centers of community life; travelers enlivened discussions with the latest news, and liquor flowed freely. De Chastellux, traveling twice through Dutchess, in 1780 and 1782, writes that he found taverns enough, but few sufficiently unoccupied to accommodate him. It is believed that by 1800 there were nine taverns in Rhinebeck alone.

By 1813 the industrial development of the county was well under way, and sloop-freighting had assumed large proportions. Of paramount importance was the commerce in flour. During the first third of the nineteenth century Dutchess County ranked first among New York State counties in wheat production, supplying one third of all the flour produced in the State. Spafford's *Gazetteer* (1813) lists 14 gristmills in the town of Poughkeepsie alone. Iron mines were in operation at Amenia, Deep Hollow,

15

Sylvan Lake, and Clove Valley. Nails were manufactured in Poughkeepsie as early as 1805. The next year saw the first of the Vassar breweries. In 1811 began the development of the textile industry. In 1814 the first iron works were founded in Poughkeepsie, ore being transported by mule teams from the mines at Sylvan Lake. *(See Tour 3, p. 134.)* Fluxing lime came from Barnegat, and charcoal from various neighboring pits. The pre-Revolutionary shipyard at Poughkeepsie has been mentioned; others sprang up at Wappingers Landing in 1812 and at Chelsea in 1828. In the former, several United States gunboats were built, in the latter several of the early steamboats. In 1812 a slate company was formed in the town of North East for the production of flagging and slate roofing. Marble quarries thrived in the town of Dover. But brickmaking at Fishkill Landing (Beacon), which was well supplied with the necessary clay and sand, is the only important early manufacturing industry of the county that has continued to the present. *(See Beacon, p. 64.)*

The Harlem Valley Railroad, the first in the county, was constructed in 1845; the Hudson River Railroad followed in 1849; both are now included in the New York Central system. Later came the Poughkeepsie & Eastern and the Dutchess & Columbia (later the Newburgh, Dutchess & Connecticut), both now a part of the New York, New Haven & Hartford lines.

The Civil War put an end to many county enterprises. In contrast to their forefathers of the Revolutionary period, in the 1860's the men of Dutchess were wholehearted supporters of the Union. Men and money were supplied freely. The 150th Infantry, mustered into service October 11, 1862, was entirely recruited in the county, and many more local men joined other units.

In the period following the Civil War industrial development in Poughkeepsie and Beacon was intensified. Dutchess turned to the manufacture of agricultural implements for the rest of the State, with Adriance-Platt harvesters, Moline plows, and DeLaval separators. Other special types of industries developed. Beacon became a center of hat manufacturing. A cotton

Van Kleeck House, built in 1702

bleachery was established at Wappingers Falls. Recently a trend to garment manufacture has appeared in Poughkeepsie. A number of small establishment, have located over Main Street stores, and several large concerns are scattered throughout the city.

Agriculture

Parallel with the rise of industry came a decline in grain production, chiefly as a result of improvements in transportation. The completion of the Erie Canal in 1825 made competition with the West impossible. The change that of necessity took place was, however, accomplished gradually. By 1860, although agriculture still led industry, Dutchess had fallen to third among New York counties in the cash value of its farms and fifth in cultivated area. Not until 1880 at the earliest, however, can it be said that wheat practically disappeared as a cash crop, and even today an appreciable amount of grain is grown for local consumption.

Meanwhile, as in industry, Dutchess turned to specialized agriculture, with the trend determined by available markets and local variations in soil. In dairying, which replaced wheat in the position of first importance, the Harlem Valley towns quickly assumed leadership. Since earliest times isolation from the river had turned them to cattle raising; and the very railroads which rendered them unable to compete with western beef encouraged them in the production of milk and milk products for New York City. By 1860 Pawling and Dover had become milk centers for the New York market, and are said to have been soon afterward the most important milk-producing section in the State.

The river counties especially, with Red Hook as a center, turned to the raising of apples. *(See Tour No. 1.)* In the northwestern section of the county the cultivation of violets was put on a commercial basis.

Thus with the diversion of land to these purposes, the last quarter of the 19th century saw the peak of agricultural expansion in Dutchess in terms of land area, accompanied, however, by a rapidly accelerated decline in relative value. In 1880 farm land, including wood and swamp sections connected with farms, amounted to 95 percent of the total area of the county.

In the 20th century, rapid refrigerated transportation exposed the Dutchess dairy industry to upstate and western competition, which it found difficult to meet because of high overhead costs. As a result dairying has in recent years suffered a marked decline, though it still holds a place of importance in the county. In 1930 the total area of farm land in the county had decreased to 65.5 percent.

With their decline in agricultural importance, the fine river lands and attractive farms were subjected to an active movement of conversion into country estates and summer homes. In the case of Hyde Park, long a fashionable New York summer resort, between 1800 and 1900 a quarter of the land came into the hands of 13 men and was developed into river estates averaging 482 acres each. This trend established itself in other sections of the county a generation later. With improved roads and a steady decrease in the relative value of farm products, New Yorkers are yearly taking over more of the rustic and now easily accessible lands and homesteads. It appears that the gradual suburbanization of Dutchess is in progress.

Population

In 1930 Dutchess County, with a population of 105,462, ranked nineteenth among the 62 counties of the State. This figure showed an increase of 13,715 over 1920. In the former year, 82.5 percent of the population was native-born white, 14.5 percent foreign-born white, and 3 percent Negroes. Of the foreign born 5,859 reside in Poughkeepsie and 2,138 in Beacon. Of the remainder, Milan and Hyde Park have the largest percentage, while Fishkill, Pawling, and Amenia have the lowest. Approximately 16 percent of the farm population is foreign born, mainly of Italian, Austrian, Polish, and Czechoslovakian origin. There are a few Dutch, British, French, and Russians, and, more rarely, Scandinavians. Italian groups have concentrated in the industrial centers, particularly in the cities of Poughkeepsie and Beacon and in the village of Wappingers Falls. The Slavic nationalities are found chiefly in Milan, Red Hook, Pleasant Valley, Hyde Park, and Stanford.

While the population as a whole is increasing, the density of population per square mile is decreasing, indicating a trend toward urbanization. In 1920, the township of Milan had a population density of 28; in 1930 the index had fallen to 17: 10 percent of the farms were abandoned during the decade.

Political Organization

Dutchess County is divided into 20 townships, the first of which were formed in 1788 from the original wards (later precincts) into which the county had been divided. They are Red Hook, Milan, Pine Plains, North East, Rhinebeck, Clinton, Stanford, Amenia, Hyde Park, Pleasant Valley, Washington, Poughkeepsie, LaGrange, Union Vale, Dover, Wappinger, Beekman, Fishkill, East Fishkill, and Pawling. Fishkill, the smallest, has an area of 24.4 square miles; Washington, the largest, 56.5 square miles. The eight incorporated villages, scattered throughout the county, are Fishkill, Millbrook, Millerton, Pawling, Red Hook, Rhinebeck, Tivoli-Madalin, and Wappingers Falls. Pleasant Valley was an incorporated village until 1926, when its charter was dissolved and it became a part of the township.

The townships are governed by the County Board of Supervisors, composed of 32 members, one elected from each township and one from each ward of the two cities (Poughkeepsie, eight, and Beacon, four wards). Dutchess County is represented in the State legislature by two members of the assembly. One senator is elected from the 28th senatorial district, which includes Dutchess, Putnam, and Columbia Counties.

Education

Education in Dutchess County was concentrated in private schools until late in the 19th century. Poughkeepsie had at one time more than a dozen,

Old Brewery at the River Front

and Beacon was the home of several. With the development of the public school system, these schools gradually disappeared. To-day in the two cities of the county there are a few business institutes, and parochial schools are connected with the larger parishes of the Roman Catholic Church. Outside of the cities, however, private schools have continued to flourish, especially colleges and preparatory and elementary schools, such as Vassar and Bard Colleges, Bennett, Fox Hollow, Pawling, Millbrook, Oakwood, and Manumit schools.

The county public school sytsem is to-day undergoing a movement toward centralization, with transportation for students to the new central schools. Large, well-constructed buildings with modern equipment and up-to-date teaching techniques are supplanting the old one-room "little red schoolhouses." There are, however, many of the latter still in use scattered about the county.

In the rural schools 60 percent of the enrollment is made up of children from farms, 40 percent from villages. Although the farm is so heavily represented, the Pine Plains High School is the only one in the county which offers courses in agriculture and homemaking. Supplementing the training offered in the rural school system are 25 4-H Clubs (Heart, Hand, Head, and Health) under the sponsorship of the Dutchess County Farm Bureau, with a total membership of 615 school children. With the aid of these clubs the children study scientific methods of farming and stock raising, canning, and many handicrafts.

Religion

The early settlers of Dutchess County showed a tendency to sectional segregation of religious sects. The Dutch Reformed Church was concentrated in the southwest, the Palatine congregations (Lutherans and German Calvinists), with a sprinkling of French Huguenots, in the northwest, the Society of Friends (Quakers) in the central and southeastern sections.

The Dutch, who then composed the majority of the population, were the first to establish church congregations. These occurred simultaneously in the three wards into which the county was then divided. The first church building to be erected, however, was the old German Church in Kirchehoek, town of Rhinebeck, which edifice had been built in 1716 as a union church for Lutherans and Calvinists. Dutch churches followed in Poughkeepsie in 1723 and in Fishkill in 1731, and the Presbyterian Church in Brinckerhoff in 1747. The Methodist and Baptist churches were organized shortly after 1800. A Roman Catholic missionary visited the county in 1781 and ministered to Acadian refugees banished from their homes in Nova Scotia. There was no Roman Catholic organization, however, until 1832, when an association was formed to raise funds for the erection of a church, Saint Peter's, in Poughkeepsie.

The younger church organizations, formed after the beginning of the 19th century, have developed rapidly and have in large part supplanted the older denominations in leadership. Union churches, in the sense of one church building serving two congregations, have with one or two exceptions ceased to exist, although it is commonly the case that suppers, parties, and entertainments for the benefit of one sect are strongly supported by all, and union services are regularly held on special days like Thanksgiving, Christmas, and Easter. This is done to promote the attendance of larger congregations than any individual church can draw. The dearth to-day is not of church edifices but rather of supporting members.

The Catholic, Methodist, and Baptist Churches, established in Dutchess after 1800, maintain organizations throughout the county. The Dutch Reformed, German Lutheran, Episcopal, and to a lesser degree the Presbyterian, hold to the sections in which they were first established. The Society of Friends has in most part been displaced, and all but seven of their meeting-houses have either been removed or are utilized for other purposes. Oakwood School, a coeducational boarding school, is maintained in part by endowments of the New York Yearly Meeting of the Society of Friends.

The Church of Christ Scientist, first established in Poughkeepsie in 1898, now maintains two churches in that city.

The Jewish congregations maintain synagogues in Poughkeepsie, Beacon, and Amenia, and elsewhere hold services in private homes.

◆ ◆ ◆ ◆

Social Life

The social life of rural and suburban Dutchess County centers in the public schools, the village church, the village grange, and the veteran organizations, and finds expression in such activities as clambakes, portion suppers, food sales, school plays, dancing, sewing bees, and horseshoe pitching contests. The 25 grange units in the county hold general meetings twice a month and frequent group meetings. While the primary object of the grange is to promote the economic interests of the farmer, it is also the center of his social life.

Sunday afternoon, formerly spent in neighborhood visiting, is now usually devoted to automobile riding or listening to the radio. The younger generation depends largely upon movies and roadside taverns for amusement. The older generation of farmers has not contracted the "movie" habit.

It has been found that in church and grange social gatherings there is a noticeable split between the farmers and the villagers, though the new centralized school system is gradually uniting the children and eliminating social distinction between these groups.

The larger towns, while clinging to many of the pleasures and customs of the countryside, have a larger variety of organizations, such as are associated with the more complicated town life. Service clubs and commercial, social, and educational societies have arisen in response to the characteristics and needs of the population groups. With the improvement in transportation facilities throughout the county, the differences between the social life of the towns and that of the country are slowly being obliterated, especially in the case of the young, who can only with more and more difficulty be kept on the farm.

Architecture

The oldest houses now standing in Dutchess date back to the days of the first settlement. They are built of rough stone, of which the settlers found an abundance on their lands. The same type of house continued to be built for about 100 years, and remains in considerable numbers, though often greatly altered and increased in size in later periods. Frame houses were built somewhat later than stone, and brick was little used before 1750. The reason for this choice is obvious. Stone was to be had for the labor of picking it up, lumber could be cut on any farmer's land but demanded more skill in its use, while brick must be either bought and transported, or else made locally, involving time and equipment. However, brick was more highly esteemed; as the country became more prosperous its use became more general, and by 1800 the practice of building in stone had almost ceased.

The early stone houses were generally one and one-half story high, with roofs of moderate pitch. The high-pitched roofs and crow-stepped gables of Albany County do not occur in Dutchess. Gambrel roofs are rarer here than in other parts of the Hudson Valley, and are found mainly on brick or frame houses built after 1750; less often on stone houses. Hip roofs are almost unknown, the plain gable being the usual type, with the roof carried over the gables, not stopped against them, as is the case in many examples in Albany and New York City.

About the middle of the eighteenth century brick and stone came to be used in combination, sometimes with brick in front and stone in the rear, sometimes with brick gable ends topping stone walls. Houses built entirely of brick were rare until after the Revolution. Frame houses were occasionally built at an early period, but until about 1750 their use was not general.

Most of the early building was done by the settlers themselves, the county then having few artisans. The stone walls are usually about 2 feet thick. Lime kilns are known to have existed in Dutchess before the Revolution, one group having been located near the present Camelot station, at what was then called Barnegat (Dutch for firehole) in the town of Poughkeepsie. A sawmill existed at Poughkeepsie as early as 1699, and there were no doubt others of not much later date. The first frame houses had thick walls filled with clay between the timbers, but brick filling was soon generally used. They were covered with wide clapboards, with shingles, or with shakes, often with rounded ends, as may still be seen in the Teller house in Beacon.

It is a matter of record that a carpenter was hired for the work on the Teller house and lodged by the owners until it was completed. For the brick houses of the post-Revolutionary period, expert masons were evidently employed, for we find many houses of this date built with a degree of skill that plainly shows the trained artisan; while others were evidently built by the settlers or by country carpenters of ability.

The first houses were small and simple. Many had but two rooms, usually with a hall between. Others had four rooms, two on each side of the hall, the front rooms usually larger than those in the rear. There were other variations, including a type with no hall, each room having its own outer door. L-shaped and T-shaped plans are represented, but these are generally the result of later enlargement. Many small old houses have been extended by the addition of larger buildings, the original house serving as a wing.

A distinctive feature of Dutchess houses is the Dutch door with its horizontal division, which was almost universal in the county, from the earliest days to the nineteenth century. The style, of course, varies: the earliest doors are of the batten type, while the later are paneled, often with considerable elegance. Bull's eyes were often introduced, and later, sidelights and overdoor panels with leaded glass. Casement windows were probably used in the older houses, though few remain. The first houses had few windows, and these were small, for glass was expensive and heating difficult.

After the Revolution the county became one of the most prosperous in the Hudson Valley, and its population increased rapidly. Many handsome frame and brick houses were built in the last quarter of the eighteenth century and the early part of the nineteenth, and many older houses were improved or enlarged. Adam mantels characterize this period, usually with composition ornaments. In many cases they have been added to older fireplaces and paneling. Another type of mantel, found also at this time, has Dutch sunbursts and reeding, cut in the wood with gouges and molding planes. Much of this work was done by country carpenters in a rather crude imitation of the designs from the popular pattern books, but some of the work done between 1790 and 1820 is equal to that in the cities. About 1820 the Empire influence began to be felt, and about 10 years later the Greek Revival became the fashion, though some good Colonial detail of later date is still extant. From the Greek Revival period on, Dutchess has followed the popular fashions in architecture, few of which have had any special merit.

With the improvement in transportation, many old estates along the Hudson have become the summer homes of wealthy New Yorkers. Some of these estates preserve old houses, usually much enlarged. Others have new houses, palatial in scale and in all manner of current styles.

In addition to dwellings, each village had one or more churches. Built of the same materials as the dwellings of the time, these were of the usual Colonial type, simple and dignified, commonly with a square tower or belfry at one end. The Lutheran stone church, built by the Palatines north of Rhinebeck on the Post Road, was of the same general type. The Quaker meetinghouses, of which several still remain, form an exception. They differ from the usual church type in being broader than deep, and in the extreme simplicity of their lines, unbroken by towers and belfries. They have separate entrances for men and women, with separate stairs leading to a balcony. The body of the church and the balcony are divided by a partition, usually with sliding panels.

The farmhouses that were used as taverns differed little, if at all, from other dwellings. A few barns and mills of the early days remain, but they are naturally simple and utilitarian, though with much charm and character.

Recent years have produced many large buildings in Dutchess County, including factories, hotels, State hospitals, churches, and government offices, but few of them have such architectural merit as to make them noteworthy. An exception is Vassar College, the buildings of which have been designed of a century, though some of them, taken individually, are decidedly better than average. The heterogeneous styes and materials are saved from discord by capable architects. As in the case of most of our American colleges, Vassar buildings present a history of architectural taste during the past three-quarters by the magnificent trees and lovely gardens that adorn the college grounds.

POUGHKEEPSIE

Railroad Stations: New York Central, Hudson River Division, entrances near foot of Main St. and at foot of Mill St. New York, New Haven & Hartford (freight only), Cottage St., near Smith St.

Bus Station: New Market St.; all lines for all points.

Airport: Poughkeepsie Airport, 5 m. SE. of city on State 376; taxi to port, $1.25; time, 15 min.

Steamboat Docks: All at foot of Main St. Poughkeepsie-Highland Ferry (R), connections with New York Central R. R. (West Shore); Central Hudson Steamboat Co. (L); Hudson River Dayline, N. of ferry slip.

Taxis: At R. R. station, 50c; all others, 25c within city limits.

City Busses: Fare 10c, 3 tokens 25c; to Wappingers Falls, 25c.

Traffic Regulations: Speed limit, 30 m. p. h. No turns on red light. Full stop at intersections with Stop signs. Parking limit in business section one hour.

Accommodations: Nelson House (E), $2.00, Market St.; Campbell Hotel (E), $2.50, Cannon St.; Windsor Hotel (E), $1.50, Main and Catharine Sts.; King's Court (E), $1.50, Cannon St.

Information: Chamber of Commerce, 57 Market St.; Nelson House, 28 Market St.

Street Order: Main St., running E. and W., divides the city into "north side" and "south side." Market St. (Albany Post Road) runs S. and Washington St. (Albany Post Road) runs N. from Main St., bisecting the city.

Theatres and Motion Picture Houses: No legitimate theatre; six motion picture houses on Main, Market, Cannon, and Liberty Sts.

Baseball: Butts Memorial Field, Church St. and Quaker Lane; Twilight League and county championship games in Eastman Park.

Horseshoe Pitching: Free municipal courts in Butts Memorial Field.

Ice Skating: Eastman Park.

Golf: College Hill Park municipal course, North Clinton St., nine holes, 40c—$1.00 greens fee; Dutchess County Golf and Country Club (*see Tour 3, p. 125*), 18 holes, $2.00 greens fee.

Tennis: Free municipal courts in Butts Memorial Field, College Hill Park, Eastman Park, and King Street Park (Corlies Ave. and King St.); Poughkeepsie Tennis Club, 137 S. Hamilton St., admission by invitation.

Swimming: Open air pool at Wheaton Park, children only, foot of Mill St. Popular swimming holes at Greenvale Park, admission 5c, 3 m. SE. on State 376, and Morello's Pleasure Park, admission 10c, 2½ m. NE. on Creek Road, continuation of Smith St.

Riding: Rombout Hunt Club, 2½ m. SE. on State 376, scene of Vassar Horse Show in May, and the Hunter Trials in October, admission by invitation; Greenvale Riding Academy, at Rombout Hunt Club, by appointment, $1 per hour with instructions; Vassar Riding Academy, 10 Raymond Ave., by appointment, $1 per hour with instruction.

Annual Events: Intercollegiate Regatta, on the Hudson, late in June. Concerts of the Dutchess County Musical Association during the winter. Concerts of the Euterpe Glee Club (male voices), Orpheus Glee Club (male), Germania Singing Society (male and female), and Lyric Glee Club (female), end of winter.

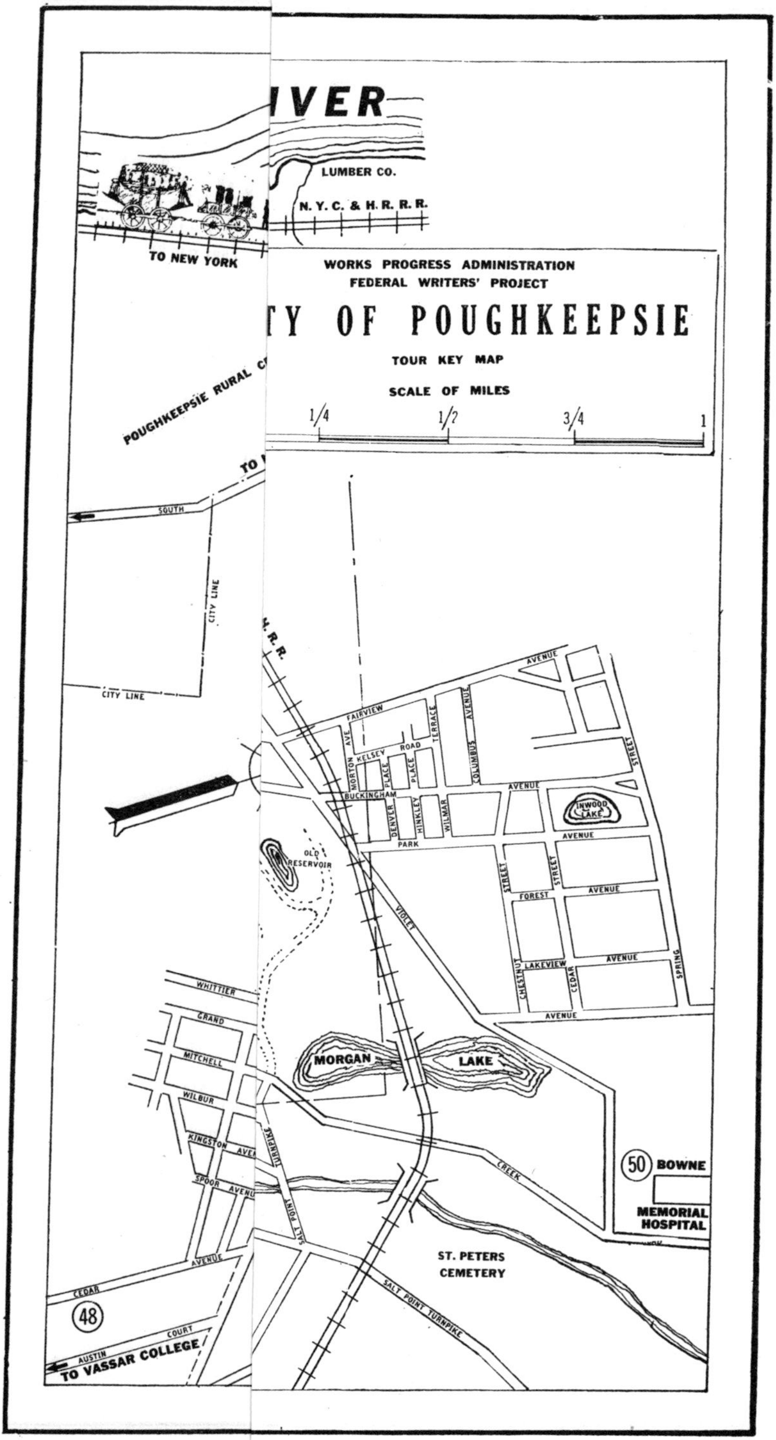

IVER
LUMBER CO.
N. Y. C. & H. R. R. R.
TO NEW YORK
WORKS PROGRESS ADMINISTRATION
FEDERAL WRITERS' PROJECT
TY OF POUGHKEEPSIE
TOUR KEY MAP
SCALE OF MILES
1/4
1/2
3/4
1
POUGHKEEPSIE RURAL C
SOUTH
CITY LINE
CITY LINE
FAIRVIEW
AVENUE
MORTON AVE
KELSEY ROAD
TERRACE
COLUMBUS AVENUE
STREET
PLACE
PLACE
AVENUE
BUCKINGHAM
DENVER
HINKLEY
WILMAR
INWOOD LAKE
AVENUE
PARK
OLD RESERVOIR
STREET
STREET
FOREST
AVENUE
VIOLET
LAKEVIEW
AVENUE
CHESTNUT
CEDAR
SPRING
AVENUE
WHITTIER
GRAND
MITCHELL
WILBUR
MORGAN
LAKE
KINGSTON AVE
SPOOR AVENU
TURNPIKE
CREEK
50 BOWNE
MEMORIAL HOSPITAL
SALT POINT
ST. PETERS CEMETERY
SALT POINT TURNPIKE
AVENUE
CEDAR
48
COURT
AUSTIN
TO VASSAR COLLEGE

POUGHKEEPSIE (173 alt., 40,288 pop.), has long been known as the "Bridge City of the Hudson" because of the older of the two great bridges which span the river at this point. *(See Water-front Tour.)* It is the county seat of Dutchess County and enjoys wide renown as the seat of Vassar College and scene of the annual Intercollegiate Regatta. During the Revolutionary period it enjoyed a brief interval of national importance. From 1777 to 1784, before it was incorporated as a village, it was the capital of New York State. The little community was then the modest metropolis of the wealthiest and most populous of the 14 counties. The outstanding event of the period—and of the entire history of Poughkeepsie—was the ratification by New York State of the Federal Constitution in 1788. *(See p. 14.)* Otherwise the city has been locally prominent as the industrial and shipping center of what was long a rich agricultural area.

Poughkeepsie is situated on the east bank of the tidewater Hudson, midway between New York and Albany. The pattern of the city is like that of many Hudson River towns. The long Main Street climbs the steep slope from the river, and, lined with offices, shops, and public buildings, extends eastward for about 2 miles. At the crest of the hill Main intersects with Market Street, which stretches north and south along the plateau. This is the center of the business district, passed by the flow of motor traffic on the Albany Post Road. The city has spread out in streets roughly paralleling these two thoroughfares, the newer sections departing from any orderly arrangement.

Architecturally, downtown Poughkeepsie presents the miscellaneous collection of buildings characteristic of older towns which grew up before the days of city planning. Brick and frame structures of varied heights are crowded together. An occasional old residence has kept its foothold, the lower floor pressed into commercial service. The residential districts in turn reflect the tastes and styles of their periods. The finest dwellings of the pre-Civil War period have almost all been destroyed or fallen into ruin. West of Market Street there are still numerous examples of the simple, substantial brick town house of the early nineteenth century. Along the water front, where the largest industries superseded the most pretentious dwellings of the city, the scene is one of alternate activity and dilapidation.

The economic life of Poughkeepsie is about evenly divided between industry and commerce, with no one trade or product predominating. In 1930, 40 percent of the wage earners were employed in manufacturing, the rest in the building and service trades, and in selling. Because of its location on the Hudson and at the junction of two great railroad systems, the city is growing in importance as a distributing point. The Dutton Lumber Company *(see p. 40),* the largest of four, stores lumber from the West Coast, the Scandinavian countries, and the U. S. S. R. for reshipment to New York and other eastern points.

The chief manufacturing concerns are the De Laval Separator Company, producers of cream separators and oil clarifiers, and the Schatz Manufacturing Company, makers of ball bearings. There is one large cigar company, one trousers factory, and two companies producing neckties. Numerous smaller shops make men's and women's garments, machine parts, woodwork, cough drops, ice cream, and loose-leaf notebooks.

The Central Hudson Gas and Electric Corporation has general offices on Phoenix Place. This corporation, with approximately one thousand employes, serves a territory of 2,600 miles, including Dutchess and Putnam, and portions of Albany, Greene, Ulster, Orange and Columbia Counties. The company operates an electric generating plant and gas manufacturing plant in Poughkeepsie.

There are many small clothing manufacturing establishments employing women almost exclusively. In 1930, 29 percent of the industrial workers in Poughkeepsie were women, almost all of them employed in these shops. Effective labor organization in Poughkeepsie is limited to the construction trades.

The Poughkeepsie retail market, in the case of its large department stores, extends beyond the Dutchess County borders, east into Connecticut and south as far as Peekskill. Merchants complain that the high tolls on the Mid-Hudson Bridge prevent the possible extension of that market to the west side of the river. Like every city feeding on industry and a large agricultural hinterland, the streets and stores of Poughkeepsie are busiest on Saturday afternoon, with Main Street east of Market carrying the heaviest burden. Though wide as streets go, and though busses have been substituted for trolleys, the normal condition of Main Street is one of congestion.

Native-born whites constitute about 82 percent of the total population of Poughkeepsie, or 34,429 persons out of 40,288. Of the remaining 18 percent, 15 percent, or 5,859, are foreign-born whites, and about 1,200, or 3 percent, are Negroes. These percentages are identical with those for the county as a whole. The Negroes in Poughkeepsie are grouped in two sections, William Street in the southwest, and Pershing Avenue, in the east central part of the city.

In the foreign-born group Italians and Slavs predominate. Employed for the most part in local factories, they make their homes in the northwestern part of the city, which lies north of Main Street and west of Washington Street. The Italian section includes the area between Main and Duane Streets and joins a region occupied by people of Slavic origin to the west of Delafield Street.

Thirty-nine churches serve Poughkeepsie and its immediate vicinity. Of these 23 are Protestant (including 2 Negro churches), 7 Catholic, 4 Hebrew, 1 Orthodox Greek, and 4 undenominational. The Catholic churches include 4 with services in a foreign tongue—Italian, Polish, German, and Slavic. The Greek Orthodox Church is a member of the Archdiocese of North America and South America, which in turn is subordinate to the Ecumenical Patriarchate of Constantinople.

The Presbyterian, dating from 1749, was the first organized English church group in Poughkeepsie. The First Presbyterian Church, a large gray stone structure in Romanesque style, at the corner of Cannon and South Hamilton Streets, is an outgrowth of this early organization.

In conjunction with the Protestant churches there are several young peoples' and social organizations, the best known being the Christian Endeavor, Boy Scouts, Girl Scouts, Young Peoples' Societies, and Ladies Aids. The Catholic churches also offer social activities to their members in the Holy Name Society, St. Aloysius Sodality, Altar Society, Children of Mary, Rosary Society, Sodality of the Holy Angels, and Sodality of the Infant Jesus. The Jewish social life is centered in the Hebrew Fraternal and Benevolent Society, the Men's Club of Vassar Temple, and the Jewish Center.

The chief social service activities in Poughkeepsie are carried on in Lincoln Center. *(See p. 46.)* The part that Vassar College plays in that work illustrates its wider significance in the community life, especially in the fields of intellectual and cultural interests.

The Poughkeepsie public school system is housed in 14 buildings. There are nine grammar schools, one high school, and two buildings devoted to high school freshmen, as well as a trade school, a continuation school, and an evening school. Incorporated in the system are medical and dental clinics. The curriculum in the grade schools includes physical education, art, music, homemaking, and manual arts, as well as the traditional three R's. The high school offers college preparatory, academic, commercial, and homemaking courses, and training in art, music, dramatics, and debating. The Poughkeepsie High School debating teams were champions of the 1932 State National Forensic League tournament, held in Albany; and in the national competition the same year at Sioux City, Iowa, the school was one of the 44 competing for the national championship.

The journalistic history of Poughkeepsie began with the career of John Holt, who published the New York *Journal and General Advertiser* in New York City until driven out by the British in 1776. He subsequently fled to Kingston, and thence to Poughkeepsie, always a step ahead of the advancing enemy, and always publishing his paper. Although printed in Poughkeepsie, it was not a local publication, but carried foreign news and items from all parts of the country.

The first distinctly local newspaper in Poughkeepsie was the Poughkeepsie *Journal,* published by Nicholas Powers. The present Poughkeepsie *Eagle-News* is a fusion of numerous newspapers going back to two principal ancestors, the Poughkeepsie *Journal* (1785) and the Dutchess *Intelligencer* (1828). Through the years the names, owners, and policies of the papers frequently changed. The Dutchess *Intelligencer* became the Poughkeepsie *Eagle* in 1834 and was united with the Poughkeepsie *Journal and Eagle* in 1844. In 1850, the name was changed to the Poughkeepsie *Eagle,* which became a weekly, and in 1860 to the Poughkeepsie *Daily Eagle,* a daily. In 1892 it was given the present name.

This paper has been closely associated with the development of the city, often having led in the advocacy of public improvements. Since the *Daily*

Eagle made its appearance on December 4, 1860, the name of **Platt** has been closely associated with it. The Poughkeepsie Railroad Bridge was first publicly proposed in an editorial written by John I. Platt in the issue of January 22, 1868. In 1889 Platt & Platt published the folio size Souvenir Edition of the *Poughkeepsie Eagle,* with its many illustrations, photographs, and historical data depicting the growth of Poughkeepsie. Its accuracy and completeness of detail still make it a valuable work of reference.

The Poughkeepsie *Eagle-News* is now published by Platt and Platt, Incorporated, and the Poughkeepsie *Evening Star* and *Enterprise* by the Poughkeepsie Publishing Corporation.

The *Sunday Courier* was first published by Thomas G. Nichols in 1872, and has continued an unbroken existence to this day. Upon Mr. Nichols's death in 1890, Arthur G. Tobey assumed control until his death in 1911, when his son, Earle D. Tobey, became the editor. Mr. Earle D. Tobey supervised for a quarter of a century, a newspaper dedicated to the best interests of city and county. The *Courier* is now managed by his widow, Florence D. Tobey. It claims the distinction of being the only Sunday publication between New York City and Albany.

Intercollegiate Regatta

The famous Intercollegiate Regatta has familiarized the nation with the name of Poughkeepsie. For two days the city is host to thousands of visitors from all parts of the country. From many years of exeperience, the plans of entertainment and accommodations have been perfected, and these days have a definite place on the municipal calendar. The outstanding competitors that have appeared in recent years include California, Columbia, Cornell, M. I. T., Navy, Pennsylvania, Syracuse, Washington and Wisconsin. The recent victories of the Washington crew have attracted a large group from the Pacific Coast.

The three races—Freshman, Junior Varsity, and Varsity are scheduled at one-hour intervals late in the afternoon of a mid-June day, the exact time determined by the tide. The setting is one of the most beautiful that can be imagined, and the scene a pageant of rhythm and color. The race course includes an imposing section of the river valley—the two bridges spanning the stream between the rocky bluffs with patches of woods on the west, and the broken slope of the city waterfront on the east. On the west shore observation cars, crowded to capacity, follow the races from start to finish. Great crowds stand on the bluffs and bridges. All available motor space is packed with cars. Yachts, launches and row boats are anchored in the river, leaving only space for the race course. Boats fly flags and the gay college banners. At the signal, a bomb fired on the railroad bridge, a slow procession starts down the river. Appearing as tiny specks in the distance the long, slender shells slip smoothly down the channel under the two bridges toward the finish, accompanied by the cheers of the spectators and the blowing of sirens and whistles from the boats.

Three times the spectacle is repeated, consuming in all about three hours. After the last race, bets are paid, the river traffic scatters, and the crowds on the shore begin a tediously slow but good-humored exodus: the crowd on foot mills around, cars move at a snail's pace; vendors of pennants and souvenirs offer their wares at sacrifice prices. In a few hours the river scene is quiet; by morning the city has resumed its normal routine.

The date given for the first modern intercollegiate regatta at Poughkeepsie is 1895. But the local history of this and allied sports goes back far beyond that year.

Crew and single sculling races have taken place here for a century. Another sport still more closely identified with Poughkeepsie was the ice yachting which flourished from 1807 to 1908, the modern form of which is said to have originated here.

In 1807 the ice yacht was first introduced as a racing craft by Zadock Southwick and was subsequently made known to the world through the activities of the Poughkeepsie Ice Yacht Club. In 1858 the skate boat was developed, and experiments were made with various kinds of steel runners and different cuts of sails. The type ultimately accepted was designed by Jacob Buckhout, who has been called the "creator of the modern ice boat." *(See Chelsea.)*

The Poughkeepsie Ice Yacht Club, representing the first formal organization of the sport, was founded by prominent Poughkeepsians in 1861. Its headquarters were in the Vassar Brewery until the brewery closed. Then it merged with the Hudson River Ice Yacht Club at Hyde Park, where all ice-boating activities have centered since establishment of the all-winter Poughkeepsie ferry in 1908.

Most famous of the old craft were the *Icicle* and the *Haze* of John A. Roosevelt and Aaron Innis, the former of which won the American iceboat pennant in 1903.

In the last 20 years, the growth of Albany as a port and the consequent employment of ice breakers between Albany and the sea throughout the winter, have virtually put an end to ice boating on this part of the Hudson. Only exciting memories of the sport remain.

The first recorded rowing regatta held on the Hudson at Poughkeepsie was rowed August 11, 1839, by the "Washington" crew of Poughkeepsie and the "Robert S. Bache" crew of Brooklyn over a 2-mile course, the Poughkeepsie crew winning. Subsequent early races were for a time rowed at Newburgh, but interest in the sport began definitely to center in Poughkeepsie after the staging here in September 1860, of a 2-day regatta in which Poughkeepsie crews won all events in both four- and six-oared races. In November of the same year occurred the celebrated race between Joshua Ward of Poughkeepsie, American single scull champion, and William Berger of Newburgh over a 10-mile course. Three thousand spectators on the riverbanks watched Ward win.

Poughkeepsie's great boat of the Civil War period was called the *Stranger,* with a crew organized from employees of local cooperages. Its last and most celebrated race, July 18, 1865, was against the boat rowed by the Biglin crew representing New York, over a 5-mile course for a $6,000 purse and the American championship. As 20,000 spectators watched from the riverbanks, the *Stranger,* after trailing over a large part of the course, reached and began to pass the Biglins, but was cut off and came in second. Because of the interference, however, the *Stranger* was declared the victor. Referee and judges were chased by an infuriated crowd into the Poughkeepsie Hotel and barely escaped with their lives. The decision was finally reversed and given to the New York crew. For days before and after this race the town seethed with unprecedented brawls and disturbances.

The Shatemuc Boat Club, the first of its kind in Poughkeepsie, was organized in 1861, with headquarters in a canal boat anchored off the Upper Landing. *(See p. 42).* In 1870, after the canal boat had been dashed against the rocks and wrecked, a new boathouse was built, which the club used until its dissolution in 1878. In 1879 the building was reopened by the Apokeepsian Boat Club, a new organization of 40 members, which, with club socials, minstrel entertainments, and regattas, soon became prominent in the social life of the town. After a long decline, this club was dissolved in 1929.

Just before the World War the advent of the motorboat and the automobile put an end to sculling as a diversion in Poughkeepsie.

Service clubs include Rotary, Kiwanis, Lions and Exchange Clubs and a Chamber of Commerce. Notable among the service clubs is the Women's City and County Club, at 112 Market Street, the former residence of the late Laura Wyley, for many years professor of English at Vassar College, and a leader in local civic affairs. The Club has a county-wide membership of 300. The social clubs include the Amrita Club, Market and Church Streets, organized in 1873, and has a present membership of 250; and the Germania Singing Society, with a membership of 370, occupying Germania Hall, 197 Church Street, organized in 1850.

History

The Indian original of the name Poughkeepsie, mentioned in early documents with a great variety of spellings, has been the subject of much research and century-old disagreement among historians. Throughout the last century it was popularly supposed to be *Apokeepsing,* translated as "safe harbor" and referring either to the little cove at the mouth of the Fallkill or to the broad indentation which originally extended from the Slange Klip· to Kaal Rock. However, *Pooghkeepsingh,* translated as "where the water falls over" and applied to the falls of the Fallkill, later came into favor. Extensive research in recent years by Miss Helen Wilkinson Reynolds, with the assistance of the Heye Foundation of New York, has, however, established the *Rust Plaets,* a small marsh opposite the Rural Cemetery, as being the *uppugh ipis ing* or "reed-covered lodge by the little water place," to which enough early documents refer to place it beyond reasonable doubt as the source of the modern name. The present spelling of Poughkeepsie, despite the numerous haphazard renderings of the late seventeenth and early eighteenth centuries, has remained uniform since about 1760.

The first record of white settlement within the city limits is a deed of 1683 conveying land from an Indian, Massany, to two Dutchmen, Pieter Lansing and Jan Smeedes. This property appears to have been centered on the river front near either the Fallkill or the Casperkill, as the intent of building a mill is mentioned in the deed. Overlapping grants and purchases, delimited in the vague phraseology necessitated by an unsettled and only half explored region, led to several territorial disputes.

Although the first settlers in Poughkeepsie, as elsewhere, clung to the riverbanks, usually where a creek provided shelter and offered power for gristmills, the location of the town center was determined chiefly by the passage of the King's Highway from New York to Albany, authorized by the legislature in 1703. The courthouse, a church, and a cluster of houses were built about the intersection of the present Main and Market Streets, which is still the business center.

The growth of Poughkeepsie in the first half of the eighteenth century exceeded that of Dutchess County as a whole, but was none the less relatively slow. The first census, 1714, numbered 170 persons, of whom 15 were slaves. Except for a dozen French Huguenots and Englishmen, this population was entirely Dutch, although all public records were regularly written in a hybrid and phonetic English. The first courthouse, authorized in 1715 and again in 1717, was probably completed in 1720. In 1725 the Van den Bogaerdt farmhouse on the site of the present Nelson House, was opened as an inn. The first ferry was established between Barnegat (Camelot station) and Milton in 1740.

In 1716 the Reformed Dutch congregations were organized in Poughkeepsie and Fishkill. The Poughkeepsie church was completed on the present southeast corner of Main and Market Streets in 1723. For 40 years, however, the English population was too small to attract even the occasional services of a missionary of the Church of England, and it was not until 1766 that Christ Church was organized, the first church edifice being built on the site of the present armory in 1774. The church glebe and glebe house which are held jointly by the congregations of Poughkeepsie and Fishkill, date from 1767.

Poughkeepsie was not involved in Revolutionary activities. No battles were fought in this vicinity, and only two cannon balls are said to have struck the town during the British invasion of the Hudson Valley. Two events, however, are memorable. On March 25, 1775, the first American liberty pole in Poughkeepsie was raised at the house of Col. John Bailey. Moreover, of the 13 frigates authorized by the Continental Congress, two, the *Congress* and the *Montgomery*, were built and launched here in 1776 at Fox's Point, and sent to Kingston for rigging. However, these ships never left the Hudson. In the fall of 1777, when the British advanced up the Hudson and burned Kingston, both ships were sent out to defend the chain across the river at Fort Montgomery, and were fired to prevent their falling into the hands of the enemy.

In 1777, after the burning of Kingston and the subsequent withdrawal of the British from the Hudson Valley, Poughkeepsie became the capital of the State. Gov. George Clinton made his residence here, where it is probable he entertained both Washington and Lafayette, and where Kosciuszko called on him to offer his services in the Revolution.

During the winter of 1778-9 a regiment of Continental troops was quartered here against the remonstrances of Clinton, who believed that the supplies of food were inadequate for both soldiers and legislators.

Possibly the chief event in the history of the town was the ratification here by the State of New York of the Constitution of the United States. This event took place July 26, 1788, in the third courthouse. In 1784 the legislature began to hold its sessions in New York, although the State officers appear to have remained in Poughkeepsie for some time longer. Fifteen years later, in 1799, a resumption of the normal growth of the little community, with its population of about 1,000, was marked by its incorporation as a village.

Among eminent Poughkeepsians of this time was Chancellor James Kent, who came here in 1781 to study law. Soon afterwards he married and established himself in what, by his own account, was a very charming cottage. In the election of 1792, Kent was an advocate of Jay, and local partisanship for Clinton was so strong that he moved, reluctantly, to New York. The next year he was defeated for Congress by his brother-in-law, Theodorus Bailey, also of Poughkeepsie. In his *Memoirs* Kent speaks of the "great men who visited there (Poughkeepsie) ....Washington, Hamilton, Lawrence, Schuyler, Duer . . ." John Adams, in his *Diary,* mentions a brief visit to Poughkeepsie.

Early in the nineteenth century the increased cultivation of the hinterland and the establishment of local factories brought Poughkeepsie into considerable prominence as a river port. From several busy landings eight large sloops sailed weekly to New York, transporting Dutchess County grain to the metropolis and bringing back supplies and settlers for the provinces. The crooked roads leading down to the river, of which only Union Street now remains unaltered, were often choked with teams waiting their turn to load or unload.

In 1814 Poughkeepsie became the first steamboat terminal between New York and Albany. The general introduction of steamboats about this time, and towboats a decade later, which permitted passengers to ride out of danger from exploding boilers, proved a further stimulation to the commerce of Poughkeepsie; and the improved "team-boat" ferries, introduced in the year 1819, gave the town an important position in the route of westward migration. With the opening of the Erie Canal in 1825, however, western competition caused a decline, continuous to the present time, in the value of Dutchess County produce, and accordingly in the commercial importance of Poughkeepsie. Passage of the Hudson River Railroad in 1850 was a further blow to local shipping interests, because, while it opened the New York market to Dutchess County dairying, it effectually ended the export of local wheat.

To counteract these changes and hasten the inevitable transition from transportation and commerce to industry, the Poughkeepsie Improvement Party was founded about 1830. Composed of prominent local business men, this group was very influential in directing the activities of the town at large, initiating industries, establishing schools, and even laying out whole streets and sections of the town. Mansion Square Park, was sponsored by the Improvement Party as a residential inducement. The Improvement Party went out of existence with the panic of 1837.

The striking development of the 1830's, one the modern visitor would scarcely guess, was the short-lived but intensive period of whaling. This industry employed at one time seven ships, kept the docks above the Upper Landing humming, and caused the erection of several of the fine water-front mansions which industrial developments were later to mar or raze.

Another short-lived but interesting enterprise of the same period was the attempt of the Poughkeepsie Silk Company to produce raw silk from silk-worm cocoons on mulberry trees planted near the junction of Delafield Street and the Albany Post Road. The company collapsed in the panic of 1837.

In the same decade Poughkeepsie acquired a reputation as an educational center by the establishment here of more than a dozen private schools. Best known were the Poughkeepsie Collegiate School, the Poughkeepsie Female Academy, Mrs. Congdon's Seminary, and Miss Lydia Booth's Seminary. *(See Vassar College, p. 54.)* In 1836 the old Dutchess County Academy moved into larger quarters in the building now occupied by the Old Ladies' Home. This sudden efflorescence induced Harvey G. Eastman of St. Louis to move here in 1859 for the purpose of founding the Eastman Business College, which, after an enrollment at one time of 1,700 students, closed in May 1933. Vassar College, the one institution of Poughkeepsie known throughout the country, was founded in 1861.

In 1854, the year Poughkeepsie was granted a city charter, Henry Wheeler Shaw, the "Josh Billings" of Yankee humor, took up his permanent residence here. Although he established himself as an auctioneer, he began here his career as a writer under the original nom-de-plume of Efrem Billings, which he soon changed to its classic form. Most of his books were written in Poughkeepsie. He contributed to local newspapers, took an active interest in civic affairs, and in 1858 was elected city alderman from the fourth ward.

The Civil War was ardently supported by Poughkeepsians who had given Lincoln an overwhelming majority in the election of 1860. Company E of the 30th Regiment, the first company raised in the city, fought at Bull Run, South Mountain, Antietam, and in other important battles. The 150th Regiment, recruited from Poughkeepsie and the vicinity, was in action at Gettysburg, where 7 of its men were killed and 22 wounded, and was also with Sherman on the famous march to the sea.

After the assassination of President Lincoln, the train bearing his martyred body passed through Poughkeepsie on its way to Illinois. Virtually the whole population of the city assembled along the tracks to stand in awed silence as it passed. Draped in black, with muffled wheels, it ran noiselessly except for the tolling of the engine's bell, and was long remembered as the "Ghost Train."

After the Civil War, Poughkeepsie entered a period of rapid industrial expansion. Factories began to spread along the water front, transforming its earlier character and substituting a multitude of warehouses, factories, and docks for the ordered system of landings, roads, and residences which had hitherto prevailed. Families of wealth and social position deserted the lively and picturesque slopes west of the Post Road for the undeveloped tracts to the southeast, entrenching themselves on the eminences of Academy Street and spreading out over the Hooker Avenue section. In Poughkeepsie, as elsewhere at this time, the "residential districts," newly created in costly and complex structures of brick and frame along new, characterless streets, established themselves in conscious opposition to the organic but unpredictable development of older quarters. Of the same period are the various philanthropic institutions, housed in the characteristic buildings of dull red brick, to be found in the various sections of the present town.

Arlington

Arlington is a vaguely defined suburb lying within the township of Poughkeepsie, just east of the city. Its center is approximately the corner of Main Street and Raymond Avenue. Its location adjacent to Vassar College has been the chief cause of its development. It is a village community with small, frame houses, stores, two churches, and two schools. Many of the residences are opened to guests of the college on weekends and gala occasions. Shops catering to college tastes line College View Avenue and the east side of Raymond Avenue. On the west, near the Main Street corner, a large modern garage stands as a monument to the march of time—its proprietor the owner of stables which for many years have furnished saddle horses for Vassar students.

In Revolutionary times the Arlington section was known as Bull's Head, a name derived from that of a local tavern. Tory and Indian raids on the other side of the Hudson are said to have caused many families to settle here. John Holt, official State printer, appears to have lived here after his escape from New York in 1776.

Among the earliest settlers were Bernardus and Johannes Swartwout, the latter of whom had a mill on the Casperkill, the small stream which is now dammed to form Vassar Lake. The same Johannes Swartwout may well have been the father of Capt. Abraham Swartwout of Poughkeepsie, who gave his blue cloak to make part of the first American flag used in battle—in the defense of Fort Schuyler in 1777.

In 1872, the name Bull's Head was condemned as undignified and replaced by the name East Poughkeepsie, and about 1900 changed again to the present name of Arlington.

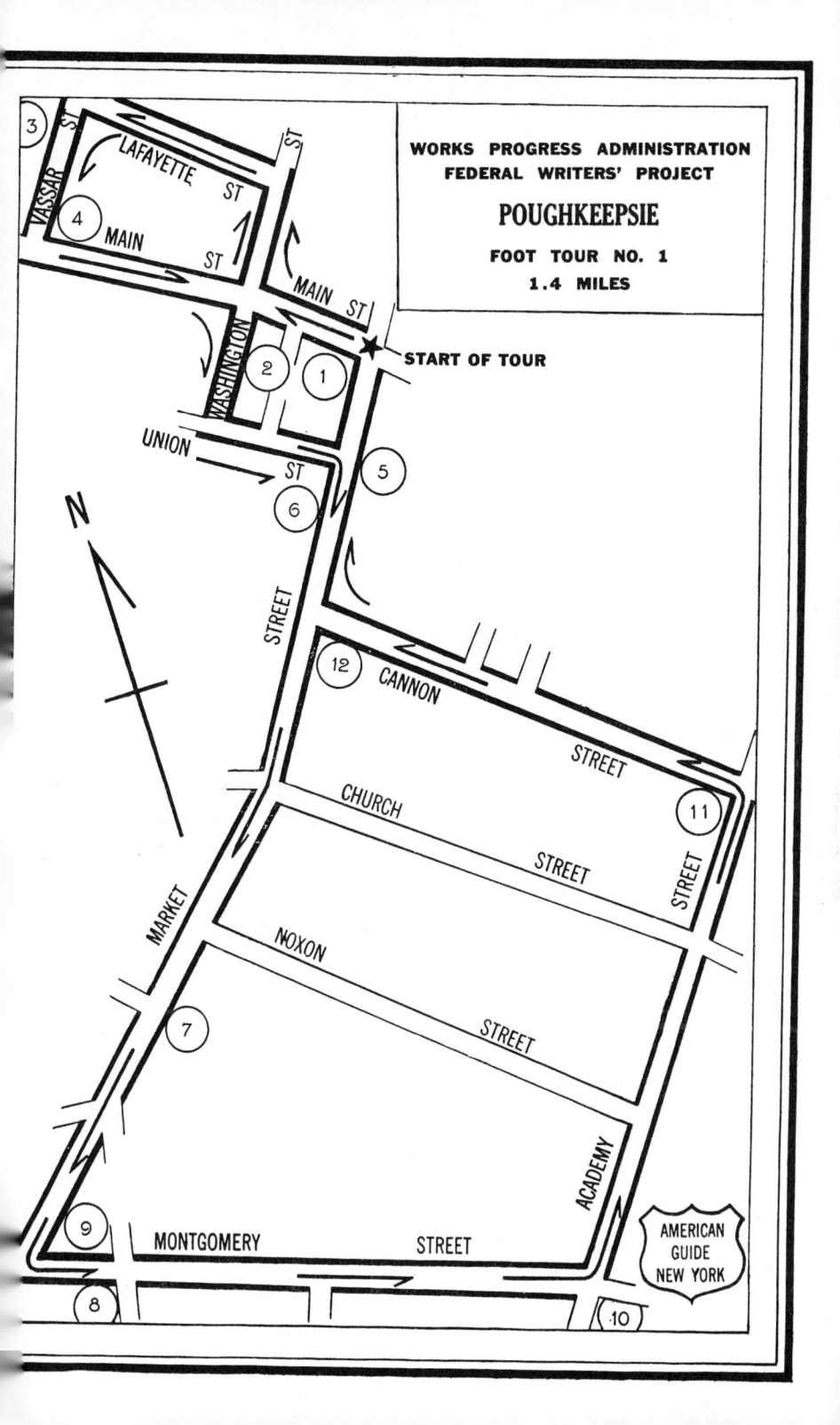

WORKS PROGRESS ADMINISTRATION
FEDERAL WRITERS' PROJECT

POUGHKEEPSIE

FOOT TOUR NO. 1
1.4 MILES

START OF TOUR

AMERICAN GUIDE NEW YORK

FOOT TOUR 1 (1.4 m.)

1. The DUTCHESS COUNTY COURT HOUSE stands at the business center of Poughkeepsie, at the intersection of Market St. (the Post Road) and Main St. It is a three-story-and-attic structure of red brick with gray sandstone trim. A mansard roof of red tile is softened by a balustrade crown. The interior walls and staircases are lined with white marble in the typical courthouse manner. Built in 1902, it stands on the site of four former courthouses, the first of which, erected before 1721, was the original Dutchess county Court House authorizen by the 16th Colonial Assembly in 1715 and 1717. The second and considerably larger structure, authorized in 1743, when the first had fallen into hopeless disrepair, became the temporary State Capitol after the burning of Kingston; this historical edifice was destroyed by fire in 1785. A third courthouse was in use by the end of 1787, and in it, on July 26 of the following year, the State of New York, after bitter and prolonged debate, ratified the Constitution of the United States. *(See p. 14.)* This building fell prey to fire in 1806, and was followed in 1809 by a fourth and still larger courthouse, which stood until razed to make way for the present structure.

From the Market St. intersection, W. on Main St.

2. The CITY HALL (L), at Main and Washington Streets, a modest gray-painted brick building of the Greek Revival type, is the only civic structure in Poughkeepsie of much architectural interest. Built in 1831, it was intended to serve as the village hall and market. The market and fishstalls which occupied the ground floor were discontinued shortly before the Civil War, and the whole interior altered. In 1865 the ground floor was reconstructed to serve as a temporary post office, and the Common Council met in the northwest room of the second floor. Part of the second floor was used for some time as a classroom of the Eastman Business College. The police station and city court in the rear were added after the Civil War.

R. from Main St. on Washington St., L. on Lafayette Pl., L. on Vassar St.

3. The VASSAR BROTHERS INSTITUTE (R), Vassar Street and Lafayette Place *(open daily 1-5; admission free),* houses a museum of natural history, a natural science and historical library, and an auditorium.

Fauna, Indian relics, and fossils collected locally are exhibited. On the first floor is a large and interesting group of insects. In the auditorium a series of travelogues and lectures on geography are given during the winter, usually on Tuesday evenings. The second floor has a large arrangement of animals, butterflies, and birds in their natural habitat, Indian artifacts, and fossils of the Hudson Valley.

The red brick building is constructed in a style which might, for local purposes, be called Vassar architecture of the Civil War period, since all the institutions donated by the Vassars are built in the same style. This building was erected in 1881 on the site of the old Vassar brewery by the brothers, John Guy, and Matthew Vassar, Jr., to promote knowledge of science, literature, and art.

4. The VASSAR BROTHERS HOME FOR AGED MEN (L), Main and Vassar Streets, stands on the site of the home of Matthew Vassar, founder of Vassar College. Established in 1880 by John, Guy, and Matthew Vassar, Jr., the institution is equipped to care for 21 elderly men. To be admitted, an applicant must be of good character, a resident of Poughkeepsie for five years, at least 65 years old, and of Protestant faith. An admission fee and the transference of all personal property to the home are further conditions.

Matthew Vassar, one of the two sons of James and Anne (Bennett) Vassar, was born April 29, 1792 in East Tuddingham, England. In 1796 James Vassar with his family migrated to America, settled in Poughkeepsie, and entered business as a brewer. Matthew Vassar followed his father in the business, and in 1813 married Catherine Valentine, who died in 1863 leaving no children. Matthew Vassar died in 1868, seven years after he had founded Vassar College. *(See Vassar College, p. 54.)* Following his example, his nephews, Matthew Jr., and John Guy, sons of his brother Thomas, became prominent in the community, founding and endowing a number of institutions in Poughkeepsie, and making further gifts to Vassar College.

L. from Vassar Street on Main Street, R. on Washington Street, L. on Union Street.

5. SMITH BROTHERS RESTAURANT, 13 Market Street, opposite Union Street, a landmark in epicurean circles, is unique in that its early development fostered the candy enterprise which later became the widely known cough drop business now conducted by Smith Brothers, Incorporated, at North Hamilton Street. The spacious dining room, with its great mirrors and portraits of the Smith brothers, "Trade" and "Mark," preserves an atmosphere of substantial dignity.

The establishment grew from a small restaurant started by James Smith, a Scotch-Canadian who came to Poughkeepsie in 1847. At his death, his sons, James, Jr., and Andrew, inherited the business. In 1876 William W. Smith succeeded James Jr., and his descendants still own it. The restaurant has always been conducted under a policy of strict temperance.

6. The NELSON HOUSE, 28 Market Street, is the oldest hotel in Poughkeepsie. Since 1777, under various names and owners, an inn has been uninterruptedly maintained on this site, and before the Revolution the Van den Bogaerdt farmhouse, which stood here, was used as an inn from 1725 to 1742.

During the years when Poughkeepsie was capital of the State (1778-83), most of the State and local officials made their headquarters in the inn opened here in 1777 by Stephen Hendrikson. Governor Clinton paid Hendrikson for a room used by the State Council of Revision in 1778.

The famous British spy, Huddlestone, after being captured at Yonkers in 1780, was brought to Poughkeepsie and hanged on Forbus Hill, behind the inn. The chief use of this hill in Revolutionary times, however, was as a vantage point for lookouts for river sloops, to ensure travelers' connections from the inn.

Hendrickson's Inn, having been enlarged from one and one-half to three stories in 1813, and, as the Forbus Hotel, to four in 1844, was torn down in 1875, and a new one, now the central part of the Nelson House, built. The following year it was renamed in honor of Judge Nelson, a former owner of the property.

Another famous hostelry, which served from 1886 to 1917 as an annex of the Nelson House, was the old Poughkeepsie Hotel. Lafayette, Henry Clay, Aaron Burr, Martin Van Buren, and many other distinguished men had been among its guests. It stood on Main Street, at the point where New Market Street now crosses. It was razed in 1917 to make way for the street.

7. The ADRIANCE MEMORIAL LIBRARY, Market Street between Noxon and Montgomery Streets, is a handsome, white, marble-faced building in French Renaissance style. It contains 85,000 volumes, the number being normally increased annually by about 1,500. Included in the library are noteworthy collections on local history.

The building, designed by Charles F. Rose of Poughkeepsie and erected in 1898, was a gift to the city from six children of John P. and Mary Adriance as a memorial to their parents. Market Street continues as a right fork at Soldiers' Monument.

L. from Market St. on Montgomery St.

8. EASTMAN PARK, an 11-acre recreational area, is entered at South Avenue (Post Road) and Montgomery Street. Its chief feature is the baseball diamond on which games of the twilight leagues and county championships are played. A field is flooded in winter for ice skating. There are two tennis courts.

Purchased in 1865 by Harvey G. Eastman, the low-lying marshy land was drained and developed as a private estate. In 1867, with a display of Chinese lanterns and fireworks, and an address by Horace Greeley on temperance, the park was formally opened to the public. Forty-two years later it became city property by gift of C. C. Gaines, who had married Mr. Eastman's widow.

The old Eastman mansion on Montgomery Street, near the entrance, is now used as the office building of the Poughkeepsie Board of Public Works.

9. The SOLDIERS' MONUMENT (L), opposite the main entrance of Eastman Park, an ornately figured fountain, was unveiled July 4, 1870, with a parade and a balloon ascension in the park, in honor of the soldiers of the Civil War.

10. CHRIST CHURCH (Episcopal) comprises a striking group of English Gothic edifices of red sandstone standing in well-shaded landscaped grounds facing Academy Street to the right of its intersection with Montgomery Street. The church building was erected in 1888 and the tower added in 1889. The Tudor rectory was built in 1903. Christ Church was established in 1766, and the first church building was erected in 1774 on the site of the present armory at Church and Market Streets.

L. from Montgomery St. on Academy St.

11. The site of the DUTCHESS COUNTY ACADEMY, (L), the first academy in the county and the first secondary school in Poughkeepsie, is at the southwest corner of Cannon and Academy Streets. Founded in Fishkill in 1769, the school was transferred to Poughkeepsie together with its original building, in 1791. Academy Street was named for the School.

Although charging for tuition, the academy was partly supported by taxation and was under a Board of Regents. Its first principal was Rev. Cornelius Brower, pastor of the Dutch Reformed Church. In 1836 the large brick bilding at Montgomery and South Hamilton Streets, now owned by the Old Ladies' Home *(see p. 50)*, was erected for the academy which continued there until 1866.

L. from Academy St. on Cannon St.

12. The building of the WOMEN'S CHRISTIAN TEMPERANCE UNION, Cannon Street, erected in 1836, housed for 50 years the Poughkeepsie Female Academy. With its immense white columns, it is a grandiose example of the Greek Revival period of architecture. The academy remained one of the best known of Poughkeepsie's many schools until it closed in 1886. In 1889 the building was purchased by the W. C. T. U., largely through the aid of William W. Smith.

L. from Cannon St. on Market St., to Court House.

MOTOR TOUR 1 (3 m.)

The Waterfront

The waterfront includes the industrialized and now partly-abandoned region lying riverward from the tracks of the New York Central Railroad, bounded by the extensive enclosures of the city's two largest industries, the Dutton Lumber Company on the north, and the DeLaval Separator Company on the south. The whole scene is dominated by the river, with its two great bridges and its miscellaneous shipping, and by the two important railroad arteries which intersect here. The four river landings of the 18th century village are still accessible as, with some restrictions, are the docks and wharves of the modern city. This region was the site of the first settlement, and has remained the seat of the chief activities of the city throughout its history. On the river bluffs, almost squeezed out by encroaching industrial plants in all stages of repair, stand the once imposing dwellings of an earlier day, while behind them on the irregular streets are grouped haphazardly the frame houses and brick tenements of more recent times. Besides the many fine views of the river obtainable here, and the concentrated local history, the Poughkeepsie waterfront is unusually interesting for its contrasts and for the picturesqueness of its subtle compositions and colors.

From Courthouse, Main and Market Sts., N. on New Market St. to Mill St., L. on Mill St. to North Perry St. Park car on Mill St. and walk (R) 100 feet up Charles St.

13. The ARNOLD COTTON MILL *(visitors welcome)*, built in 1811, still stands in tolerable repair on the Keating lumberyard on

39

Charles Street. The old mill, built of field stone, is now the lower part of the central section of the main building. The waterwheel has been removed, and the course of the Fallkill, which powered it, gradually diverted to the north. The original cross timbers of oak and the one-piece oaken window frames remain. Cotton fabrics were manufactured here during the War of 1812, when the cessation of American coastwise trade necessitated the carting of raw cotton in wagonloads from Georgia. The mill failed because of the flood of imported goods consequent upon the peace treaty in 1815.

Return to car. At Dongan Monument Mill St. bears (R), and at next traffic light, (L).

14. The yellow walls of SAINT PETER'S CHURCH (R) AND SCHOOL (L), foot of Mill Street, stand amid tumbledown environs on a bluff above the tracks of the New York Central Railroad. This was the first Roman Catholic church in Dutchess County. The original structure, dating from 1837, faced west overlooking the river, and has been retained as the transept of the present church, erected in 1853, with additions made later. Of painted brick in a Renaissance style, this is one of the most strikingly situated of the city's buildings. A fine view of the railroad bridge, rising above power plant and gas tanks, extends to include the Mid-Hudson Bridge (L) outlined gracefully against the Highlands.

L. from Mill St. on Dutchess Ave.

As the road curves right beneath Saint Peter's and turns left into Dutchess Avenue, an impressive prospect of industrial structures opens to view. Along Dutchess Avenue, one of the oldest streets in the city, a number of picturesque old frame and brick houses are passed.

Across the railroad overpass, the route turns sharp (L) into North Water St.

The route here enters the water front proper, where dwellings have almost disappeared before the demands of commerce and manufacture.

15. The route proceeds left, but a right turn on North Water Street, into the short dead end of Hoffman Street, affords the best view of the docks and yards of the DUTTON LUMBER COMPANY, largest of their kind in the eastern United States. The company is an important distributor of domestic and foreign lumber. Ocean-going ships, huge cranes, and stacks of lumber spread along the half mile of water frontage, create maritime impressions rare at such a distance from the sea. These yards play a major part in the American building industry: vessels of all draughts ply here from the West Coast, Norway, and the U. S. S. R. And the sense of activity and the color of the scene are enhanced by the immediate presence of the busy railroad tracks and sidings.

As the route proceeds south along North Water Street, extremely slow driving will be repaid by views of a complex and vivid scene—bridge and gas tanks on the right, and left, across the tracks, the string of colorful houses along Dutchess Avenue, the desolate slope with its automobile graveyard, and beyond, Saint Peter's Church crowning the background.

(R) from North Water St. on Dutchess Ave.

16. The DUTCHESS AVENUE DOCK, a public landing, adjoins the long wharves of the Dutton Lumber Company. The scene from this point,

Dutch House, known as "Old Hundred," New Hackensack

Reformed Dutch Church at New Hackensack

Poughkeepsie Railroad Bridge from the Waterfront

Interior Woodwork of the Lewis DuBois House, Grays Riding Academy

doubtless one of the finest in Poughkeepsie, includes a splendid vista of the broad, busy river bounded by the smoke-plumed trains of the West Shore Railroad, behind which the horizon rises abruptly with the Highlands. Mile long freight trains cross the lofty bridges overhead in silhouette against the sky.

The Dutchess Avenue Dock had a brief but intense period of activity in the 1830's, when, at the height of the great American whaling industry, the Poughkeepsie Whaling Company was established here. This company was followed by a larger enterprise, the Dutchess Whaling Company, which maintained a fleet of seven ships, one of them, the *New England,* mentioned in Dana's *Two Years before the Mast.* The romantic calling was abandoned in 1844.

Back track to North Water St.; R. (S) on North Water St.

North Water Street continues a short distance between the railroad tracks (L) and the Slange Klip *(Dutch, snake cliff)* (R), crowned since 1894 by the power plant of the Central Hudson Gas and Electric Co., and then dips quickly to the historic Fallkill Creek, which empties at this point into the Hudson.

Pass under the Railroad Bridge.

17. The RAILROAD BRIDGE, by reason of which Poughkeepsie was long known as the "Bridge City of the Hudson," is part of the New York, New Haven & Hartford Railroad system. Begun in 1873, it was at the time a notable engineering achievement. The width of the river at this point is 2,608 feet, and the length of the bridge 3,094 feet. The roadbed is 214 feet above water level. Six masonry piers support the steel towers that carry the cantilever trusses of the river spans.

The erection of the bridge was the culmination of a quarter century of railroad construction linking Poughkeepsie with the four points of the compass. Promotion of the great enterprise was chiefly the work of Harvey G. Eastman, founder of the business college, and John I. Platt, editor of the Poughkeepsie *Eagle,* who conceived its possibilities as a link between the coal fields of Pennsylvania and the manufacturing cities of New England. A company was formed and incorporated under authority of a special act of Congress dated May 11, 1871. John F. Winslow, partowner of the first patent on the Bessemer steel process and the chief financial backer of Ericsson when the first *Monitor* was built, became president of the corporation. The act provided for a suspension bridge, but this, after thorough consideration, was judged impracticable because of the long span. In the face of strong opposition from the river-towing interests, Eastman succeeded in getting a bill passed authorizing the erection of piers in the river.

At this time the Pennsylvania Railroad, looking for an eastern connection, subscribed $1,100,000 of the total $2,000,000 required. Subsequent repudiation, caused by the panic of '73 and the death of the president of the road, resulted in delay. In 1876 the American Bridge Company of Chicago, accepted the contract, and built three timber caissons and one stone pier on the west shore. An accident to this pier proved so expensive that it ruined the company.

41

A Manhattan bridge company was subsequently organized to carry on the project, and the construction was sublet to the Union Bridge Company of New York City. The success of the cantilever bridge which this company had already built at Niagara Falls suggested the combined cantilever and deck-truss construction; Arthur B. Paine was general supervisor. On August 29, 1888, the last pin was driven in the cantilever span between Pier 5 and the east shore. The approaches were finished a few months later, and the first train crossed the bridge on December 29, 1888.

In 1904 the bridge and the lines connected with it came under the control of the New York, New Haven & Hartford Railroad. Three years later it was found necessary to make repairs and reconstruction at a cost of $1,500,000. Since its period of greater activity, during the decade before the World War, traffic over the bridge has registered a gradual decline. It is now used for freight only.

18. Directly north of the Fallkill, within the enclosure of the gas and electric company, stands the old, neatly painted stone and brick HOFFMAN HOUSE, which was bought by three Hoffman brothers from Col. R. L. Livingston in 1800. In its stone foundation and walls something may remain of the house of Col. Leonard Lewis, built in 1717. The interior has been completely altered.

19. Within the same enclosure, a few feet left, stands the OAKLEY MILL, a plain, gray-painted three-story building, a typical sturdy millhouse, built in 1810 by George P. Oakley. It is now used as a garage.

From the little bridge that spans the Fallkill *(Dutch, Val Kil, stream of falls),* there may be seen two of the conflicting sources from which the name Poughkeepsie has been traditionally derived. On the right, the mouth of the creek, which is said originally to have had three times its present flow, once afforded enough shelter to Indian canoes for the place to be named *Apokeepsing,* or "safe harbor"; on the left is the FALLS, called by the Indians *Pooghkeepsingh.* The old course of the stream has been diverted to the north by a factory building.

20. The mouth of the Fallkill (R) is the site of the old UPPER LANDING, at one time the busiest on the water front. This was the ferry dock from 1798, when the first regular service was introduced, until 1879. (From 1740 until the end of the century ferries also ran occasionally from Barnegat, 4 miles south of Poughkeepsie, to Milton). The first regular ferry, which plied from the Upper Landing to New Paltz, was a barge propelled by sail and oars in the hands of slaves. In 1819 a team-boat was introduced, which was propelled by four horses in a treadmill, making the crossing in 10 minutes. Strongly built and easily operated, the team-boat was considered a great advance over the earlier ferries. A lively expectation that it would prove commercially important to the town as a link in the route of the contemporary migration westward reached its peak in 1825 when an unfruitful movement was started to make New Paltz Landing the terminus of a great State highway to Buffalo.

The place became known as the Upper Landing about 1800, when it had become a center of freighting and manufacturing. For a score of years, sloops carrying freight and passengers sailed daily to New York. Barges, towed by steamboats, replaced the sloops in 1821, and in 1837 regular steamer service was introduced. Falling gradually into disuse through the mid-century, the landing became inactive after 1879.

The old mills gathered about the falls were razed by the New York Central Railroad to make way for its tracks, and the storehouses near the old landing followed in 1894 when the power plant was built on the site.

21. Just past the Fallkill are the huge brick buildings and yards of the ARNOLD LUMBER COMPANY (R), established in 1821, the only survivor of the many early industries of the Upper Landing.

22. The ARNOLD HOMESTEAD (L), 58 North Water Street, a weather-beaten frame house with central gable, was built about 1840 during the whaling boom. It rests on a terrace hemmed in by a brick retaining wall which is patched with stone where the stairway once descended.

23. Directly beyond, the yellow clapboard OAKLEY HOUSE (R), rooted on a bluff against the irresistible encroachment of industry, was built in 1807. Oakley was a local politician and businessman, best known as the chief promoter of lotteries in Dutchess County. The main entrance, with its original door frame to which a two-story porch has been added, now faces the north. Originally it was part of the western facade overlooking the river. This and the Arnold homestead, across the street, with all their dilapidation, still retain traces of their past splendor.

North Water Street continues between the railroad tracks and a vacant space which was once the site of the Matthew Vassar brewery. The approach to Main Street is of little interest except for occasional views of the Mid-Hudson Bridge.

R. from North Water St. on Main St.

24. The POUGHKEEPSIE-HIGHLAND FERRY, foot of Main St. on the river front. *(Two alternate ferries operate on half hour schedule. Rates: car, driver, and one passenger, 40c; additional passengers, 10c; children 5c.)*

25. MAIN STREET LANDING, foot of Main St. adjacent to the ferry slip on river front, is the only one of the four 18th century landings continuing in active use. Although noted under the name Caul (Kaal) Rock Landing on maps as early as 1744, it did not become important until 1811, when sloops were already sailing to New York from all the other Poughkeepsie landings. The landing proper is the chief public dock of the city. Adjoining it are the ferry slip and the dock of the Hudson River Day Line (R), and the office of the Central Hudson Steamboat Company (L). The last named occupies the old Exchange House built in 1834 and conspicuous for its rounded shingles.

Backtrack on Main St. (a short block) to Front St.; R. on Front St.

26. The new MID-HUDSON BRIDGE *(tolls: passenger automobile, including driver, 80c; extra passengers, each 10c; maximum fare, $1.00; trailer on passenger automobile, 20c; motorcycle with side car, 35c; children,*

43

seven years and younger, free. Book tickets at reduced rates) unites the east and west banks of the Hudson River at a point midway between New York City and Albany. The eastern approach is from Church and Union Sts. Immediately west of the bridge the highway spreads to form a Y. Its northern branch connects with Highland and the southern with US 9W on the west bank of the river.

The official permit for the building of the bridge was granted June 6, 1924, and the structure was formally opened in August, 1930. It was designed by Ralph Modjeski and Daniel E. Moran; the steel superstructure was erected by the American Bridge Company of New York City. The bridge is of the long suspension type, with the two river piers 1,500 ft. apart; each side span is exactly one-half the length of the center span; the entire length of the bridge is 4,530 ft. The west approach is by a highway 1½ miles long. The cables are suspended on steel towers rising 280 ft. above the piers, and surmounting these are large oval lights, the rays of which are visible for many miles. The design of the towers produces an impression of strength as well as of grace and beauty of line.

The river piers supporting the two steel towers are massive concrete columns faced with granite to a point 35 ft. below water level. The bridge has a 30-ft. roadway and a 4-ft. sidewalk on either side. The bridge floor is of concrete slabs with expansion joints.

27. **KAAL ROCK** (R), Front St. (Park car just S. of bridge and R. of highway and walk 150 ft. (R) to top of rock.) Both this bluff on which the Mid-Hudson Bridge rests, and the one a little north of it, are known as Kaal (older Caul) Rock (pr. *call; Dutch, Kaele Rugh,* bare back.) An erroneous tradition has it that passing ships were signalled or "called" from this eminence, and that the name was thus attached to it. In any case, one may well wonder in what way it is a rock at all, until considering the actual Dutch name "bare back," which describes the precipitous and naked fall to the river, and realizing that the present English name is merely a case of false etymology. In 1824 the visit of Lafayette to Poughkeepsie was celebrated with a great bonfire on Kaal Rock and salvos of artillery.

This, the highest point on the waterfront, affords a sweeping view of that part of the Hudson known to early Dutch settlers as the *Lange Rak,* or Long Reach, a straight sailing course of about 11 miles between Crum Elbow *(see Hyde Park, p. 89)* and a flat promontory called the Dannammer, on the west bank opposite the mouth of Wappinger Creek.

28. The **UNION LANDING**, a dead end at the foot of old, winding Union St. (right fork), was for 47 years after the Revolution the chief shipping point of Dutchess County wheat and other produce. In 1831 a steamboat still carried freight and passengers daily from this landing to New York, but soon afterwards it was entirely superseded by the Main Street and Upper Landings. The sequestered dock shows nothing of its old importance and activity.

In the hollow of Kaal Rock is a cluster of gasoline tanks, beyond which the rock juts forth again, supporting the square, gray building of the old brewery. Here again is a close-up view of the strong, graceful suspension bridge and the cantilever trusses of the railroad bridge.

The Poughkeepsie Yacht Club, tucked in at the south end of the old landing, is officially designated as the half-way point in the annual speedboat races from Albany to New York.

Backtrack on Union St. to South Water St.

29. The GREGORY HOUSE (L), Union and South Water Sts., built in 1841, is stranded stepless on its high bare basement in the wired enclosure of a factory. Long abandoned, the weatherbeaten brick house designed in the Greek Revival style consists of a receding two-story center fronted by a Doric-columned portico and flanked by one-story wings. The fine doorway still bears the street number. The interior has been altered to serve as a factory warehouse.

R. (S) on South Water St.

30. The route passes through the deep shadow of the grim, deserted red brick factory buildings (R. and L.) formerly occupied by the MOLINE PLOW COMPANY, well known as manufacturers of harvesting machinery. Inactive since 1922, it was at one time Poughkeepsie's largest industry.

31. The old SOUTHWICK HOUSE (R), South Water St., just beyond the Moline factory, stands among trees in one of the few early 19th century gardens remaining in Poughkeepsie. The large yellow frame house with its gambrel roof was built in 1804 or 1805 by John Winans. In 1807 he sold it to Zadock Southwick, an early tanner and builder of the first Hudson River ice-boat. The Southwick family still lives in it. The garden remains substantially as it was laid out by Zadock Southwick. In it is a thorn-locust tree more than 14 feet in circumference.

A short dead-end road (R) around the Southwick house leads to the old Southwick Landing. Here is an excellent view of the southern half of the Long Reach and of the two bridges to the north.

32. The DELAVAL SEPARATOR COMPANY (R) *(visitors welcome)*, at the end of South Water St. on the site of the LOWER LANDING, is the largest Poughkeepsie manufacturing establishment. The main product is the centrifugal separator used by dairy and oil industries.

The DeLaval property includes the sites of the old Henry Livingston estate of the 18th century and of FOX'S POINT SHIPYARD, where the Revolutionary frigates were built. *(See p. 31.)*

Sharp L. from South Water St. on Pine St.

> Pine Street leads through a long underpass to the intersection with Tulip Street (L) and Prospect Street (R). The tour here leaves the waterfront proper, although Prospect Street for almost a mile skirts the river behind long areas of factories and warehouses.
> A pleasant route back to the Court House is by Tulip and Union Streets. The latter winds from the Court House down to the Union Landing. Laid out in 1767, it penetrates the heart of the old and picturesque south side of the city.

45

33. LINCOLN CENTER, Lincoln Ave. and Pine St., a stark yellow frame structure standing on a low bluff in a small recreational park west of Eastman Park, is the settlement house of Poughkeepsie. It provides recreational guidance and facilities to the underprivileged children of this crowded district.

The first floor of the building contains a gymnasium, a playroom for babies, and a child welfare clinic. On the homelike and friendly second floor are a dining room and kitchen for the use of members, a game room, a small club room and a larger recreational room, and a radio room, for the use of young people unable to entertain at home. On this floor are displays of the handicrafts of members. A small club room and a pool room are on the third floor.

In 1936 the Mayor and Board of Aldermen authorized a **WPA** project for a gymnasium for boys which will leave the original house for girls' and children's activities. Other renovations and repairs have been financed by the **TERA** and the **WPA**.

The center is open to all residents of the city, children or adults, with no discrimination as to race, creed, or color.

Lincoln Center was started by Vassar students in 1917 as a play group for children. A house rented on Church Street provided space for handicrafts, games for little children, and gymnasium work for older boys, together with quarters for a city health nurse. In the influenza epidemic of 1918 it was the only social agency in the district prepared to meet the needs of the sufferers and report cases to the Board of Health.

In 1925 the old Riverview Academy building, a city-owned structure, was assigned by the common council to Lincoln Center for an indefinite period, with the provision that part of it be reserved for use as a city clinic. The reconditioning of the large frame building, which had been abandoned for 10 years, was accomplished by voluntary labor supplied by the unions of Poughkeepsie. Neighboring families assisted in cleaning the grounds.

Three paid workers, aided by various Poughkeepsians and by 60 Vassar students under weekly assignments, direct the activities of the 1,100 members. The older boys and girls are trained to assist the younger groups.

A striking instance of the effectiveness of Lincoln Center is shown in the reduction of juvenile delinquency in the district, which formerly had the highest percentage in the city and now has the second lowest, standing next to the privileged area. This is believed to have resulted entirely from the introduction of these recreational facilities.

L. from Pine St. on Market to Court House (end of tour).

MOTOR TOUR 2 (5.5 m.)

From Court House, Main and Market Sts., E. on Main St., L. on N. Clinton St.

34. Largest and by far the best known of the parks of Poughkeepsie is the COLLEGE HILL PARK, with main entrance on North Clinton Street, a finely landscaped area on the highest eminence of the city (375) ft.), offer-

ing unsurpassed views of the city and the surrounding country in a complete panorama bounded by the Highlands, the Catskills, and the Berkshires.

Facilities for public amusement include a nine-hole golf course, open daily from 7 a. m. to 8:30 p. m. on the northeastern slope of the hill. The course is kept in excellent condition for play. A tennis court adjoins North Clinton Street Picnic grounds, with tables and fireplaces, overlooking city and river on the west slope.

The drive up the hill offers a succession of expanding views. Below, to the southeast, lies Poughkeepsie spreading around to Arlington on the east with the Gothic turrets of Vassar College just visible in the southeastern distance. East and north, the broad plains and hills of Dutchess County extend to the distant Berkshires and Taconics, visible on clear days, which form the natural divide between New York and New England. The giant Catskills are banked in huge masses 40 miles to the northwest. On the south stands high Mount Beacon, its inclined railway and casino visible on clear days, from which the long Fishkill or Breakneck Range runs easterly along the southern horizon.

At the summit of the hill stands a STONE SOLARIUM of conventional Greek Doric design, a monument to Guilford Dudley, a local financier, who left a bequest to be used for the erection of a shelter at this spot. Additional funds were provided by the TERA and WPA. The architect was John P. Draney, of Poughkeepsie, and the work was completed in 1936.

The solarium stands on the site of the famous colonnaded building, an imitation of the Parthenon, which for 30 years housed the Poughkeepsie Collegiate School. This school in 1866 was renamed the Riverview Military Academy, military instruction having been instituted four years previously, and in 1867 was transferred from College Hill to a new site on Lincoln Avenue *(See Lincoln Center)*. The hill itself had already been sold to George Morgan in 1865 under the gavel of Josh Billings, auctioneer, *(see p. 33)*, and the building was reopened, though unsuccessful, as the College Hill Hotel. The subsequent plans of John Guy Vassar to establish posthumously an orphan asylum on the site were frustrated by the invalidation of the relevant clauses of his will.

South of the monument, on a large pedestal, is a bust of William W. Smith, cough-drop manufacturer, who in 1892 purchased the College Hill property and gave it to the city.

Rock gardens and greenhouses, in which plants for all the city parks are raised, lie on the slope east of the solarium. The most noteworthy display is of dahlias in August and September. Below the main greenhouse, the Clarence Lown Memorial Rock Garden contains, besides many more or less rare European plants, a bed at the base of which is calcareous tufa, in which Alpine and rock garden plants flourish.

The open reservoir on the north slope of the hill was formerly the main water supply of the city but now supplies only hydrants. A new reservoir, higher on the slope, is concealed from view. Both draw their water from the Hudson River.

L. from College Hill Park on North Clinton St., L. on Oakley St.

35. The FENNER HOUSE, Oakley St. (L), one and one-half story Dutch Colonial homestead with gambrel roof and dormer windows, was built by Thomas Fenner prior to 1815. Though the walls are weatherbeaten, the house is well preserved; and the fine, simple lines of the Colonial style still give it a real distinction.

R. from Oakley St. on Smith St., L. on Main St.

36. The CLEAR EVERITT HOUSE (L), White and Main Sts. *(open weekdays, 10 a. m.-12 m. and 3-5 p. m., admission free)*, a historic house-museum under the direction of the Daughters of the American Revolution, has been popularly believed to have been the residence of Gov. George Clinton from 1778 to 1783. Research by members of the Daughters of the American Revolution has failed to confirm the tradition, but it is said that original documents supporting it were destroyed by fire in Albany. Other sources indicate 448 Main St. as the Clinton residence.

According to early records, for a number of years the Clear Everitt property belonged to Udny Hay, an officer in the Continental Army, and the present house was built by him under remarkable circumstances. In 1780, Hay resigned his post in the army and, with his wife, came to Poughkeepsie as purchasing agent for the State of New York, buying at this time the Clear Everitt property from Hugh Van Kleeck, who had inherited it from Clear Everitt, his wife's father. A house then stood on it. Two years later this house was destroyed by fire, and the Hays rented the Glebe House *(see below)* while building a new one. Masons and carpenters being scarce during the war, Hay wrote General Washington for permission to use workmen from the army. This permission was granted and the present house was accordingly erected. In the cellar of Hay's rebuilt house as it stands today are huge hand-wrought beams, some of them charred; it may reasonably be assumed that these beams were saved from the original house built by Van Kleeck and used again when the army workmen reconstructed the building. A stone in the front wall marked "VK" doubtless also came from the older house.

Although dating from 1783, the Clear Everitt House is externally in the style of an earlier period. The attic section, like those of many early Dutchess County houses, is constructed of wood; the foundations, 2 feet thick, are of rough field stone, crudely laid, and held together with a mixture of clay and gravel with a minimum of lime. The walls of the house are of the same materials and workmanship as the foundations, though pointed up recently on the outside; and the typical Dutch doors are also suggestive of pre-Revolutionary Dutchess County.

The first floor is divided by a broad central hall, with a dining room and parlor on one side and a large reception room on the other. One of the four rooms on the second floor is a museum-bedroom, which contains 18th century furniture, including a canopied bed and two heavy armoires. The downstairs rooms, though fitted out roughly as a museum, do not represent any attempt at a reconstruction of the actual period scene. A number of original state documents and papers with signatures of both Governors George and DeWitt Clinton, pictures, Revolutionary relics and weapons, and 18th and 19th century furniture, are exhibited in the various rooms. The furniture includes Windsor, Hepplewhite, Sheraton, and Empire pieces, as well as two square pianos of early American make. There is also a large collection of household implements and dishes of Colonial days.

Probably the most notable piece in the collection is the south mantelpiece in the large reception room, saved from the pre-Revolutionary house of Henry Livingston (site of the present office of the Phoenix Horseshoe Works) when it was torn down in 1910. Slender double columns, narrower at their bases than at their tops, ornament each side of the mantel, and Greek urn designs are carved in the cornice board. The north mantel in this room, as indicated by the pineapple carvings, is probably from about 1800. The mantel in the east reception room is said to date from 1812, and that in the dining room has the oakleaf and acorn carving typical of American furniture of the period of 1790 to 1815.

The Mahwenawasigh Chapter of the Daughters of the American Revolution, chartered in 1894, obtained possession of the house in 1900 and transferred it in the same year to the State of New York. The society has restored and somewhat altered the exterior, installed and arranged the collection, and maintains the museum.

37. The GLEBE HOUSE, 635 Main St. *(admission free)*, built in 1767 as the rectory of the English Church, later Christ Church *(see p. 38)*, is probably the most charming house in Poughkeepsie. The simple story-and-a-half structure of red brick in the usual Flemish bond reveals indoor room and hall proportions that give an illusion of spaciousness common to the houses of its period but later lost. Two fine, large, cheerful rooms flank a broad central hall, well lighted by large window sashes with finely made and inconspicuous wood mullions, each with its ample fireplace. The rear room and the large square kitchen show an equal regard for space and freedom. A Dutch oven in the kitchen lies in the large chimney above another Dutch oven and firehole in the cellar. Upstairs a four-room attic split by a broad hall-landing presents a variety of floor levels and wall proportions due evidently to the numerous additions and remodellings to which the house has been subjected.

Under the custody of the Dutchess County Historical Society and the Junior League, much interior restoration has been carried out and the beginnings of a historical collection undertaken. Of the few pieces of furniture at present in the carefully painted and papered rooms, the most important is a large and very beautiful Hepplewhite sideboard. An equally beautiful handrail, strikingly suited to the gracious simplicity of the hall, though it dates probably from about 1810, borders the stairs.

The exterior of the house, showing at close view many restorations, conforms generally to the original. The lean-to in the rear and a small extension on one side, both of frame, are evidently later additions. The recessed front door and its porch, of Colonial design, are part of a recent restoration.

One of the oldest houses standing in the city, the Glebe house was built on land of the English Church in 1767. Its first tenant, the Rev. John Beardsley, was exiled 10 years later because of his Royalist leanings. For a few years thereafter it was occupied by Revolutionary officers, and served again as Christ Church rectory from 1787 to 1791. In 1796 Christ Church sold the house, which, under various owners, remained a private residence until 1929, when, by a popular subscription, it was purchased for the city. *Sharp R. from Main St. on Church St., R. on Market St. to Court House.*

Additional Points of Interest

38. The OLD LADIES' HOME, Hamilton and Montgomery Sts., occupies the large colonnaded red brick building of the old Dutchess County Academy. It is open to Protestants over 60, in good health, who have lived in Poughkeepsie at least 5 years. The admission fee is $500, and residents must transfer all their property to the Home.

The institution was founded in 1871, chiefly through the efforts of Miss Alice M. Fowler. The building and a permanent endowment fund of $20,000 were donated by Jonathan A. Warner. In 1897 the Home was enlarged and the endowment fund increased by W. W. Smith.

The building was erected in 1836 to house the Dutchess County Academy and was used by the Academy until its close in 1866. From 1866 until 1871 it was rented by the city for use as a public high school. Many of the original panes of glass, marked by the initials and scribblings of former Academy pupils, remain in the windows.

39. SMITH BROTHERS, INC., 134 North Hamilton St. *(visitors welcome),* are doubtless the best known cough drop manufacturers in the country. The business was established before 1850 by William Wallace Smith and Andrew Smith, the famous bearded "Trade" and "Mark." The two well-known faces were actual representations from photographs. The cough drops were first made in a basement by hand; now hand labor is eliminated, and they are manufactured by the ton in this modern factory built in 1914.

40. The DIVISIONAL PRODUCE MARKET, Smith St. just south of College Hill, a PWA project, providing a central distribution point for local produce, occupies 2 acres of graded and paved land easily accessible to all nearby State roads and adjacent to the Central New England Railroad. It was completed in the winter of 1936-37 as an adjunct to the considerably larger primary or regional PWA market in Newburgh.

41. The CITY HOME AND INFIRMARY occupies 32 acres of ground at Maple St. and Jewett Ave. North and east of the tree-shaded buildings in the style of the Civil War period lie 10 acres of cultivated fields bounded by a rocky slope used as pasture land. The group of buildings, of various dates, constructed to provide a cheerful and comfortable atmosphere, comprises the largest public institution of the city. The latest addition, completed under the PWA in 1936, is the infirmary, which was carefully planned to equal a modern private hospital in comfort and efficiency. The capacity of the Home, exclusive of the infirmary, is 120.

The City Home was placed in 1930 under the supervision of the Board of Public Welfare. From 1854 to 1900 the board which directed this work was known as the "Almshouse Commissioners," and from 1900 to 1930 as the "Board of Charities." In 1901 the old "Almshouse" became the "City Home." The purpose of the institution, little changed during the years, has been to care for people in temporary or chronic need, investigate cases of poverty, place the mentally or physically ill where they may receive care, and attend to transients. Since the enlargement of the infirmary, many cases of non-contagious diseases formerly sent to local hospitals have been adequately attended to in the Home.

42. The DUTCH REFORMED CHURCH, Hooker and Hanscom Aves., was built in 1922. Of native stone, it is in a style known as English Parish Gothic. The square tower appears to have been a tradition in the Dutch church buildings in Poughkeepsie, of which the present church is the fifth.

43. The PRINGLE MEMORIAL HOME, 153 Academy St., a three-story, yellow clapboard frame building with wide, white verandas, was organized in 1899 by Clarence Fenton as a home for "aged, indigent, literary and professional gentlemen." Originally a private house, it has nothing of the appearance of an institution. The name was given in memory of Mr. Fenton's aunt and uncle, who had left funds for the establishment of such an asylum. Membership is limited to nine. Applicants are required to be between the ages of 65 and 80 and in good health, and must pay an admission fee of $1,000.

44. HOUSE OF TIMOTHY COLE, 39 Ferris Lane. In this tiny gray stucco house with unusual rolling roof, Timothy Cole, world-renowned wood-engraver, lived from 1917 until his death in 1931. Cole was born in London, England, in 1852, and when 4 years old was brought to America by his parents. He was educated in New York and Chicago, but was a self-taught engraver. Developing his own technique, he became the great master of the white-line engraving. In 1875 he became a member of the staff of the *Century Magazine,* and was assigned by the publishers to make engravings of the paintings of the great European masters. He is best known for these reproductions, which have been published in book form with comments by the engraver.

The type of art Cole represented was brought to an end by the introduction of process engraving, but in the quality of his work, as in the delicacy and softness of his medium, he remains unsurpassed.

45. The QUAKER MEETING HOUSE, Hooker Ave. and Whittier Pl., is a simple, square red brick structure set in a neat lawn, shaded by a grove of Norway spruces. Designed by Alfred Bisselle of New York, it was erected in 1927. The general style of the 18th century Quaker meeting house has been followed, with its broad, harmonious proportions. The lines of the building, the Flemish bond, white marble trim, and white shutters, with the main architectural effect produced not by decoration but by proportion and tone, all approximate the Georgian type. The buff and white interior is neat and inviting.

Adjoining the meeting room on the left is a large Sunday school room, separated by an adjustable partition which permits the whole to be converted into a single commodious auditorium when occasion requires. The old practice of separating the sexes, usual in the prototypes of this meeting house, has been abandoned, so that the meeting room, with its attractive white pews and pulpit, is similar to the interiors of other churches.

The simple yard has been laid out with the same care apparent in the construction of the building. Well groomed conifers shade the street front. A low brick-and-marble terrace, before which stand two dainty Chinese poplars, bounds the shrub-planted lawn at the entrance.

46. VASSAR BROTHERS HOSPITAL, Reade Pl. and Lincoln Ave., stands in 32 acres of pleasantly cultivated grounds overlooking the Hudson. The red brick buildings are bordered by a limestone wall on the river side. It was founded by Matthew Vassar, Jr., as Vassar Hospital; but, in accordance with the provisions of his will, the name was changed when his brother, John Guy Vassar, added an endowment. The hospital was incorporated in 1882, and the main building erected in 1884. A library and laboratory building was erected in 1899, and the hospital capacity was nearly doubled by additions in 1907. The hospital maintains 225 beds and the usual services, carried on by a staff of 38 attending surgeons and physicians.

47. The LANE BROTHERS HARDWARE COMPANY, near the foot of Prospect St., was the third manufacturer of steam automobiles in America. Following the expensive Stanley and White steamers of 1894-5, the Lane machine, a lighter and cheaper model, appeared in 1900. Automobile manufacturing started here as a result of the delay of the Stanley Company in filling an order of William L. Lane, who, becoming impatient, decided to make his own machine. In 1901 the Lane car was awarded a first class certificate by the Automobile Club of America in the New York-Buffalo endurance contest. With the increase of gasoline powered automobiles, production of the Lane car was discontinued. The company, under another management and under the name Lanebro, continues other manufacturing in the same plant.

POINTS OF INTEREST IN ENVIRONS

48. The KIMLIN CIDER MILL, Cedar Ave., 1.3 m. from its intersection with Hooker Ave. *(open 10 a. m.-8 p. m. except Mondays; admission free)*, a local show place with "atmosphere," is a favorite rendezvous of Vassar College students. It houses the largest miscellaneous exhibit of historical and antiquarian collections in the vicinity of Poughkeepsie. Many of the mounted birds and animals have been acquired from Vassar Brothers Institute. *(see above.)* The innumerable antiques crowd the low-ceilinged rooms. Refreshments are sold, with cider a specialty.

49. The POUGHKEEPSIE RURAL CEMETERY occupies about 150 acres of woodland between the Post Road and the Hudson River, 1.5

miles south of the Court House. Non-denominational, this is the only large cemetery of Poughkeepsie. It was incorporated in 1853 and is privately owned by a plot-owners' corporation.

Attractive plantings, a charming pond, the partly cleared oak woods, and the magnificent views of river and city from the river bluff, more than compensate for the relative lack of historic interest in this cemetery.

In Section L, due west of the entrance gate, is the Vassar Acorn, so called from the sculpture adorning it, where lie the graves of Matthew Vassar, founder of the college, and his wife. The Livingston plot is surrounded by a hedge on the high ground in the northwest corner of the cemetery. The grave of Henry Livingston, an early land owner and a prominent figure in the Colonial history of Poughkeepsie, is surrounded by those of about 70 of his relatives and descendants, among them the eminent jurist, Smith Thompson. Nearby is the nursery, where many varieties of ornamental trees, shrubs, and grasses are grown.

A road winds up from the pond to Mine Point, a high bluff overlooking the river and offering an unsurpassed view of the entire long reach of the Hudson, 5 miles north to the bend of Crum Elbow and 6 miles south to the west bank promontory, Danskammer. This splendid expanse is framed on the west by the highlands of Orange and Ulster Counties; on the south and beyond Newburgh Bay, by Mount Beacon and the Storm King; and in the north distance, by the towering Catskills, visible on clear days. From this eminence the entire waterfront of Poughkeepsie is visible in clear perspective, with the two great bridges spanning the river to the left and the city spread out in wooded undulations eastward. Directly opposite, the high bluff on the west bank is the Juffrouw's Hook mentioned in many early documents.

The white marble mausoleum on the summit of Mine Point, conspicuous from the river and from the southern waterfront of the city, was erected recently as a private memorial. It was designed in a semi-modern style by Presbery Leland of New York. A railed terrace beneath the monument has been designated as the Lovers' Leap of popular tradition. Two young Indian lovers, thwarted by the chiefs of the tribe, are said to have leaped to death from this point.

50. SAMUEL W. BOWNE MEMORIAL HOSPITAL, Pendell Rd. just off Violet Ave. (State 9 F), *(visitors admitted 3-5 p. m. daily)* is a city-owned hospital for the treatment of tuberculosis. The hospital buildings are situated in a commanding position on a high knoll, the grounds including 32 acres of land. The present capacity is 135 beds, 52 of which, housed in the Preventorium, are for children, and 83 for adults. The hospital was opened in 1909 as a camp for those suffering from tuberculosis. In 1911 Mrs. Bowne, widow of Samuel W. Bowne, who had been a partner of Scott & Bowne, makers of Scott's Emulsion, erected the first of the present buildings in memory of her husband.

The Nettie Bowne Hospital on the same plot of land is a private sanitarium with 50 beds. Opened in 1928, it specializes in the treatment of chest diseases and cardiac troubles.

VASSAR COLLEGE

The Vassar College campus is open to visitors, who may inspect the buildings and grounds, including the gardens and arboretum. Upon application to the Message Center in the Main Building, a guide will be provided. The campus of the college is closed to automobiles on Sundays and holidays. This regulation is a tradition of the college in the interest of maintaining an atmosphere of quiet one day a week. Parking space is provided outside the college gate for the convenience of visitors.

Vassar College was founded by Matthew Vassar, a Poughkeepsie brewer, in 1861. The breaking out of the Civil War delayed the opening of the college until the fall of 1865. Though lacking a formal education himself, Mr. Vassar's innate wisdom led him to provide for others the advantages he had never enjoyed. He was influenced in his decision to found a college for women by his niece, Lydia Booth, and by Dr. Milo P. Jewett, head of the Cottage Hill Seminary in Poughkeepsie. Although he had many far-reaching ideas about the education of women which he expressed with complete freedom, at its first meeting Mr. Vassar transferred to the Board of Trustees all the funds for the college without restrictions or reservations.

One year before the opening of the college, Dr. Jewett resigned from the presidency and from the Board of Trustees; and the Board elected John H. Raymond, then president of the Polytechnic Institute, Brooklyn, as his successor. Since the organization of the college, the choice of faculty, and the determination of policy fell on Dr. Raymond, he is often spoken of as the first rather than the second president of Vassar.

The enrollment for the first year was over 300. In the second year four women received the A. B. degree: the two survivors of this class attended their 70th reunion in June 1937.

For three years Mr. Vassar enjoyed close touch with the college and the company of his "daughters." On the day before the commencement of 1868, he died while reading his annual address at a meeting of the Board of Trustees.

Dr. Raymond died in 1878. His successor, Dr. Samuel L. Caldwell, served for 7 years. During the 28-year (1886-1914) administration of Dr. James M. Taylor, the enrollment increased so rapidly that it was necessary to limit the student body to 1,000. In 1915, Dr. Henry Noble MacCracken was elected to the presidency, which he still retains.

The distinctive feature of the administration of Vassar College is its liberal democratic organization. The faculty is in control of educational matters. The students have self-government, an uncensored press, and are largely consulted in curriculum content. Through joint and advisory committees much responsibility is delegated to the community as a whole. The Students' Association, of which all students are members, charters various clubs, such as the Glee Club, the Art Club, and Le Cercle Francais, as well as the student publications, which include the *Miscellany News,* a semi-weekly newspaper, the *Vassar Review,* and others. There are no sororities at Vassar College.

Between classes the campus hums with bicycles operated under a system of licenses and traffic regulations administered by the students. There are no student-owned automobiles.

The religious life of the college centers in the Vassar Community Church. In accordance with the intention of Matthew Vassar, the college, while distinctly Christian in government, has no denominational affiliation. Attendance at all chapel services is voluntary. The daily chapel services are led by the faculty and students. For the Sunday services the church brings to the college prominent leaders of religious thought.

During the summer months the Vassar Institute of Euthenics provides six weeks of study, chiefly for college graduates who, as parents, teachers, or social workers, are interested in the problems of rearing children and the conduct of the family. During these six weeks the Wimpfheimer Nursery School holds a summer session, and trained teachers care for the children of mothers who are attending the summer Institute.

Among the 9,021 (1927) living alumnae of Vassar College are included women of distinction in various fields. Poetry has been represented by Adelaide Crapsey and Edna St. Vincent Millay, and literature by Constance Rourke. Pioneers and leaders in their chosen fields were Ellen Swallow Richards, Julia Lathrop, and Katherine Bement Davis. Administrative and executive positions are occupied by Josephine Roche, Ruth Taylor, and three college presidents: Katharine Blunt, Constance Warren, and Mildred McAfee.

From the time of Harriet Stanton Blatch, '78, a pioneer, through that of Inez Millholland Boissevain, '09, until suffrage was an accomplished fact, members of the college took an active part in the campaign for the enfranchisement of women. In addition to their contribution to the general field of education, Vassar students and alumnae have increasingly participated in social and civic affairs.

The Vassar student body is now limited to 1,150. The faculty numbers 180 members, who teach in 31 departments. Vassar draws its students from private and public schools throughout this country and from abroad. The curriculum, several times revised, maintains the principles of distribution and concentration as essentials in liberal education, but leaves the choice of particular subjects and of special fields to individual election. The curriculum is divided into four groups of subjects: the Arts, the Foreign Languages and Literature, the Natural Sciences, and the Social Sciences. Credit is given for applied art and music, for the writing and production of plays in the Experimental Theatre of the English department, and for participation in the Nursery School, used by college students as a laboratory for child study.

The aim of the plan of study is to secure for the student powers of self-direction, and to avoid the cramping effects of regimentation. The scope of the curriculum may establish direct connection with whatever life work the student may choose. If she plans a career in one of the professions, she may lay the foundation for further study. If her next step is to be a job, she may obtain training which will be invaluable when she comes to the problem of earning her living. If she looks forward to marriage, she may prepare herself fully for the responsibilities of a home and family and citizenship.

Tour of Campus

The 950 acres of land owned by the college include, beside the campus proper, a 9-hole golf course, two small lakes, a large farm, two large faculty residences, and 27 other buildings. On the campus are 18 academic buildings, 4 social buildings, and 8 residence halls, as well as gardens and an outdoor theatre seating more than 3,000. The Vassar College buildings, erected over a period of 70 years, are notable for their variety of architectural style.

The triple-arched gateway running through Taylor Hall (L) on Raymond Avenue, is the main entrance to the campus. TAYLOR HALL (1) houses the art department. Loan exhibitions are shown throughout the college year. Outstanding in the permanent collections are three bronze portraits by Jo Davidson; a bronze figure of a woman by Lachaise; several notable Rembrandt prints; water colors by Turner from the personal collection of John Ruskin; and a collection of the paintings of the Hudson River School, including some of George Inness. The most important paintings in the large gallery are: Taddeo Gaddi's *San Taddeo; St. John the Baptist* by Bartolomeo Vivarini; two Ulysses panels from the school of Piero di Cosimo; *View of the Scuola di San Rocco* by Marieschi; Mattia Preti's *Erminea and the Shepherds;* a *Landscape* by Salvator Rosa; a portrait by Pourbus; Courbet's *Jumping Jack;* and a *Landscape* by Wilson.

The gray, pinnacled THOMPSON MEMORIAL LIBRARY (2) was donated by Mrs. Mary Clark Thompson in memory of her husband, Frederick Ferris Thompson, a late trustee and friend of the college. Warmth of color is added to the gray stone and oak interior by five 17th century Flemish tapestries which tell the Cupid and Psyche story, and by a stained glass window in the west wing which represents the conferring of the doctorate upon a young Venetian woman by the University of Padua in 1678.

The library contains 200,000 volumes, including several valuable collections: the Justice collection of material relating to the periodical press, the Village Press collection printed by Frederic W. Goudy, of Marlboro, N. Y., and a Browning collection.

VAN INGEN HALL (3), a new wing connecting the Thompson Library and Taylor Hall, provides additional space for the art department and the main library.

The MAIN BUILDING (4) is one of the academic buildings completed before the opening of the college in 1865. James Renwick, Jr., architect of St. Patrick's Cathedral in New York, based his design on the famous Tuileries palace. To this old building clings much of the history of the college, and old graduates returning, although delighting in improvements to the interior, feel very much at home at the sight of old Main. Until 1893 practically all the students and many faculty members lived in this building.

Blodgett Hall Arch, Vassar College

Students' Building, Vassar College

Now it accommodates about 350 students, business and administration offices, the post office, the Cooperative Bookshop, the Raymond Reading Room, and several reception rooms.

ROCKEFELLER HALL (5) was designed by York and Sawyer of New York in modified early English Renaissance style. This building contains class and lecture rooms and offices for many of the academic departments.

Rockefeller Hall forms the southern end of the dormitory quadrangle with RAYMOND (6) and DAVISON HOUSES (7) on the west, and STRONG (8) and LATHROP (9) on the east, all very similar in architecture. Each houses about 95 students. Since 1933 Raymond has been a cooperative house, the students doing all the housework except the cooking. This plan was started because of the depression, but has proved so satisfactory that it is being continued indefinitely. Since no student may live in Raymond who is not doing satisfactory academic work, to be assigned to this house is an honor.

The quadrangle enclosed by these buildings is said to be the site of the field in which the daisies were picked for the first daisy chain carried by sophomores on Class Day.

MILO P. JEWETT HOUSE (10), another dormitory, closes the quadrangle on the northern end. It is constructed of red brick with white stone trimmings. The central tower, originally built to support a tank for the college water supply, was not tall enough to provide the necessary water pressure, but its height, compared with that of the other buildings, has brought it much unfavorable criticism. It commands a remarkable view of the surrounding country.

OLIVIA JOSSELYN HOUSE (11), which accommodates 132 students, was given by Mrs. Russell Sage in memory of her granddaughter. This dormitory, a red brick building, was designed by Allen & Collens in a modified Gothic style. Back of Josselyn to the north are tennis courts and a hockey field, shielded from the street by rows of lilac bushes.

The STUDENTS' BUILDING (12) reveals its purpose in its name. Designed by McKim, Mead, & White of New York, its architecture is as simple and dignified as the Colonial town hall from which it was derived. The interior is finished in white paneled wood. The auditorium, seating 1,200, is used for concerts and lectures. It contains a stage fully equipped for the plays given by Philaletheis, and furnishes ample space for the "junior prom" and other important dances. The auditorium is flanked by offices for the various student organizations, and the Council Room, for small student meetings, is on the second floor.

Students' Building faces the CIRCLE (13), a lawn encircled by flower beds, shrubs, and pine trees. In the early days of Vassar a Floral Society cultivated these beds. At a time when athletics as practiced today would not have been considered "ladylike" and yet one hour daily outdoor exercise was required, this work in the garden was very popular. Today, under the supervision of the Superintendent of Grounds, the Circle is one of the most beautiful spots on the campus. The lawn which it encircles is used as an athletic field for track, baseball, and archery.

CUSHING HOUSE (14), designed by Allen & Collens, is the newest dormitory. The exterior, constructed of red brick and half timber, is of Tudor design. The rooms, almost all single, accommodate 125 students.

HELEN KENYON HALL OF PHYSICAL EDUCATION (15), named for a member of the class of 1905, is of red brick and built on the unit plan. One of the four great wings built around the central dressing rooms is used for individual exercise and rhythmic work. In the other wings are basketball, tennis, handball, and squash courts and a large swimming pool. Under these courts run bowling alleys and an archery range.

The MILDRED ROSALIE WIMPFHEIMER NURSERY SCHOOL (16), a small gray stone building, provides classrooms and play equipment for about 30 children from the ages of two to five, who come from the families of the faculty and of residents of Poughkeepsie. The Nursery School serves as a laboratory for students taking courses in child study. In this school Vassar has made a very successful experiment in co-education.

The MINNIE CUMNOCK BLODGETT HALL OF EUTHENICS (17) furnishes facilities for education and research in the field of euthenics, a word which has been defined as "the application of knowledge to the betterment of human living." Blodgett Hall contains a demonstration theater, a large lecture hall, classrooms, laboratories for research, and studios for design and interior decoration. The north wing houses the physiology department with classrooms and a well-equipped laboratory. In this building a group of about 30 students live under a cooperative system. Under the supervision of the director of euthenics they order the food, which they cook and serve, plan the menus, and control entirely the expenditure for food.

The WARDEN'S HOUSE (18), with its cedar-hedged garden, is the private residence of the college warden.

The OBSERVATORY (19) is the only academic building beside Main finished before the opening of the college. First professor of astronomy was Maria Mitchell, distinguished, not only as a scientist, but also as an ardent advocate of woman suffrage. She was the first woman whose bust was placed in the Hall of Fame in New York. The first years of her life were spent on her native island, Nantucket, where she got her early training in the observatory of her father, William Mitchell. At the age of 10 she was both teacher and pupil in his school, and in her thirteenth year she was keeping records of his observations. Before she was 30, international fame came to her through discovery of a comet for which she received a gold medal from the King of Denmark. The degree of LL.D., conferred upon her by Hanover College, was probably the first degree of its kind ever conferred upon a woman by an American college. Professor Mitchell withdrew from active duties at the age of 70, less than two years before her death. A bust of her, the work of Emma Brigham, a former student, stands in a niche in front of the Observatory.

METCALF HOUSE (20) was given to Vassar in 1916 by former United States Senator and Mrs. Jesse Metcalf, of Providence, R. I., as an expression of gratitude to the medical department for the care given their daughter Cornelia during a serious illness. Miss Metcalf became the wife of New York State Senator Frederic H. Bontecou, of Millbrook. The building contains a pathological laboratory, an apartment for the resident physician, and rooms for convalescents and rest cases.

The SWIFT MEMORIAL INFIRMARY (21) is the hospital for members of the college family.

ELY HALL (22) is now the health center, with offices for the medical staff and the nurses' suite. It houses also three art studios and class rooms, offices, and a laboratory for the geology department. Its name recalls to those who knew her, one of Vassar's distinguished graduates, Achsah M. Ely, professor of mathematics, 1887-1904.

Back of Main are the buildings classed as the business group, including the laundry, the service building, and the heating plant. This last was the first central heating plant constructed in America. Nearby is the little ELEANOR CONSERVATORY (23) and the GOODFELLOWSHIP CLUB HOUSE (24), built by the Students' Association in 1902 as a club house for the employees of the college, both men and women. Here a trained supervisor lives, creating a home atmosphere for the members. She is assisted by students, who conduct classes, direct the annual Goodfellowship Club play, and often share in the social life of the house.

The Lombard Romanesque ALIDA C. AVERY HALL (25) is one of the three oldest buildings on the campus. Although it has borne several names and has been used in many different ways, its exterior is scarcely changed since the time it was built during the first year of the college. It was then called Riding School and Gymnasium, but contained also a bowling alley, rooms for the department of music, and rooms for the families of employees. The New York *Times* reported the Riding School as "the most beautiful in this country, second in size only to that of West Point." But in 7 years it proved a financial failure; and the student paper of January 1873, contains the following mournful item: "The glory of Vassar has departed. Its Riding School is no more. False economy. Would the Art Gallery be abolished if it did not pay?" Today the building contains the Experimental Theatre; its director, Hallie Flanagan, has been granted an extended leave of absence to carry on her work as National Director of the Federal Theatre Project under the Works Progress Administration. The building houses also the classrooms and offices of the Greek and Latin departments with their fine collection of ancient vases, glass, coins, armor, and household utensils;

the offices of the English department, and the classrooms, offices, and workshop of the classes in Dramatic Production.

South of Main stands the science quadrangle, the ground sloping away behind it to the Outdoor Theatre and the Shakespeare Garden. The earliest of these buildings is VASSAR BROTHERS LABORATORY (26), given for the use of the departments of chemistry and physics by the two nephews of Mr. Vassar, Matthew Vassar, Jr., and John Guy Vassar, both charter trustees of the college until their deaths.

The SANDERS LABORATORY OF CHEMISTRY (27) contains laboratories and lecture rooms and has special laboratories for water analysis, study of foods, electrolysis, and physical chemistry.

The HENRY M. SANDERS LABORATORY OF PHYSICS (28) contains laboratories and lecture rooms.

Directly west of Vassar Brothers Laboratory is the NEW ENGLAND BUILDING (29), the gift of the New England alumnae. Over the door is set a piece of Plymouth Rock broken off prior to 1859, when the canopy was erected over it. The name of the vandal who procured this relic is not known. The building houses the departments of botany and zoology as well as the museum of natural history.

The PRESIDENT'S HOUSE (30) stands near the southwest corner of Main Building.

The CHAPEL (31) was dedicated in the fall of 1904. It is constructed of yellow Weymouth granite trimmed with limestone. The exterior is designed like an English parish church in the Norman style. The interior is Gothic with hammer-beam trusses copied from Westminster Hall, London. The stained glass windows are from the Tiffany studios, three of them designed by LaFarge. The organ of 4,538 pipes has been rebuilt as a gift from the donors of the chapel. A rose window on the west was given by the trustees to commemorate the twentieth year of the administration of President Taylor. The facade of the chapel faces north, with a square three-story bell tower on the western side. The tower contains a memorial room with tablets commemorating members of the college who have rendered conspicuous service to the college or to the outer world. In the upper part of the tower is a room used for religious services by the students. Here visiting preachers hold weekly conferences on Sunday evenings.

The BELLE SKINNER HALL OF MUSIC (32) is designed in modified French Gothic after Mont St. Michel in France. It contains a large recital hall, classrooms, offices, rooms for instruction and practice, and a collection of old musical instruments. A library of books and music includes the Chittenden Pianoforte Library and the Dannreuther Collection of Chamber Music. The building is equipped with an auditorium and a sound-reproducing system, a four-manual concert organ with self-playing attachment, phonographs, player pianos, and a stereopticon.

South of Skinner Hall are the COLLEGE GREENHOUSES (33), and across the street is a FARM (34) stretching over more than 900 acres, which supplies the college with many of its vegetables, poultry, and dairy products.

To the north along Raymond Avenue and extending up College Avenue are KENDRICK HOUSE (35) and WILLIAMS HOUSE (36), faculty residences, and the DEAN'S HOUSE (37).

ALUMNAE HOUSE (38) is on the Rock Lot between Raymond and College View Avenues, overlooking the campus. Both this house and Williams are in early half-timbered style. Alumnae House was given by two sisters, Mrs. Blanche Ferry Hooker, '94, and Mrs. Queene Ferry Coonley, '98. Many of the rooms have been furnished in memory of classmates and friends. A Japanese room was given in memory of the Princess Oyama, formerly Stematz Yamakawa of the class of 1882. The living room is a copy of a room in the Davanzatti Palace in Florence, and is furnished with antiques, reproductions of Spanish furniture, and a cryptic painting by Violet Oakley. The house is under the management of the Alumnae Association and is the home of its executive secretary.

The OUTDOOR THEATRE (39) takes advantage of the hillside to form an amphitheatre and makes use of the pine trees and Sunset Lake as a backdrop for its stage. It was first used in 1915 to present a pageant during the fiftieth anniversary, which was celebrated that year.

West of the theatre and enclosed by tall hedges is the terraced SHAKESPEARE GARDEN (40), begun in 1916, the year of the Shakespeare Tercentenary, by Shakespeare classes and classes in botany. At the foot of the hill is a tree said to be grown from a slip of the willow over Napoleon's tomb on St. Helena. Along this brook are cultivated, for experimental purposes, most of the plants native to the county. The strip is known as the DUTCHESS COUNTY OUTDOOR ECOLOGICAL LABORATORY (41).

On the hillside south from the Shakespeare Garden and sloping down to Sunset Lake are the azaleas and rhododendrons planted for the class of 1875 ARBORETUM (42).

Most of the college buildings have been gifts from alumnae, trustees, and other friends of the college, who have not only contributed in this substantial way, but have identified themselves with the activities and progress of the institution.

The following paragraph, in the formal language of the day, appeared in a student magazine issued in 1873: "The artist who sketched the picture of our college as shown in the first page of the catalogue must have looked with the eye of faith to see waving elms and flourishing maples. The eye of flesh sees only here and there amidst the growing corn and trailing pumpkin

61

vines a few slender twigs. We can never picture our great great grandchildren wandering under spreading boughs." So spoke a pessimist, little realizing that not only her grandchildren but she herself might now walk for hours over the well-kept lawns and under the beautiful trees of the Vassar campus.

BEACON

Railroad Stations: New York Central, Ferry Plaza, foot of Beekman St.; New York, New Haven & Hartford, (freight only), 501 Main St.; connections with West Shore (N. Y. Central) and Erie at Newburgh via ferry.

Bus Stations: Pizzuto Bus Lines, Bank Square, to Wappingers Falls and Poughkeepsie. *City Busses:* Ferry Plaza, to Glenham and Fishkill. Special bus service to U. S. Veterans' Hospital and Camp Nitgedaiget.

Taxis: Ferry Plaza; independent lines, three zones, 25c, 40c, 50c.

Steamboat Docks: Newburgh Ferry, foot of Beekman St., 6 a. m. to 1:45 a. m. Hudson River Dayline, via ferry to Newburgh, during summer after May 1.

Accommodations: Hotel Holland (E), 217 Main St., at South Elm St.; Dillon House (E), opposite new postoffice; Beacon View Hotel (E), 426 Main St.; Bennett Hotel (A & E), 248 Main St., at Walnut St.; Mount Beacon Cottages (E), on west spur of Mount Beacon, reached by incline railway.

Motion Picture Houses: Two.

Recreation: Mount Beacon, via incline railway. *(See Point of Interest No. 32.)*

Playground: Hammond Memorial Field, Verplanck Ave., N. side.

Skiing: Junior ski course, along mountside, NE. Beacon. Ski-run, Mount Lane-Howland Ave. triangle, E. Beacon.

Golf: Southern Dutchess County Club, North Ave., nine-hole. Greens fees $1.50; Sat., Sun., holidays $2.

Tennis: Southern Dutchess Country Club; Hammond Memorial Field.

Baseball: Wilke St. (Tompkins) Field, off Fishkill Ave. (State 52).

Trap-Shooting: Southern Dutchess Sportsmen's Assn., oven-works range, Glenham (State 52).

BEACON (350 alt., 11,933 pop.), the county's second largest community, marks the spot where Fishkill Creek flows into the Hudson. Mills and factories line the creek and river shores. The streets of frame cottages sheltered by elms and maples wind up and down and along the steep slopes of the two valleys. The better homes lie along the slope of the Hudson; those of the middle class cover the slopes above the Fishkill; and the poorer homes alternate with the mills along the creek-edge or hug the terraces which rise to the rugged side of Mount Beacon on the south. The city line extends far beyond the compact city streets, so that much of the corporate area is distinctly rural.

Beacon is essentially a manufacturing community; bricks and hats are now, as they have been for generations, the principal products, though the list exceeds 50. The brick industry is concentrated in one large plant at Denning

Point on the Hudson. *(See Points of Interest.)* Of the few remaining hat factories, one occupies the site of Madam Brett's gristmill *(See Point of Interest No. 12)*, and another a building in which handcut files were first manufactured in the United States. *(See p. 66.)*

While almost every European nationality is represented, the Italians are by far the most conspicuous, comprising one-sixth of the population; and their activities are those of the city. Americanization has been so rapid that old world customs are but faintly traceable. The influence of the early Dutch, Huguenot, and English settlers has been lost, other than in surviving names and buildings. An exception are the "mountaineers," who live on the flanks of Mount Beacon and look down upon the valley dwellers as "water-rats." These descendants of early English residents of Fishkill Landing and Matteawan, the two villages which were welded together in 1913 to form Beacon, are largely odd-job and day laborers and small-scale truck farmers, though some of them work in the city factories.

Beacon has the distinction of being the first commission-governed city in New York State, as well as one of the first in the United States. The government is managed by a board of five commissioners, each of whom has charge of specific details. The city council controls all public affairs excepting the department of education, which is under the supervision of the school board appointed by the mayor. A municipality owned water supply of three reservoirs is maintained in the nearby mountains. The climate is temperate and the coolness of the mountains makes a summer resort of the city and vicinity. Over 70 percent of the city's 2,400 houses are owned by the occupants.

River, creek, and mountains made of the site of Beacon and the surrounding area a favorite resort of the Indians; and not far from the mouth of the creek was located the village of a sub-chief of the Wappinger Indians. This good hunting, fishing, and trapping ground was called by the Indians *Matteawan* (Mat-te-a-wan), the name later applied to one of the white men's villages. The Highlands were known by the Waranoaks of this section as the Matteawan Mountains. The name has been interpreted as "the place of furs," referring to beaver, once plentiful along the creek. Another claim is that it is derived from *metai,* a magician or medicine man, and *wian,* a skin, hence "a place of enchanted skins." It is said also to have been derived from the stream passing through this area, from the nearby mountains, and from the region itself. Interpretations are various: "river of shallows," "the large water in the valley," "a good beaver ground," "good furs," "country of good fur," and a term applied to a junction of a stream with another or with a lake.

The site of Beacon was included within the territory covered by the Rombout Patent; the land was purchased from the Indians in 1683. *(See p. 6.)* It is said that in the bargaining the Indians agreed to transfer to Rombout all "the land that he could see," but did not specify that his view was to be confined to the valley where he stood. Rombout led them to the summit of

South Beacon mountain, and extending his arm toward the northward and eastward, laid claim to the vast expanse of rolling hills and forests that lay beneath their gaze. The Indians had made their bargain and they held to it. The patent was based upon the wide boundaries of this purchase.

The earliest recorded mention of this locality by a European was that made by the mate of the *Half Moon,* which on the trip down the river was compelled by the whims of the weather to lie for a day in the vicinity of the present city of Beacon. *(See p. 6.)* The log of the voyage mentions the mountains and refers to the site of Beacon as an admirable townsite.

For nearly three-quarters of a century after the visit of the *Half Moon* there were no permanent white settlers in Dutchess County. The first was Nicholas Emigh, who settled at the mouth of Fishkill Creek, within the present city limits, in 1682. Emigh, a Hollander and a soldier under Prince Rupert in the warfare against Cromwell, came to America with Robert Livingston about 1672. He was married on shipboard, and, with his wife, settled in this nearly unbroken wilderness. Their daughter was the first white child born within the precincts of Dutchess County. The next permanent settler was Peche Dewall, a squatter, who located at Fishkill Landing in the spring of 1688. His wife helped him to clear the forest and till his land. In the fall he had a tolerable crop; and in the winter he built a handsled and went to New York, bought a half-bushel of salt and a side of sole leather, and drew it home over a road then but an Indian trail.

Development was slow. More Dutch, a few Huguenots, and some English settlers joined the trailbreakers; but for many years Fishkill Landing played a mute role as the port of Fishkill Village, transporting flour and produce to New York and receiving foreign and manufactured goods.

Active in the stirring preliminaries to the Revolution was Nathaniel Sackett, described by tradition as a jack of many trades and man of mystery who did his work under cover. He lived up on Fishkill Creek, in what became Matteawan. He served as financial officer of the Committee of Conspiracies, member of the Flax Committee and of the Provincial Congresses and Assembly. When the news came to the Provincial Congress in New York of the Battle of Lexington, Nathaniel Sackett hastened back to Fishkill like another Paul Revere, to spread the general alarm and organize the Committee of Observation. At the first meeting of this committee a Spartan woman declared with patriotic zeal that if exigencies required it her own sex would take up arms.

In the summer of 1776 and on into 1777, the problem of the refugees and the poor from the city of New York was of considerable concern to the Colonials. A large number of these people were removed to Dutchess, and many were brought by water to Fishkill Landing.

The war came close to the locality when the British moved up the Hudson in 1777. Almost all the men went to the defense of the Highland forts. When these fell and the British sailed up the river to burn Kingston, the people of the neighborhood hid their valuables in the woods. The approach of the fleet was made known by the kindling of signal fires on the mountain tops. The present city takes its name from the fiery beacons that blazed forth from time to time on the summits of Breakneck Ridge to warn the Revolutionary armies of the movements of the British.

At the end of the war, when the proclamation of the end of hostilities was received, the people obeyed Washington's order and held an appropriate celebration. At night beacon lights proclaimed the news to the surrounding country.

For nearly 30 years after the close of the Revolution the region continued its quiet rural life, the grist mills continued grinding their grain and the saw mills sawing their wood. The War of 1812 ushered in a new era. The Schenck mill on the creek at what later became Matteawan took on the added task of grinding grist for the fighting forces, and the flour industry hummed. But the influence of the war was much broader than that: it brought a consciousness of self-sufficiency and internal strength; forward-looking investors and speculators began casting about them, seeking new resources and opportunities. And the war provided a field of activity by serving as an embargo against English textiles and giving domestic manufacturers a virtual monopoly of the home market for the time being. It was the beginning of the industrial age in America.

To the attention of a small group of men was presented the possibilities of developing the power of Fishkill Creek, which drops rapidly from Glenham to the Hudson, with a fall of 40 feet in a short section where Schenck's gristmill already stood. Flour was nearly forgotten in the rush to turn out textiles. The first big mill was built at Glenham in 1811. The Matteawan Company, organized in 1812 by Peter A. Schenck, Philip Hone, John Jacob Astor, and others, erected a cotton mill in 1814 on the creek directly above Schenck's gristmill. Shortly thereafter they built a foundry on the east side of the creek, devoted largely to the production of cotton machinery. With the spread of the cotton craze, their machinery was distributed far beyond the bounds of the United States.

Around the Matteawan factory grew Matteawan village, the name of which was originally restricted to the mills. The founders are reputed to have been Schenck and Leonard of the Matteawan Company. The Brett influence was represented in this development of the new country, since Peter A. Schenck's wife, Margaret Brett, was a granddaughter of Madam Brett.

Fishkill, five miles back from the river, had long been the important village of southern Dutchess. The lower settlements near the river did not amount to much, except for Fishkill Landing, where the sloops docked with merchandise and passengers to be hurried inland by wagon and coach. The new cotton mills stimulated the growth of the river communities. Another fillip was given by the introduction of steam, as a result of which river traffic grew in volume and importance. The Bretts *(See Teller House, p. 74)* and their associates were quick to turn to the new mode; and the lower settlements began to outrun Fishkill.

65

The power sites that were the chief stimulus to the development of Matteawan attracted other industries besides the textile mills. John Rothery, of Sheffield, England, built his file works in 1835 near the Matteawan factory. Various other industries located in the neighborhood: an oil mill, a clay mill, cooperages, tanneries, a leather belting manufactory, a shoe factory, soap and candle makers, and a brewery.

Quantities of clay and sand of good quality were at hand, and brickyards were established near the landings in the late 1830's. At Gowdy's yard, and its successor, the Lomas yard, the pace was set in brickmaking: here was first introduced the circular pit and wheel, with horses on a sweep, for mixing materials, and a hand-press for moulding the brick. Previously the clay and sand had been mixed by driving oxen through it and moulding it by hand, a slow and laborious process. The next stage in the development of the industry was the use of the Adams contrivance of circular pit and wheel, mixing and moulding in one operation; then the Chambers machine, mixing and die-cutting the brick in a continuous stream.

After the financial crisis of 1837 the forties ushered in a golden age. The cotton craze continued, and in '41 and '42 a dam and factory devoted to cotton spinning were erected at Wiccopee, below Matteawan, now included in Beacon. At Byrnesville, the southern section of the present Beacon, flour mills were dismantled and cotton machinery installed. Freighting at the landings was stimulated by this industrial boom. About 1844, Alfred Lomas, operating a pin factory near the "Five Corners" (Bank Square), invented a machine to turn out 150 pins a minute. At Wiccopee in 1851 was begun the manufacture of rubber goods. In 1853, at the Upper Landing, a foundry was started for the manufacture of stationary and marine engines. The famous Fishkill Corliss engines were made here. During the Civil War this foundry turned out ordnance: and from the landing nearby, the steamboat *William Kent* went into service carrying troops.

After the war, in a new era of iron and steel, industry took another spurt. Railroad development helped, first the New York Central, and in 1868 the beginning of lines eastward from Fishkill Landing into New England. Thus Fishkill Landing became a railroad terminal point. The New Haven built docks and yards and operated a ferry freight transfer to the Erie across the river. In 1860 Jackson started his carriage works; his wagons became known afar. At Matteawan in 1864 the manufacture of wool hats began. The knife and cutlery industry also started there, but moved to Walden, where it was developed. The wealthy Winthrop Sargent brought from England for use on his country estate the first lawn mower on American soil. Coldwell saw it, and worked at Matteawan on the first American machines. A. T. Stewart started his carpet mills at Groveville in 1873.

Fishkill Landing was incorporated as a village in 1864. Matteawan was considerably larger than the Landing, but was not officially incorporated as a village until 1886. In the nineties the twin villages ranked next to Danbury, Conn., in the manufacture of hats. In that decade the British patent holders established their American plant at Matteawan for the manufacture of fuel economizers and ventilating systems. The Corrington plant turned out air brakes. Benjamin Hammond came from Mount Kisco with his patented formulas for insecticides, fungicides, and the like. Potter invented and manufactured wagon brakes. The Van Houten brothers invented brakers' machinery and set up a factory. The silk industry thrived. The two villages expanded and finally grew together, uniting in 1913 to form the city of Beacon.

The present century brought a slowing up and a decline. The railroad terminal and transfer were removed; the hat industry shrunk; silk mills closed. But the diversity of industries held the community together and the storms were ridden out. And in the midst of all the industrial ups and downs the old Schenck gristmill, begun in 1800, continued grinding grist almost until the day it burned in 1915. The growth of the city has continued steadily. Between 1900 and 1930 the population showed an increase of 25.8 per cent.

MOTOR TOUR (7.4 m.)

The tour begins at Bank Square.

W. on Main St.

1. Site of UPPER LANDING, foot of Main St., which for many years was Fishkill Landing's front door. Peter Bogardus built the dock and storehouse, and in 1765 opened a ferry which ran from here to Newburgh across the Hudson. At the opening of the Revolution it was known as Bogardus Dock, and during the war the storehouse contained military supplies. The ferry was an important link in a military artery, the "middle road," which crossed the river at this point.

In 1853 a foundry was built here for the manufacture of stationary and marine engines, the famous Fishkill Corliss steam engines. During the Civil War the foundry was converted into an Army ordnance shop; and the landing became a troop center. The Hudson River Railroad had a station stop here after its completion in 1849-50; and the Connecticut and Dutchess Railroad made the landing its western terminus in 1868. Extensive docks and yards were built at a point south of the present ferry; and a freight car ferry made connections with the Erie Railroad at Newburgh.

L. from Main St. on River St.; R. on Beekman St.

2. The BEACON-NEWBURGH FERRY (L), foot of Beekman St., was established at the LOWER LANDING in 1743. The original charter, which forms the basis of the charter under which the ferry now operates, was granted by King George II on the petition of Alexander Colden of Fishkill Landing to the Hon. George Clarke, then Lieutenant-Governor of the Province of New York. The first ferry consisted of sail and row boats.

Today there are four modern boats, sturdily constructed for ice-breaking and especially equipped for passenger and motor car transportation. Since 1881 ferry service has been continuously maintained throughout the year.

The river between Beacon and Newburgh is about 1 mile wide. This expanse, once known as Fishkill Bay, is now called Newburgh Bay. The ferry boat offers an excellent vantage point from which to view the much-praised scene at the north portal of the Hudson Highlands. When he was Governor of the State, Franklin Delano Roosevelt often travelled on this ferry, describing it as "one of the most historically colorful ferries in America."

Directly below, and adjoining the ferry slip, is the historic LONG WHARF, built between 1812 and 1816. A promoter put a small fortune into this dock. The older portion of a yellow wooden building standing at the tip of the wharf was at one time an inn. Erected about 1830, it was an important hostelry in the heyday of river traffic.

Backtrack on Beekman St.; Sharp R. on 2nd opening of Ferry St., western entrance to Bank Square.

3. The REFORMED CHURCH (R), Ferry and Academy Sts., is the city's oldest standing church. A massive edifice of somewhat peculiar, modified Gothic architecture, it is built of red brick with locally quarried stone capping the buttresses. In 1859 it replaced the original one built in 1813. In 1820, a negress, Margaret, was baptized and received into the church; and seats were thereafter provided for her race. Liberated slaves in 1857 established a school nearby in the Academy Street neighborhood and later built their own church.

John Peter DeWindt, wealthy trader and slave owner, was one of the founders of the Reformed Church. Millard Fillmore, as ex-president, attended services here. Henry Ward Beecher preached here in the years before the Civil War, when he was being subjected to violent attacks for his strong anti-slavery stand.

At the rear of the church an old graveyard extends down the slope to the old plank road. In this somewhat neglected burial ground, dating back to the 18th century, families are interred in rows, not in plots. Unusual also in this region are vaults built into the steep bank. On the headstones are the names of Tellers, Wiltses, and Boyces, and others who figured prominently in the early history of the section. The oldest inscriptions are those on the markers of Henry Schenck (1743-1799), William Sebring (d. 1814), and Dr. William Forman (d. 1816).

L. from Ferry St. on Park Ave.

4. SPY HILL (L and R), Park Ave. between Ferry St. and Wolcott Ave., gets its name from the eminent service it performed as a lookout point during the Revolution. Commanding an unbroken scene up and down the Hudson for many miles, it offers a view of the Highlands in the south with Storm King and Sleeping Indian Mountains looming against the horizon. Westward on the river terrace is the city of Newburgh, with the

Along Wappinger Creek

Shawangunk Mountains in the distant background. In the northwest the Catskills tower 4,000 feet above the Hudson. The artist-historian, Lossing, speaks of the "broad and beautiful bay," its surface broken by a solitary rock island, Polopel. He sketched and published views made from this point. One of them includes lower Newburgh, the mouth of Quassaic Creek, and the villages of New Windsor and Cornwall. Private residences now crown the hill where blue-coated patriot soldiers once camped.

L. from Park Ave. on Wolcott Ave.

5. WHITE HOUSE SANITARIUM (R), Wolcott and South Aves., a large house with white pillared porches, was once the home of Prof. Charles Davies (1798-1876), mathematician, author, and instructor at West Point and later at Columbia University. Charles Dickens was among the distinguished guests entertained here. Between the Davies occupancy and the advent of the sanitarium, the house was used as a school conducted by Benjamin Lee Wilson, educator, English scholar, and cousin of President Woodrow Wilson.

6. The LOUIS A. GILLET HOUSE (R), 263 Wolcott Ave., was built in 1836 and is famous for its door, removed from the DePeyster House. *(See Point of Interest No. 11.)* This second-oldest doorway in the county shows the Georgian influence in the grooved and reeded pilasters and raised bevelled panels. The bulls-eyes at the top of the door are typical of the style; and the small panes of colored translucent glass in the side lights are unusual. The inside of the door has horizontal boards and long, iron strap hinges.

R. from Wolcott Ave. on Sargent Ave.

7. The LARCH TREES (R), along Sargent Ave., which are interspersed with hemlocks, are notable for their unusual height. Larch is the one conifer that sheds its needles in the winter—the one evergreen that is not an evergreen.

8. The MARIANIST PREPARATORY (L), opposite the larch trees, conducted by Brothers of the Order of the Society of Mary, trains young men for the priesthood and as religious educators. The main building was once the residence of William Kent, son of the Chancellor and Justice of the Supreme Court of New York State. The recently altered house is covered with cream, beige, and brown siding, suggesting stone.

9. WODENETHE (R), opposite and a little farther on *(public may drive through the grounds)*, was formerly the home of Winthrop Sargent, an early 20th century philanthropist. It is now one of the properties of the Craig House Sanitarium. *(See Point of Interest No. 14.)* The house is a large two-story structure painted yellow with white trim. A three-story section is topped by a 4-hipped, curved pyramidal roof. The grounds were embellished by the elder Sargent; and although he was an amateur, he may be called the originator of landscape gardening in the United States. Sargent was a friend of Downing, the famous horticulturist and architect. The gardens, and especially the Roman Garden, are renowned.

L. *from Sargent Ave. on South Ave.*

10. The BYRNESVILLE CEMETERY (L), corner of Sargent and South Aves., above the road cut, contains the unkept graves of early settlers: Roger Brett, Myer Thomas Pierce, and others. The earliest date on any of the dozen remaining stones is 1797.

R. *under railroad tracks.*

11. The DE PEYSTER—NEWLIN—BYRNES HOUSE (R), close to the railroad, was erected about 1743 and was occupied for a time by Abraham de Peyster, nephew of Madam Brett. It later passed through the hands of Newlin and Byrnes, and is now occupied by several families.

It is a fine example of gambrel-roofed, Colonial brick house. The basement story is of Hudson River blue stone, and runs back into the hillside. The story and one-half above the basement are red brick laid in Flemish bond, pierced by three windows in the gable ends. The high stoop fronting the main entrance is not the original; the first Dutch door was moved to the Gillet House. *(See Point of Interest No. 6.)*

After the burning of Kingston, the British fleet dropped down the Hudson and anchored in Newburgh Bay. Lieut. Philip Hamilton, so the tale runs, came ashore with other officers of his ship and wandered into the forest alone. When he returned to the river, the boat that brought him ashore had gone; and the ships were under sail. He ran down the river bank in a vain endeavor to signal them. Dusk was setting. Seeking shelter, he knocked at the door of Abraham de Peyster. Frankly confessing his identity, Hamilton was admitted and invited to join the family at the evening meal. Katrina, the daughter, presided; and the young officer fell in love with her at once. With characteristic Dutch caution, Abraham de Peyster conducted Hamilton to a room on the top floor, turned the key, and the following morning escorted him to Fishkill to face a military tribunal, which paroled him in de Peyster's custody for the period of the war. The romance and courtship thus begun ended in his marriage with Katrina in the fall of 1783, after the surrender of Cornwallis.

12. The site of MADAM BRETT'S MILL (R), occupied by the Tioronda Hat Works, is beside the Fishkill at the foot of a falls which furnished the necessary water power. The gristmill was built in 1708 by Roger and Catharyna Brett, who also built a dwelling nearby and set aside 300 acres to go with the two buildings. No trace of the house remains, as it was probably abandoned within a year, when they moved to a new house. *(See Point of Interest No. 23.)* The mill stood at the head of navigation on the Fishkill. Here an eyebolt, still visible, was set in a large stone by which to tie up ships.

ROGER BRETT, a native of Somersetshire, England, was one of a coterie of young Englishmen who came to America at the time Queen Anne sent her young cousin, Lord Cornbury, to be governor of the province. He lived in New York in 1703, and after his marriage to Catharyna Rombout in that year, was listed as "a Master of Family in the City of New York." In 1703-06, his name appears as a vestryman of Trinity Church. He was on intimate terms with Lord Cornbury and entertained him at his home. Brett had married well, for his wife had fallen heir to the great Rombout Patent *(See History)* up the Hudson. Less fortunate was his death. In 1716, coming from New York in his own sloop, he was drowned when the boom of his ship swept him overboard not far from the Brett mill.

13. The FISHKILL (since kil is Dutch for creek, Fishkill Creek is a tautology) (R and L) bounds down the side of the Hudson Valley and enters the tidewater Hudson at this point. The prosaic sucker, which is here in large numbers, has lent its name to the cascade immediately upstream. Between Sucker Falls and the road is the small FAIRY ISLAND. The Indians believed a manitou dwelt here, and they often came to admire and worship. Painters of the Hudson River School and other later artists have pictured this scene of foaming water and mossy, tree-shaded banks.

L. from South Ave. on Grandview Ave., L. on Howland Ave.

14. CRAIG HOUSE SANITARIUM (General Howland House) (L), first beyond intersection, was the home of Gen. Joseph Howland from 1834 to 1886. Howland was a Civil War officer and a philanthropist. Eliza Woolsey Howland, his wife, and Georgeanna Woolsey Bacon, his sister-in-law and author of *Handbook of Nursing,* were both nurses in Civil War hospitals. The property and house, known as Tioronda, have been purchased by the sanitarium corporation, which has taken over many another South Beacon estate for the treatment of mental patients. A private institution, it caters to those who can afford to pay for the elegance and care the various units offer.

71

15. The UNIVERSITY SETTLEMENT (New York City) SUMMER CAMP (CAMP STOVER) (R), just beyond the sanitarium, is a well equipped vacation resort for 700 boys and girls and some adults from New York's lower East Side. Facilities include a swimming pool and various buildings for camp use. Mountain Rest, the main building, is the remodeled former HOME OF REV. HENRY WARD BEECHER. The original house, which forms the nucleus of the present structure, was the 18th century ANNAN HOUSE, one of the first dwellings in this region. Annan, later a lieutenant in the Revolution, purchased a tract of land from the Brett Estate between 1757 and 1761. The present building, with its white clapboard siding, green trim, and red roof, gives little if any clue to the appearance of the original.

R. from Howland Ave. on dirt road.

16. The MOUNT BEACON INCLINE RAILWAY (L), end of road, *(30¢ round trip),* climbs the west spur of Mount Beacon, giving access to the mountain top resort of the Mount Beacon-on-Hudson Association. This cable railway, powered by electricity, is reputed to be the steepest of its kind in the world; it is 2,200 ft. long, with a vertical rise of 1,200 ft. The two observation cars are built on a tilt to correspond with the slope of the hill. A single cable, attached to each end of a car, passes over a rotating drum in the power house at the summit. While one car rises, the other descends; and they pass on a midway switch. The road was opened on Memorial Day in 1902, carrying more than 60,000 people the first season. *(For Casino see Point of Interest No. 32.)*

Backtrack to Wolcott Ave.

17. ST. LUKE'S EPISCOPAL CHURCH (R), Wolcott Ave. between South Liberty and Rector Sts., is a plain English Gothic structure of stone, erected in 1868. The building with its high gables, buttresses, and arched doors and windows, is a copy of an English church visited and admired by General Howland, one of the chief subscribers to the St. Luke's building fund. The Rectory and Parish House are set apart from the church, separated from it by a broad park which is studded with magnificent beech trees, imported from England. A chestnut-oak, the only oak in the line along Wolcott Ave., was propagated from one of the "Washington Oaks" which stood on Dennings Point in Revolutionary days, and under which Washington rested after ferrying from New Windsor.

On both sides of the rocky knoll north of the church is a cemetery which contains the graves of many famous persons. Here are buried James Kent, Chief Justice of Supreme Court, Chancellor of the State of New York, and author of *Kent's Commentaries;* Smith T. Van Buren, son of the president; Dr. Frank M. Tiernan, Civil War drummer boy; and many others whose names hark back to early settlement: Van Vliet, Tillot, DuBois, Van Kleeck, Schenck, Wolcott, Sargent, and Knevels. The northeastern part of the cemetery is the Presbyterian section, older than the Episcopal section, and contains a marker dated 1812.

R. From Wolcott Ave. on Spring Valley St.

18. MARY ANN'S BRIDGE (L), spanning the Fishkill, is named for a woman who kept a tavern at this crossing before the Civil War. The new concrete arch bridge replaces spans dating back a hundred years and offers a fine view of the lower valley of the Fishkill, a sight often described, photographed, and painted. The creek cuts between the high banks, tumbling over several falls before it reaches the Hudson.

Spring Valley St. becomes Mill St. Straight ahead on East Main St. to Howland Ave. Main tour turns L. on Howland Ave.
A side-tour continues on East Main St., locally known as "Mountain Lane."

Right on Annan St. is the diminutive MOUNTAIN CHAPEL (R), a gray painted frame building which looks like a one-room country schoolhouse. For many years it has served the mountainside people as an undenominational church. The "mountaineers," as they are called, are a peculiar folk group which has resided at the foot of the mountains for many generations, adhering to primitive traditions and customs. Although a large number of them work in Beacon as factory hands or odd-job men, they spend a great deal of their time in the hills, know every foot of the rough ground, and are natural woodsmen. Some of the older ones pride themselves on their wood-chopping ability. These people appear to have descended from some of the finer early families. A tradition among them avers that a British soldier was a progenitor of a representative family. Scotch settlers also came into the mountain fastnesses nearly a hundred years ago, a hardy people, who believed that elves, fairies, and gonomes inhabited the hills.

At the end of East Main St., a bridge crosses Dry Brook.

The HIKER'S TRAIL ascends an ancient road beyond the bridge. Early maps indicate that this was an important highway of the early 19th century, and one of the pioneer roads of southern Dutchess a century earlier. It is understood that this is the old Danbury Road that left the Hudson at Willet Landing and crossed the mountains here to the Clove, thence continuing into New England. This route to the east was the most direct from the West Point vicinity and was used for military purposes during the Revolution when troops and supplies were transported back and forth across the Hudson between Fishkill Landing and the west shore.

As it rises above the city, the trail leads up a deep ravine north of Mount Beacon and skirts the slope of Bald Hill (L).

The character of the vegetation changes rather abruptly as the higher elevations are reached. At 700 to 1,000 ft. are thickets of laurel, azalea, and scrub-oak. Trailing arbutus, once plentiful, has become scarce. The rattlesnake and the copperhead are rarely met.

At *1.25 m.* (R) is a side trail to Beacon reservoir and Mount Beacon. Straight ahead the main trail leads to the head of the ravine and the abandoned Greer farm.

A rough trail (L) leads along the ridges of Bald Hill and beyond, following the general trend of one of several roads constructed nearly a century ago for exploiting iron ore deposits. Near Bald Hill was located the 19th century property of the Manhattan Iron Works.

Bald Hill (over 1,200 ft.) is named for its barren and rocky slopes which have only a thin covering of stunted trees. It is sometimes called Burnt Mountain, for it has repeatedly been swept by forest fires.

At *1.5 m.* is HELL HOLLOW (Boulder Glen), a 1,000-ft.-deep gulch in the eastern mountainside. Its bottom is choked with huge boulders, which,

73

combined with the precipitous sides, make the cleft practically inaccessible. A foot trail descends to the Albany Post Road (US 9), in the valley to the southeast.

L. on Howland Ave.

19. HIDDENBROOKE (R), Howland Ave. opposite green barn, is occupied by the Ursuline Novitiate. It lies in a little valley at the base of the mountains, and is surrounded by lawns and gardens. The institution is devoted to the training of novices for lives of religious work. The Novitiate chapel, erected in 1925, is of Gothic architecture. The exterior brick is laid in an irregular manner, and the roof is of heavy slate. A somewhat Spanish touch is evident in the stuccoed outer wall of the vestry. The nave, roof arches, hewn beams, oak paneling, and cloister are Gothic in design.

R. from Howland Ave., on Washington Ave.

20. GROVEVILLE PARK (L), Washington Ave. and Park St., once an amusement resort, is now the assembly grounds and cottage colony of the Nazarene Camp Meeting Association. The park is owned and operated by the Nazarene Society of the Nazarene Church. The members, recruited from a wide area, gather here in large numbers during the summer months to receive religious education and attend daily services. About 50 one-room cottages are scattered about under the trees for the use of visitors who have no camping equipment.

L. from Washington Ave. on Park St., keep R.; L. on Liberty St.

21. The GROVEVILLE FLATS (R), across the creek, are a narrow flood plain of the Fishkill. The mill and tenant houses were erected in 1873-75 by A. T. Stewart, merchant prince of Manhattan. The mills were a carpet factory; but now they are occupied by several small manufacturing concerns.

R. from Liberty St. on East Main St.

22. The EAST MAIN ST. BRIDGE (Fountain Square Bridge) offers a view of the Mill Rapids (R) at the center of the old mill district of Matteawan. Factory walls rise abruptly from the Fishkill. The extensive yellow brick buildings (R), formerly the plant of the Matteawan Manufacturing Co., makers of wool hats, are now occupied by the Braendly Dye Works.

L. from East Main St., on Main St., L. on Tioronda Ave., R. on Van Nydeck St.

23. The BRETT-TELLER HOUSE (L), corner Van Nydeck St. and Teller Ave., is the oldest standing building and one of the first to be built (1709) in Dutchess County.

This home of romantic and historic memories is a noteworthy landmark of the Hudson valley and a splendid example of the simple, solid Dutch architecture of its period. It is a story-and-a-half high; three long, graceful dormers on each side of the house, project from the gently sloping peaked roof. The house has thick stone foundations; and the frame of massive timbers is held together by wooden pins. The main body of the house is sided with scalloped cedar shakes 4 feet long, varying from 5 to 9 inches in width and fastened with handwrought nails. The east wing has wide clapboards.

The interior, staircase, and woodwork details are representative of the better homes of the Colonial period. A mantel in the dining room is very plain, with a fluted pattern beneath the shelf; another, which was put in prior to 1800, replacing one faced with old Dutch tile, is of elaborate design with marble facing. The dining room has two alcoves with graceful arched and fluted columns. A large fireplace in the old beamed kitchen still has the crane and large iron pot. The cellar door is hung on wooden hinges and is fastened by a wooden latch which is lifted from the outer side by a string.

The 4 acres of land on which the homestead stands was part of the large tract of 85,000 acres acquired by Francis Rombout and Gulian Verplanck. Verplanck died before the patent was issued. *(See History.)* Title to these 4 acres has never been transferred and still rests on the original patent. When Francis Rombout died in 1691, his share of 28,000 acres "in the Wappings" passed to his daughter, Catharyna, who married Roger Brett. *(See Point of Interest No. 12.)* The Homestead is still owned and occupied by their descendants.

After Roger Brett's early death, Madam Brett possessed and managed her vast heritage. She presented a commanding figure as she rode on horseback over her land, administering its affairs and promoting its development until well advanced in years. On church and gala days she rode in her coach-and-four, with three Negroes in attendance. She was a friend of the Indians, and was active in community affairs, holding a partnership in the Frankfort Storehouse, the region's first freighting establishment, at the Lower Landing. She died in 1764 and was buried in the cemetery of the Dutch Church at Fishkill, which she helped found. *(See p. 82.)* She left two sons, Francis and Robert.

During Revolutionary times the Homestead was occupied by Maj. Henry Schenck, who in 1763 had married Hannah, daughter of Francis Brett and granddaughter of Madam Brett. As Quartermaster in Washington's Army, he stored military supplies here. The Homestead was then famed for its hospitality and was a frequent resort of Army officers. Washington, Lafayette, Von Steuben, Abraham Yates, and other distinguished patriots were guests.

The name Teller Homestead was applied to the house as a result of the marriage of Alice Schenck, second daughter of Maj. Henry Schenck, to Isaac dePeyster Teller in 1790. The latter purchased the property in 1800 in the settlement of the estate of Major Schenck, who died in 1799. One of Teller's daughters, Margaret Schenck Teller, who married Rev. Dr. Robert Boyd Van Kleeck, inherited the Homestead, which upon her death in 1888 passed on to their daughter, Agnes Boyd Crary, wife of Rev. Dr. Robert Fulton Crary, oldest grandson of Robert Fulton. It is now held in her estate. The present occupants are the seventh generation in direct line to own and occupy the Homestead.

R. from Van Nydeck St. on Teller Ave., which becomes Fishkill Ave.; L. on Verplanck Ave.

24. MATTEAWAN STATE HOSPITAL (R), Verplanck Ave. and Canon St., *(admission 1-4 weekdays only)* is devoted to the incarceration and treatment of the criminal insane. The buildings, which are on a reservation of about 900 acres, reflect several periods of construction in their varied but harmonious architecture. All are of red brick with many barred windows. The main unit is in the state institutional, pseudo-Romanesque style. Another unit has red tiled roofs; and another has small, white-trimmed windows and a gray slate roof of low gable. The officers' residence unit suggests Elizabethan architecture with half-timbering and leaded windows. A farm colony and various service buildings complete the plant.

The hospital contains 1,348 patients (Aug., 1936). Completion of the building under construction will increase the capacity to 1,421. The number of patients has been increasing at the rate of 30 to 40 annually.

Before the State acquired the property, it was the home and training ground of the famous John J. Scanlon trotting horses, winners and record holders of Hambletonian races. *The Abbott* ($2:03\frac{1}{4}$) and *Kentucky Union* ($2:07\frac{1}{4}$) are buried beside the road just back of the present fence. The pyramid which marked their graves has been removed.

L. from Verplanck Ave., on North Ave.

25. The SOUTHERN DUTCHESS COUNTRY CLUB (R), facing Verplanck Ave., has for its nucleus an old Dutch building; date of erection is unknown. It is a low built, plain stone dwelling with a wide sweep of roof and thick walls. Early in the 19th century, it was slightly remodeled by John Peter DeWindt *(see Point of Interest No. 3)* for the use of his son, and was called "Stone Cot."

At this point is a stretch of sandy beach, rare along the river. This is a small popular bathing place. Benches and tables are provided for picnic parties.

Straight on North Ave. to Bank Square.

Additional Points of Interest

26. EUSTATIA, on Monell Place, is the Monell-Van Houten House, an Elizabethan-American country home built in 1867 by Andrew Jackson Downing, the landscape artist and horticulturalist who was lost in the *Henry Clay* steamboat disaster. This was Downing's first practical example of his conception of an American country home. Downing's widow, who was a daughter of John Peter DeWindt, married Judge John Monell.

A short distance S. of Eustatia stood the DeWindt house. DeWindt, who was called "the Firebrand," was a West India trader, prominent in Hudson River commerce, and helped to develop Fishkill Landing as a port. Under his patronage, James Mackin, a poor boy, rose later to be Senator and State Treasurer. Mackin's wife, nee Countess Sally Britton Spottiswood, known as the "Belle of St. Louis," was an authoress and philanthropist. On the DeWindt grounds lived Clarence Cooke, an art critic of the last century. His studio, *Copy Cotte,* is now in ruins.

27. The BOGARDUS-DEWINDT-VAN HOUTEN HOUSE, 16 Tompkins Ave., is a picturesqne dwelling, almost hidden from view by lilac bushes. Erected before 1800, it was first the home of Peter Bogardus, a local merchant, was acquired by John Peter DeWindt about 1825 and occupied by his widow; and was later purchased by the Van Wagenen family. It is a good example of the story-and-a-half frame Dutch homestead of Revolutionary times. The house has interesting details of window frames, original trim, and original fireplaces. Except for the addition of a wing and dormers and the removal of a Dutch oven, it is little changed.

28. The KNEVELS-STEARNS HOUSE (Sunny Fields), 75 Knevels Ave., erected in 1835, is a weathered shingle house of frame construction with plain gabled roof. Gertrude Knevels, a modern novelist, lived here early in the 20th century. According to tradition, the ghost of an Indian chief, stalking from the trees under which he used to live, frequently visits the grounds.

29. DENNINGS POINT was early known as "the island" in Fishkill Bay. It was in possession of Peter DuBois under a life lease from Madam Brett. Later, when the DePeysters came into possession, it was called DePeyster's Point. The Verplancks owned it for a time. William Allen, a grandson of William Allen, founder of Allentown, Pa., built a mansion here about 1814. Only the walls remain, on the high ground at the center of the point. This house contained an octagonal room, an eccentric form of architecture fashionable in that era. William Allen and his wife, according to tradition, lived here in such a lavish scale of elegance and hospitality that they became financially embarrassed. At the end of nine years they were obliged to sell the estate to the Dennings, who built a causeway to the mainland and called the promontory Presqu' Ile *(almost an island).* Denning's famous cider mill, a large brick structure, still stands on the inner shore. Nearby is a fisherman's cottage; and huge reels for shad nets are spread on the stony beach where the shoals stretch out into the little bay between the point and the mouth of Fishkill Creek. Washington was in the habit of landing on this promontory after crossing from his headquarters at Newburgh. Under large oaks on the river shore he found an orderly waiting with his horse and rode to the highway leading to New England.

The DENNINGS POINT BRICK WORKS, at the foot of Dennings Ave., on the "neck" of the point, is one of the more complete and up-to-date of the electrical machine-operated yards in America. This concern began making the widely known Hudson River common brick here in 1880. Nearby are sites of pioneer brickyards.

30. The HOWLAND LIBRARY, 477 Main St., was established in 1872. The brick building of the Norwegian chalet type was built from plans brought to this country by General Howland. There are 15,000 volumes available to the public.

31. The SURVEYOR'S OFFICE, 181 Main St., is probably the oldest surveyor's office in continuous operation. It contains a file of old deeds and maps, including local charts drawn by Simeon DeWitt, official geographer of the Revolution.

Points of Interest in Environs

32. The CASINO, at the head of the Incline Railway *(See Point of Interest No. 16)*, besides being famous as a resort, is noted for the view it commands. Under the flank of the 1,200-ft.-high mountain spur, the course of the Fishkill can be traced to the bay. Southwest, the vista extends to the north portal of the Hudson Highlands. To the west are Cornwall Bay, Sleeping Indian Mountain, and the terraced city of Newburgh, backed by Snake Hill. A blue barrier on the far horizon, the Shawangunk range forms a curtain in the west. The 4,000-ft. crests of the Catskills loom in the northwest.

Rising still higher above the Casino is the crest of MOUNT BEACON (1,500 alt.), reached by a foot trail, *1 m.* This peak has gone by the names of Solomon's Bergh, Beacon Hill, North Beacon, and Old Beacon. The name "Beacon" dates back to 1777 when signal fires were lighted on the mountain as a means of communication with military outposts in Connecticut, Westchester, and Sandy Hook. The city has borrowed the name of the mountain. The summit duplicates the view obtainable at the Casino.

From Mount Beacon a trail extends to SOUTH BEACON PEAK (1,635 alt.), *1 m.*, the highest in the Highlands of the Hudson. It is called South Beacon Hill by the United States Geological Survey, and was named New Beacon or Grand Sachem in Hayward's *Gazetteer* of 1853. Hayward writes: "The river is visible from West Point to Tappan Bay on the south, and for an extent of 50 miles on the north. The surrounding rich and highly cultivated country, dotted with villages, and wanting in nothing that renders so extensive a landscape lovely, lies as a picture before the observer." From the fire tower which rises 75 ft. above the summit, the skyscrapers of Manhattan are visible on exceptionally clear days. The Empire State Building can be seen with the naked eye, but binoculars are necessary to bring out the New York outer and inner harbors.

VILLAGE
NEW

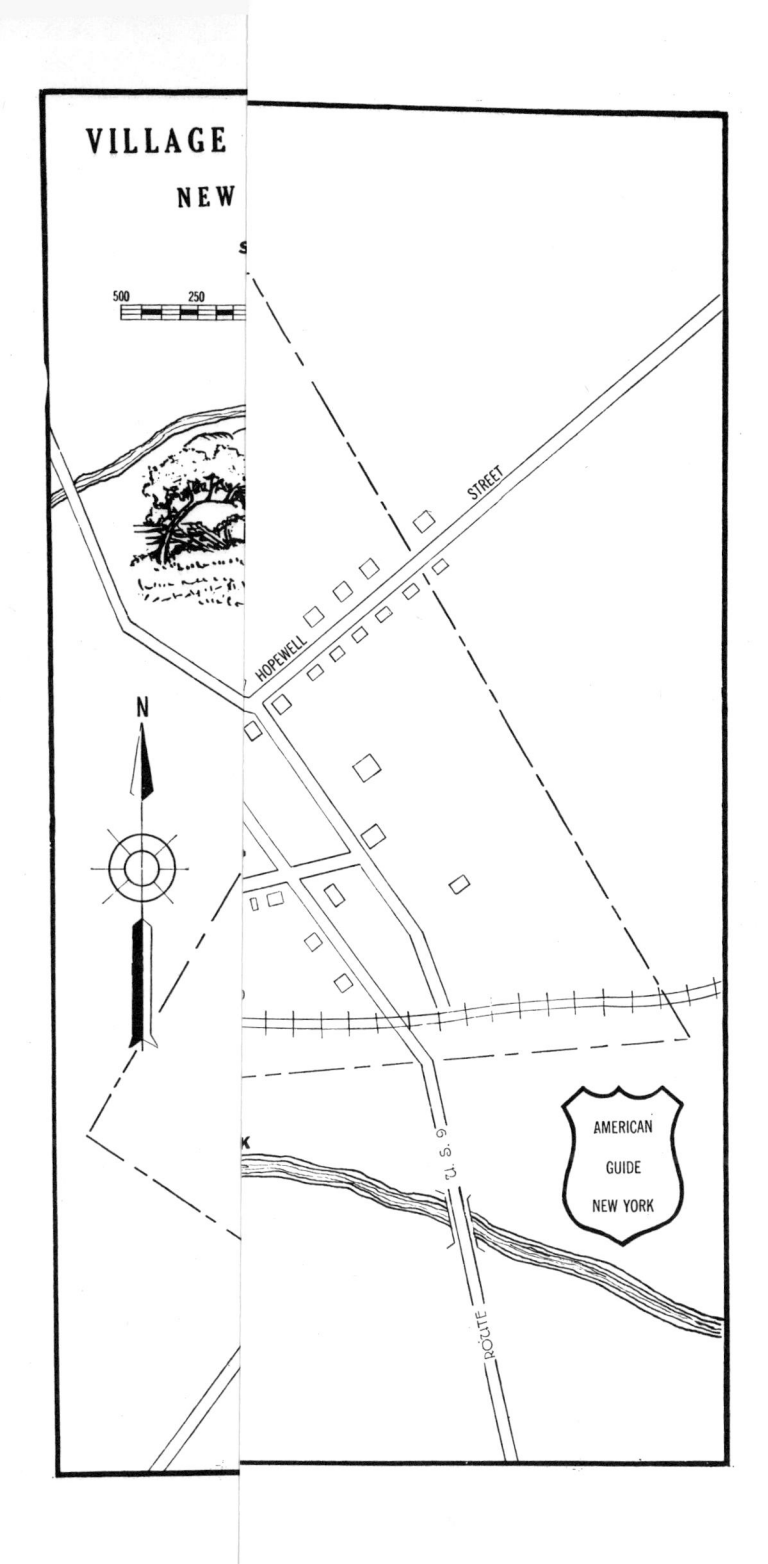

500 250

HOPEWELL STREET

U.S. ROUTE 9

AMERICAN GUIDE NEW YORK

FISHKILL VILLAGE

Railroad Stations: New York, New Haven & Hartford R. R. (freight only).

Busses: Beacon-Fishkill Bus Line, New York-Montreal Bus Line, Mohawk Bus Line.

Taxis: To Beacon, one to four passengers, $1; each additional passenger, 25c.

Accommodations: Union Hotel (E); Ye Olde Fishkill Inne (A and E); Elm Lodge (A and E); Old Post Road Inn (A and E).

Recreation: Hiking trails over nearby mountains. Swimming in Fishkill and Clove Creeks (stocked with fish). Skiing at Norway Ski Jump and on trails over the mountains.

Annual events: Middle Atlantic Ski-Jumping Tournament, winter, when condition of snow permits.

FISHKILL VILLAGE (200 alt., 553 pop.) is a residential community at the junction of US 9 and State 52, 4.5 miles east of Beacon, 13.5 miles south of Poughkeepsie. Sheltered by the sturdy Fishkill mountain range, this secluded little village still pursues serenely the placid life of its Dutch pioneers. Main Street, most important of the village thoroughfares, is broad and gracious, arched by great elm trees. To the east and west of the restricted business section, stand fine old dwellings and historic churches. Neat white houses, some with Dutch doorways opening upon the street, lend an atmosphere of neighborliness suggestive of an earlier day. Several more spacious mansions are set in deep lawns bordered by old fashioned gardens and white picket fences. Among these relics of the past there are few tokens of today's world and never an intimation of tomorrow's.

Fishkill was settled by the Dutch a few years after the granting of the Rombout Patent in 1685. English colonists from Ulster County across the river had seen the low, swampy land of the Fishkill valley and had scornfully rejected it as worthless; but the Dutch, accustomed to the lowlands of their native country, were undaunted. Gradually they moved in, cleared the wilderness, drained the swamps, and built their homes. To the stream which flows through the valley they gave the name *Vis Kil* (Dutch, *fish creek*), which, in its Anglicized form, Fishkill, was applied in time to the village, the township, and the nearby mountains.

The first to occupy the land now comprised within the village limits were Johannes Ter Boss and Henry Rosecrance, whose names appear in a list of freeholders of Dutchess County prepared in 1740. Ter Boss was an eccentric man. When a controversy arose in the Dutch church, Ter Boss transferred to the Presbyterian church at Brinckerhoffville, to which he took his Negroes one Sabbath and sat among them, to the consternation of the congregation.

The village probably owes its existence to the fact that here in 1731 the settlers built their first church, in which on alternate Sabbath mornings the people gathered for worship, many coming from as far as Hopewell and New Hackensack. De Chastellux, the French traveler, who visited

Dutchess County 45 years later, found in Fishkill only one Dutch and one English church, 12 to 14 dwellings, an inn, and a schoolhouse. Nevertheless, he rated Fishkill as the only village in the county, outside of Poughkeepsie, deserving mention.

This was Fishkill at the outbreak of the Revolution: in that struggle the little village played an important part. It lay on the only practical military route through the Highlands of the Hudson, as well as upon the most direct route from the mid-Hudson valley to New England; it was readily accessible to the river and to West Point; and it was the center of a highly productive agricultural area capable of provisioning an army.

It was early anticipated that the British forces in New York would attempt to establish direct communication with Quebec through the Hudson-Champlain valleys and thereby isolate New England from the other rebellious Colonies. Their path would lie through Wiccopee Pass, the narrow defile immediately south of the village, which might easily be held by a small army against a much larger attacking force. Quick to recognize its strategic importance, Washington had the pass fortified; three batteries of artillery were stationed there in 1776 and redoubts were built. On the plain to the eastward of Fishkill, and across the creek, barracks were erected for the quartering of troops, while Washington and his aides were quartered in and about the village in homes, some of which still stand. Storehouses were built for military supplies, and Fishkill became the military base and supply depot for Dutchess County, and headquarters for a year of the State clothing stores. On the good-hearted Dutch wives devolved the self-imposed task of making additional clothes for the poorly clad soldiers and preparing supplies for the military hospital.

The Dutch Church was converted into a prison in which Tories, deserters, and British prisoners were confined. The English Church became the Army hospital, in which victims of smallpox, then raging in the ranks, and men wounded in the battle of White Plains, October 28, 1776, were cared for. According to an eye-witness, after the White Plains engagement the dead were piled like cordwood in the Fishkill street between the two churches.

The New York Provincial Convention, evacuating New York City on August 29, 1776, before the threatened invasion of the British, came to Fishkill. Its first sessions in the village were held September 5 of that year in the English church, and later sessions were held in the more commodious Dutch church until February, 1777, when it removed to Kingston.

To add to the burden of the villagers, numerous refugees, the "poor and distressed," from New York and White Plains fled to Fishkill, where they found asylum in the already overcrowded community. Among these was Samuel Loudon, the Whig printer, who set up his press in the house of Robert Brett *(see Obadiah Bowne house, p. 84)*, and issued on October 1, 1776, the first number of the New York *Packet and American Advertiser,* the first newspaper to be printed in Dutchess County. In this house he also printed the

Reformed Dutch Church at Fishkill

Road to old landing near mouth of Wappinger Creek

first copies of the Constitution of the State of New York, drawn up by John Jay, the *Journal of the Legislature,* and most of Washington's military orders. The State Constitutional Convention met in the Bowne house in 1776, and the following year ratified Jay's Constitution in Kingston. Loudon continued his paper until the end of the war, when he returned to New York.

After the war, the Dutch Church, emptied of its prisoners, was in such disrepair, that it was deemed unfit for use as a House of God. Accordingly, poor as they had become after bearing the burdens of war for seven years, the congregation decided to rebuild their church. The work, begun in 1785, required 10 years to complete. All stone, timber, hauling, and labor were donated by members of the congregation. When the building was half done funds failed, and the villagers were obliged to borrow money from their relatives in Long Island to carry on.

Although in 1789 Fishkill was considered important enough to be granted a post office, one of but seven then in the State, it appears that from the Revolutionary period to the Civil War the village grew slowly. The construction of the Dutchess and Columbia Railroad in 1869 brought the village a fresh impulse. A paper bag mill and other factories were built and the town's population mounted to almost 1,000. At that time Fishkill had four churches, a "select" school, a free school, two banks, and a weekly newspaper. Such prosperity, however, was not destined to endure. Within four years the factories closed their doors, and in December, 1873, the year of the panic, a fire, said to have been the work of an incendiary, destroyed many of the historic buildings. From this disaster Fishkill never recovered. By 1880 its population had decreased to 800, and today numbers but half that of 1870. The "select" school, one of the two banks, and the weekly newspaper are gone, and only the churches, the free school, and the savings bank remain. Most of the Revolutionary landmarks in the vicinity of Fishkill are included in Tour No. 3.

Contemporary Fishkill is primarily the home of retired farmers and professional and business men, and the village has known some development as a suburb of Beacon. Foreign-born families, although they settle in the countryside, have avoided the village itself.

FOOT TOUR (1 m.)

The tour begins at the western entrance to the village on Main St. (State 52).

1. Adjoining the now unused airplane landing field (R) on the outskirts of the village is the WHITE HOUSE (R), approached by a long, straight, tree-lined driveway. Dr. Bartow White, who built it in 1805, called it "Avenue Farm." A frame building, two stories high, with a service wing at the east end, it is a good example of the Dutchess County house of its period. Silver hardware was used throughout.

Dr. White served as a member of Congress from 1825 to 1827 and as a presidential elector for New York State in 1840. In this house he reared his ten children, one son and nine daughters, the last two of whom he humorously named Octavia and Novenia.

On both sides of the street are substantial houses set in spacious grounds, varying in architecture from the simple Dutch Colonial to the more ornate style of the nineties.

2. The edge of the business section is marked by the small brick BANK BUILDING (R), now Dean's, the shop of the village historian. The building is little changed since the banking business was suspended in 1877.

3. East one-half block is the JAMES GIVEN HOUSE (L), a white house with green shutters, and fenced along the street front by white wooden pickets. It is a solid frame building of generous proportions. Its doorway is Georgian, the pilasters of the frame grooved in the upper portion. Given, the builder, came to Fishkill from Ireland in 1798. Prospering as a merchant, he built this dwelling in 1811, naming it "Shillelagh," after the town in which probably he was born. It is related that a bottle of wine used in christening the house failed to break, an incident which was taken to be an omen that the structure would never burn. The house was in fact spared by the 1873 fire. Given's memory is also perpetuated in the elms which he set out along Main Street the year he built his house.

4. The ELM at the entrance to VAN WYCK HALL (L) is the pride of Fishkill. Planted about 1790, it now measures over 4 ft. in diameter. The hall is a large frame building used as a community center.

5. Across the street is the UNION HOTEL (R), a red brick building occupying the site of an inn kept in Revolutionary days by James Cooper, which may have been for a time the headquarters of Washington during the encampment in the village. Prisoners of war were tried here. The inn perished in the great fire.

6. Just beyond is YE OLDE FISHKILL INNE (R) formerly the Mansion House, built by Cornelius Van Wyck in 1820. Though altered, it retains its stout oak timbers, original doorway, and triple windows in each gable end. Major Hatch, later manager of the Poughkeepsie Hotel *(See Poughkeepsie, p. 38)* was the first host. Among the noted men who have stopped here were President Martin Van Buren, Henry Clay, Aaron Burr, Washington Irving, and Benson J. Lossing.

7. Across the street is the REFORMED DUTCH CHURCH (L), the embodiment of Fishkill's life and history. The oldest building in the village, it was enlarged in 1785 around the original church of 1731. Decidedly Dutch in character, it is a solid structure of stuccoed stone with brick-trimmed corners. Its walls are 3 ft. thick, and its steeple, 128 ft. high, has supported the same weather vane since 1795.

In 1716 a congregation was organized in Fishkill by the Rev. Petrus Vas, fifth pastor at Kingston, in conjunction with one at Poughkeepsie. These two congregations were in the charge of one pastor until 1772. In 1731 the members of the Fishkill congregation petitioned Governor Montgomery for permission to solicit funds with which to build a church. Permission was granted, and the church was immediately erected on land which was not formally deeded to the congregation until 1759. Early prints of this building show a heavy rectangular stone edifice with a hip roof surmounted at the middle by a bell-tower and weather vane. Window lights set in iron sash frames were very small, and the upper story walls showed port holes, used in defense against the Indians. Some of these port holes can still be seen. Much of the labor on this structure was performed by slaves of the settlers, and the materials came from the hills and fields about Fishkill.

One of the pastors of the church was the Rev. Isaac Rysdyck, who served the congregation from 1765 to 1790 and whose reputation for learning and charm long survived him. He lies buried in the churchyard of the Dutch Church at New Hackensack. *(See Tour 2, p. 113).* In the Fishkill churchyard are tombstones with Dutch inscriptions which antedate the church. The grave of Catharyna Rombout (Madam Brett), daughter of the patentee, formerly in the cemetery, was enclosed under the pulpit when the church was enlarged.

This church figures in Cooper's novel, *The Spy*, the hero of which, Harvey Birch, was in real life Enoch Crosby, an American secret service agent. Crosby was held here among Tory prisoners, whom he had tricked into captivity, and by prearrangement with the guards was permitted to escape.

8. The BLODGETT MEMORIAL LIBRARY (R) stands across the street a short distance beyond the church. This small stone building was given to the village in 1934 by John Woods Blodgett in memory of his father. It is an example of modern Colonial architecture. The library was at first opposed, it is said, on the grounds that "everyone in town has a library of his own."

9. The FISHKILL GRILL (R) on the SE. corner of the junction of Main St. and US 9, is a lunch wagon of interest principally because it is a stopping place of President Franklin D. Roosevelt when en route to or from his Hyde Park home.

10. One block beyond US 9 is the historic TRINITY CHURCH (R), erected in 1769 and known locally as the "English Church." It stands today, a Colonial frame structure, very little altered except that a tall steeple, deemed unsafe, was removed in 1803. The high, many-paned windows are noteworthy.

The church congregation was founded in 1756 by the Rev. Samuel Seabury. In that year, Seabury, a missionary of the Society for the Propagation of the Gospel, came riding into the village of Fishkill on a sorrel horse. Ordained a priest in 1730 by the Bishop of London, he had been rector of an English church in Hempstead, Long Island, but disgusted with the constant bickerings between his congregation and that of a neighboring Dutch church, he resigned and set forth. In Fishkill the Dutch received him cordially, readily granting his request to preach in their church. It is said that more than 300 persons gathered from miles around to hear his first sermon. He soon formed his own congregation, which included Dutchmen whom he had converted.

In 1776 Trinity Church, jointly with Christ Church of Poughkeepsie, had the Rev. John Beardsley as its rector. *(See Poughkeepsie, p. 38).* Another rector, the Rev. Philander Chase, who served here from 1797 to 1805, afterward became Bishop of Ohio and of Illinois and founded Kenyon College in Ohio and Jubilee College in Illinois. The son of the founder of the church, also named Samuel Seabury, became the first Episcopal Bishop in the United States. This name and line are carried on by Justice Samuel Seabury of New York City.

The gravestones in Trinity churchyard date back to 1770; many Revolutionary soldiers and their enemies were buried here side by side in unmarked graves. A vault contains the bodies of several members of the family of Gulian Verplanck, one of the three joint holders of the Rombout Patent.

Gulian Verplanck, grandson of the patentee, presented to this church and to the Dutch Church identical tankards, which are still used in the celebration of the Lord's Supper. These tankards are inscribed in memory of Englebert Huff, a Norwegian, who, once attached to the Life Guards of the Prince of Orange, died in Fishkill at the age of 128 years. A story is still in circulation that when Huff was 121, he and a young man, 100 years his junior, simultaneously courted the same young lady. The story does not relate which of the lady's suitors won her favor.

11. At the English Church, Main St. curves R. The OBADIAH BOWNE HOUSE (L), now a frame structure, vacant, stands on a steep bank beside the railroad crossing. Obadiah Bowne built the house in 1818. It is set in a grove of old trees, which include a red beech reputed to be the first in the locality. The elaborate detail of the mantels and interior wood trim show, according to an authority, the hand of a traveling carpenter who was hired at a dollar a day plus board and lodging.

A plaque set in a boulder in front of the house was placed conjointly by the Melzingah Chapter of the Daughters of the American Revolution and the State of New York to commemorate the uses of a previous house, which stood here during the Revolution. In this earlier house, owned by Robert Brett, son of Madam Brett, Samuel Loudon, the patriot printer, lived and worked, and here the State Constitutional Convention first met. Later the building served as the first post office in Fishkill.

The junction with US 9 marks the end of the foot tour.

Dutchess County Motor Tours

NOTE ON MOTOR TOURS

Motor tours are divided into sections for the tourist's convenience; at the beginning of each section it is necessary to set the speedometer at *0.0 m*. Such parts of the tours as are on the main route are printed in larger type. Side-trips, leaving the main route, usually for only a few miles, are in smaller type, indented. The mileage on the side-trips is computed from the point of leaving the main route, which point is considered as *0.0 m*. Upon returning to the main route, it is necessary to set the speedometer back to the main-route mileage given for that point in the text.

TOUR NO. 1

Poughkeepsie—Hyde Park—Rhinebeck—Red Hook—Pine Plains—Amenia—Millbrook—Washington Hollow—Pleasant Valley—Poughkeepsie. US 9, State 199, US 44.
Poughkeepsie—Poughkeepsie, *77.2 m.*
The road in section a is 3-lane concrete; section b, 2-lane macadam; section c, 3-lane concrete. Between Poughkeepsie and Red Hook, local and interstate busses; in other sections, local busses.

This route follows main roads through northern Dutchess, exhibiting the variety of interests offered by the county. It winds up the historic

Hudson valley through sleepy villages, past grand estates, and between orchards of apple trees; then sweeps east across northern and southwest across central Dutchess through a typical rolling and hilly countryside devoted to dairying and a quiet life.

Section a. Poughkeepsie—Red Hook. US 9. 21.6 m.

From the Court House, Main and Market Sts., Poughkeepsie, the route turns W. on Main St. toward the river, and R. on Washington St. (US 9).

This section follows the heavily traveled Hudson valley route between New York and Albany. Today the highway runs well above the river-level. In an earlier day, when river transportation was of primary importance, the road dipped down at intervals to the villages along the waterfront; these sections of the old Post Road are now side-roads leading to such sleepy villages as Camelot, Chelsea, and Staatsburg.

The road on the east shore of the Hudson was first laid out from King's Bridge, New York, to the ferry opposite Albany, following closely an Indian trail which had existed long before the coming of the white man. Begun in the reign of Queen Anne, the road was at first known as the Queen's Road, later as the King's Highway, and since the Revolution as the Albany Post Road.

The heavy traffic includes not only private cars and busses, but also a large number of trucks; much of the New York City milk supply is shipped along this route. Day-driving is not dangerous or unpleasant, but at night, when a majority of trucks do their traveling, caution is necessary.

At *1.6 m.* is the entrance (L) to WOODCLIFF RECREATION PARK, the principal playground of Poughkeepsie. Shaded picnic grounds, an outdoor boxing arena, an outdoor dance floor, and a modern swimming pool *(adults 25c, children 15c, including lockers)* are among the facilities offered. Overlooking the Hudson, the pool is supplied by a continuous flow of filtered river water.

In the 1860's this was the estate of John F. Winslow, partner in a large iron foundry at Troy, holder of the first American rights for the manufacture of Bessemer steel, and staunch patron of John Ericsson. Plans for Ericsson's *Monitor,* the famous "cheesebox on a raft," were drawn in Winslow's home, now the Park Inn.

At *1.9 m.* is the entrance (R) to the HUDSON RIVER STATE HOSPITAL, an institution for the insane opened in 1871. It has 83 buildings and occupies 1,730 acres. Twenty-eight doctors and 1,100 employees care for an average of 4,400 patients. Ample provision has been made for the practice of recreational therapy.

At *2.9 m.* is the entrance (L) to the estate of Miss Ellen Roosevelt, cousin of Franklin D. Roosevelt. The house, 500 ft. from the road, is not visible from the highway.

The ST. ANDREW'S NOVITIATE (L), trains young men for service in the Jesuit Society. Established in Maryland in 1833, the Novitiate was moved to its present location in 1903. The wooded grounds surrounding the five-story, red brick building are dotted with shrines.

North of this point, between the highway and the Hudson River, are large, well-kept estates hidden by trees. To the right are farms on gently rising hills. Old trees raise a green arch over the Post Road as it crosses a broad plain, still called by its 18th century name, the Flats. The plain was once thickly forested and some of the early woodland remains, especially several magnificent oaks. Portions of the cleared ground have been under cultivation since before the Revolution. The broad lawns, tilled fields, and meadows have been likened to the countryside of southern England, the riverside mansions to the manors of the English gentry. Westward, terraces drop from the tableland to the river's edge, and the heights command a view of the Hudson as it sweeps southward into the LONG REACH, the 11-mile straight sailing course from Hyde Park to New Hamburg, named in 1609 by Robert Juet in his log of the *Half Moon* and known to the Dutch as the *Lange Rak*.

At *4.4 m.* is the ESTATE OF MRS. JAMES R. ROOSEVELT (L), widow of the half-brother of Franklin D. Roosevelt. The two-story clapboarded house, painted dark red with black trim, is visible through the trees. It was built between 1833 and 1835 by Joseph Giraud, but the original plan of the interior, with a central hall and stairway and two rooms on each side, was modified late in the 19th century.

Included in the Great Nine Partners Patent of 1697, the land was first settled in 1748 by Charles Crooke, a New York merchant, who came here to remove his blind son from the difficulties of city life. Within the next 75 years the estate changed hands several times. Edward and Joseph Giraud and Henry Kneeland, New York merchants, held the property until 1852, when it was purchased by Mrs. Walter Langdon (Dorothea Astor) for her daughter. James Roosevelt acquired the estate in 1868, leaving it to his son, James R. Roosevelt, whose widow is the present owner.

At *4.7 m.* is the entrance (L) to CRUM ELBOW, the estate of Mrs. Sara Delano Roosevelt and the birthplace and home of Franklin Delano Roosevelt. The entrance can be identified by a red sandstone marker, the 86th milestone from New York, which stands at the left of the road between this and the James R. Roosevelt property. (This marker is one of a series of sandstone tablets, now encased in fieldstones, which were erected in the 18th century along the route from lower Broadway, New York, to Albany). A guardhouse, in which state troopers are stationed when the President is in residence, stands inside the gate.

When there are no leaves on the trees a glimpse of the house can be caught from the highway. It stands at the edge of a steep, wooded slope overlooking the river. Southward is a sweeping view of the Hudson and the two bridges at Poughkeepsie. Groups of old trees shade the lawns, with hedges of dense hemlocks and rhododendrons on the north.

The house, built in 1748-51 by Charles Crooke, is a typical country residence of its period, 3 stories high and stuccoed, to which a semi-formal front and two stone wings have been added. A flagged and balustraded terrace leads to the curved Doric portico fronting the original building.

Milestone near entrance to Crum Elbow

Entrance drive to the Roosevelt estate

Crum Elbow, the Roosevelt Estate

The balustraded deck on the rooftop is a copy of the "Captain's walk" commonly found on houses in New England ports. The projecting wings, of gray stone 2 stories high, are crowned with simple cornice and balustrade. On the first story of the north wing is an arcade, in one aperture of which hangs an old Spanish bell. Around the house is a mass of evergreens, ivy, and honeysuckle.

The interior is simple and dignified. The library, in the south wing, is a large paneled room, with carved mantels at each end; the walls are covered with prints of figures in American naval history and early battles. The family interest in the sea finds further expression in the valuable collection of books on naval history. The west windows of the library overlook the lawn and the river. On the screened porch at the south of the library stands the tiller wheel of U. S. S. *Gloucester,* which took part in the battle of Santiago in 1898. The wheel was also used on the *Mayflower,* the presidential yacht during the administrations of Theodore Roosevelt, William H. Taft, and Woodrow Wilson.

At *5.6 m.* is the entrance (L) to CRUMWOLD, the Col. Archibald Rogers estate. The son, Herman Rogers, present owner of the estate, was born here. Mr. and Mrs. Herman Rogers have for many years been friends of Mrs. Wallis Simpson, and during the crisis that resulted in the abdication of Edward VIII, entertained her in their villa in Cannes.

HYDE PARK, *5.8 m.* (150 alt., 738 pop.).
Railroad Station: New York Central, .4 m. W. of center of village.
Busses: Twilight Bus Line, New York-Montreal Bus Line, Hyde Park Bus Line.
Accommodations: Zeph Hotel.

Hyde Park, founded in 1741, was originally known as Stoutenburg for Judge Jacobus Stoutenburgh, Gentleman, the first white settler. Later, the name was changed to Hyde Park, in compliment to Edward Hyde, Lord Cornbury, who was Governor of the Province of New York from 1702 to 1708.

The village lies on a plateau at the edge of a bluff a half-mile from the Hudson. On all sides except the west, it is hemmed in by landed estates. Crum Elbow Creek forms the north village line. The older houses are neat, well-kept frame buildings clustered near the crossroads. East of the village and roughly paralleling the highway, an outcrop of Hudson River shale topped by a scanty growth of scrub oaks forms a rugged background.

The village founder, a religious refugee and heir to a large estate, came from Holland at the beginning of the 18th century, moved north from Westchester and built three stone houses near Hyde Park village, on the tract known as the Nine Water Lots, one of which he owned. The big house of the Stoutenburghs and its extensive servants' quarters stood west of Park Pl. near Market St. Stoutenburgh erected a dock and boat-landing by the river on the site of the present landing. In October, 1777, the village was cannonaded by Gen. Sir John Vaughn as he retired down the Hudson after burning Kingston; marines came ashore to plunder and punish the Whigs, burned Stoutenburgh's landing, a shop, and an Army storehouse, and departed.

In the 19th century Hyde Park was the home port of sturgeon fishermen. The fish were dumped in pens anchored near the village shore; the meat was shipped to Albany to be sold as "Albany beef"; the roe was prepared here for exportation. Porpoises and shad were also attracted by the reefs and natural breeding grounds along the river. An occasional whale sent the entire local fleet in a chase upstream.

Throughout the two centuries of its existence, Hyde Park has witnessed the comings and goings of many celebrities and men who have been prominent in governmental affairs: Alexander Hamilton spent much time here; Washington Irving was an intimate friend of James Kirke Paulding, who lived nearby; Morgan Lewis, the Livingstons, the Pendletons, and Dr. Bard, founder of Bard College, were guests or residents.

One block S. of the crossroads is the JAMES ROOSEVELT MEMORIAL LIBRARY (L), Colonial in design, built in 1927 with stone from the Roosevelt estate. The library was given to the village by Mrs. Sara Delano Roosevelt in memory of her husband. Among the books on the shelves is a compilation of town records by Franklin D. Roosevelt.

Just W. of the crossroads (L) stands a building, now used in part as a plumber's shop, which was a 19th century inn. A long upper porch overlooks the road; a covered way leads through the lower story to an open yard and sheds where the horses of the Post Road stage-coaches were changed.

North of the crossroads, on US 9, is the REFORMED CHURCH (R), established in 1789. The white frame building of simple Colonial design, with a square tower over the main entrance, has high, arched windows at the front and old-fashioned small panes and memorial windows at the sides and rear. In the yard behind the church, grave markers date back to that of "Mr. Noah Bunnel, 1790."

At *6.8 m.* is the ornate stone entrance (L) to the estate of F. W. Vanderbilt.

At *7 m.* is ST. JAMES' CHURCH (R), built in 1844 and long attended by the Roosevelt family. English Gothic in style and set back from the road in a handsome grove of trees, it has the grave dignity and beauty of its forebears in the English shires. The chief feature of the front is a tall, square tower, with a low pitched roof that is more Italian than English. The interior, consisting of a nave and chancel, without aisles, is plastered, and has simple woodwork in black walnut, and hammer-beam trusses. The first two windows, with clear diamond panes, are from the original church, built in 1811. Two others, of simple stained glass, were brought from the Church of the Ascension in New York City.

Dr. Samuel Bard, a famous New York physician and president of the College of Physicians and Surgeons in New York, donated land for the first structure. The tract had been granted to his family by Queen Anne. The 125th anniversary of the founding of St. James' Parish and the erection and consecration of the original church was celebrated October 25, 1936, at a service attended by President Franklin D. Roosevelt and his family.

North of Hyde Park the contrast between the formal estates and the natural beauty of the countryside is striking. The highway here is flanked by concrete and steel fences.

At *7.5 m.* is the SITE OF PLACENTIA (L), the home of James Kirke Paulding, Secretary of the Navy under Martin Van Buren. Paulding was Washington Irving's biographer and collaborated with him in the *Salmagundi Papers,* a satirical literary periodical published in 1807. He was author of many books and for a time an editorial writer for the *New York Evening Post* under William Cullen Bryant. The house was occupied by Paulding from 1846 until his death in 1860.

A view of ST. JOSEPH'S NOVITIATE (L), across the Hudson River, appears at *9.1 m.* The massive stone structure, with its many spires, is situated on a high bluff overlooking the river. Since bluff and river are invisible from the road, St. Joseph's appears to be across the meadow.

MARGARET LEWIS NORRIE STATE PARK, *9.5 m.* (L), was donated to New York State by Geraldine Morgan Thompson in memory of her sister, Margaret Lewis Norrie. The 312 acres of ground, with wooded hills, slope down from the highway to the river front. In 1937 a large Civilian Conservation Corps Camp housed the young men who were developing the area into a recreational center. Plans have been drawn for a large swimming pool and picnic grounds with parking fields, and paths radiating from the highway to the Hudson River.

At *9.75 m.* is junction (L) with the old Post Road, macadam. *(See Tour No. 1A.)*

US 9 swings R. up a long, easy grade with views left across the meadows to the river. Twenty miles away tower the Catskill Mountains, their rounded blue bulk filling the Northwest horizon.

At *13.1 m.,* north of a white mansion, is the PARTHENON (R), a small wooden reproduction of the Greek temple. It was built by J. W. Gardner, a corporation lawyer, and houses his valuable law library. A collection of first editions of Blackstone is shown occasionally to visitors. Behind the Parthenon is an original Dutch windmill, imported from Holland.

The Rhinebeck line is crossed at 16.3 m.

At *16.4 m.* is the junction (L) with the OLD MILL ROAD.

> Left on this dirt road is GRASMERE (Fox Hollow School), *.75 m.* (L), the home of the late Maunsell Crosby. The dignified mansion of red brick overlooks wide lawns and rolling wooded hills extending toward the Hudson. This was the birthplace of W. A. Duer, president of Columbia College (1829-1842).
>
> Grasmere was begun in 1773 by Gen. Richard Montgomery and completed by his wife after his death. The many locust trees on the grounds grew from seeds scattered by Mrs. Montgomery in her walks about the estate. In 1828, the 700-acre estate was purchased by Peter H. and Lewis Livingston, who lived here until 1850. It was purchased by Mrs. Fanny Crosby in 1894. It is now a private school for girls.
>
> Beyond the Fox Hollow School is ELLERSLIE, *2.7 m.,* the former home of Levi P. Morton, elected Vice President of the United States in 1888 and Governor of New York State in 1894. The home is now occupied by his daughter, Miss Helen Morton.

WILDERCLIFF, *4 m.* (R), is an estate owned by R. B. Suckley. The name is an example of the fusion of the Dutch and English forms in many place names in the Hudson Valley. With slight variations in spelling, it appears to have clung to the estate for 200 years, and may have had its origin in the Dutch *wilden,* wild men or savages, and *clif,* old Dutch for rock.

On the northern end of the river cove on the estate is an INDIAN PICTURE ROCK, dating from at least 1686, when the Indians sold the land. Originally the rock showed a cutting of two Indian warriors; today only one figure can be seen. The tomahawk which was in the left hand is gone, but the calumet in the right hand can still be made out. The carvings were apparently chipped in the rock by a tool with rotary motion. The picture rock is difficult of access and can be reached only by canoe or by wading knee-deep through water.

RHINEBECK, *16.9 m.* (203 alt., 1,569 pop.).
Railroad Station: At Rhinecliff.
Ferry: Rhinecliff.
Bus Line: Twilight Bus Line.
Accommodations and Information: Beekman Arms Hotel.
Motion Picture House: One.

As it approaches Rhinebeck, the road is bordered by large shade trees. The village has an air of age and substance, with dignified buildings close to the highway. In 1670 William Beekman, an employee of the Dutch West India Co., purchased land in this vicinity. In 1697 his son, Henry, secured a patent for a vast tract of land lying opposite Esopus Creek, which included the site of Rhinebeck. This section of the land passed to William Traphagen in 1700. Among the early settlers, mainly French Huguenots and Dutch, was a group of Palatines, who are credited with naming the village for Rheinbach, a village in the Rhine valley. Other sources give the name as a German combination meaning "Rhine-like"; still others contend it is of local invention and merely means "Beekman's Rhine."

Early in the 18th century the village was a change station for stage-coaches; during the Revolution it was an active military center. Modern Rhinebeck is engaged in dairy farming and fruit raising. The cultivation of violets, for many years an important industry in this section, recently declined, but is again on the rise.

In RHINEBECK CEMETERY (L), at the extreme southern end of the village and bordering US 9, is the grave of Levi P. Morton.

VINCENT ASTOR CONVALESCENT SCHOOL FOR GIRLS (L) is at the southern end of the village. It was established in 1901 at Rhinecliff by Miss Mary Morton, daughter of Levi P. Morton, to provide a suitable environment and recreation for convalescent under-privileged children of New York City, and was later taken over by the Vincent Astor family, patrons of Rhinebeck, who moved it to its present location.

Built in 1809, the REFORMED CHURCH (R), on US 9, one block S. of the village center, is painted white, except for the ivy-covered north side and the brown cornice and blinds. The south end has a pediment with a bulls-eye filled with louvres, surrounded by a wooden tower and belfry. On this side are both round and elliptical arches, with the usual Colonial keystones; while the east and west sides have high windows with pointed arches and interesting sectional outside blinds.

The sides of the building facing the two streets are of brick, while the east side, away from the road, is of stone. According to local tradition, this construction grew out of a dispute between factions as to which material should be used. Those who could furnish stone did so and demanded that the building be built of stone; others who could furnish money demanded brick construction. They compromised.

The history of the church goes back to 1730. In that year Henry Beekman gave a deed for 2 acres of land to the inhabitants of North Ward (Rhinebeck) for the purpose of erecting a church or meeting house within 3 years; and he gave the minister, elders, and deacons the right to cut timber or carry away stones from his land. In accordance with the provisions, a church was completed in 1733. Henry Beekman was buried in 1776 in the church of which he was the benefactor.

The BEEKMAN ARMS HOTEL, at the SW. corner of the intersection of US 9 and State 308, is the largest and most prominent building in the village. It claims to be the oldest operating hotel in the United States. The original inn was a one-story stone house with two rooms and a loft, built shortly after 1700 by William Traphagen on this land which he bought that year. His grandson, Arent Traphagen, enlarged the business, which at his death in 1769 occupied a building 2 stories high and covered the area of the present main structure. It was built like a fortress, with heavy stone walls; and the arrangement of the cellar indicates that it was intended to serve that purpose. The present third story was added in 1865. The wooden wing on the north, the brick wing on the south, and the pillared portico across the front are later additions. The original building is stuccoed, painted white, producing a harmonious general effect. The modern taproom has a fireplace said to date back to the original building. The entrance hall retains its old beamed ceiling, but the post and knees ostensibly supporting it are apparently modern. During its long history the hotel has entertained such distinguished guests as George Washington, Alexander Hamilton, Aaron Burr, De Witt Clinton, and Theodore Roosevelt. Adjoining the hotel on the S. is a courtyard, used during the Revolutionary War as a parade and training ground for soldiers.

The BOWERY HOUSE, a short distance E. (R) on State 308, is a frame structure painted yellow, with brown trim and small-paned windows. The main entrance is set off by a porch with Doric columns.

This inn was erected about 1800 on the land of the Old Dutch Church, which served as the dominie's farm (Dutch, *bouwerie*). Abram Brinckerhoff, the first proprietor, was succeeded by Pieter Pultz, after whom it is often called the Pultz Tavern. It was once the stopping place of the Yellow Bird Coach line, and rivalled in fame the old hotel (Beekman Arms) on the Post Road.

Right from the center of the village runs State 308, an alternate route between US 9 and State 199. This new concrete road winds through a thinly settled farming country, the wooded sections interspersed with small truck farms.

At *5.2 m.* is the entrance (R) to LAKE SEPASCO (open), with an area of 25 acres. CAMP RAMAPO is located on the southern tip of the lake. Large picnic grounds surround the lake, which is ideal for swimming and fishing. Boats may be hired at the northern end of the lake.

At ROCK CITY, *6.5 m.* is junction with State 199. *(See section b.)*

The CHURCH OF THE MESSIAH (R), just above the intersection, is a low stone structure, Gothic in style, artistically comparable to St. James' Church at Hyde Park. Built in 1897 with funds donated by the family of John Jacob Astor, it was designed by Stanford White as a miniature of an English cathedral. Episcopal in faith, the church is a center of worship for the owners of estates in the region, and serves as music center for the village.

At *16.9 m.* is the junction (L) with a dirt road. *(See Tour No. 1B).*

At *17 m.* is the NORTHERN DUTCHESS HEALTH CENTER (L), a red brick structure of the hospital type, which was built in 1931. Thomas Thompson of Boston, a frequent visitor in Rhinebeck, founded the Center 35 years ago. It is operated by a board of managers under the Thompson Trust and maintains clinics and emergency and isolation wards for the northern towns of the county. Miss Helen Morton donated the operating room in memory of her parents, Mr. and Mrs. Levi P. Morton.

Opposite the Health Center are the ETHAN COONS GREENHOUSES (R). The plant consists of 25 greenhouses which specialize in double English violets. It serves a nation-wide market; flowers are sent by air to points west of the Mississippi. The Princess Mary, a semi-double, dark violet was developed here.

Just beyond the greenhouses, a road runs R. to where the Dutchess County Fair is held during the first week in September. The chief attractions are the agricultural exhibits in which the juvenile grange and 4-H clubs join. Special features of the fair are the horse and automobile races.

At *17.3 m.* US 9 enters ASTOR FLATS, a 2-mile straightaway used 20 years ago as a testing ground for automobiles. It is a section of the vast local estate of Vincent Astor; the house and outbuildings lie on the river front. Tenant farmers care for the fruit orchards and guard the wooded game preserve.

At *19.4 m.* the road curves around the yellow, somber Evangelical Lutheran Church of St. Peter the Apostle, known for more than a century as the OLD STONE CHURCH (L). The edifice was built in 1730. In 1729, Lutheran residents in that neighborhood applied to Gilbert Livingston, the husband of Cornelia Beekman, for a lot for a church near "Kirchehoek," and near the Old German Church, then standing. Livingston gave the site upon which the stone church was built and also that of the adjoining cemetery, providing in the deed that the land should forever be used for church purposes only. The oldest stone in the cemetery, dated Jan. 25, 1733, is that of Carl Neher, who was actively employed in the building of the early church. In 1824 the church was remodeled and enlarged and its present tower added.

North of the Old Stone Church, US 9 passes through a wide and level area of rich soil devoted to the apple and grape industry. Orchards line the highway at intervals from Rhinebeck north to the county line. This is a favorite drive in the spring when the trees are in bloom. In late summer innumerable roadside stands carry on a brisk trade in vegetables, fruits, and preserves.

RED HOOK, *21.2 m.* (200 alt., 996 pop.).
Railroad Station: New York Central at Barrytown, 3 m. W.
Bus Line: Twilight Bus Line.
Accommodations: Red Hook Hotel.
Motion Picture House: One.

The first settlers in this region were Dutch, who came to what is now Upper Red Hook, 3 miles N. of the present village, between 1713 and 1727. As the result of a village quarrel, the postmaster moved the office to the site of the present village. The name is said to have been given the region by early Dutch navigators, who saw a hillside covered with red berries near Tivoli and called the place *Roode Hoeck.* The village is today the center of the northern Dutchess fruit belt.

The RED HOOK COLD STORAGE CO. WAREHOUSE (R), just S. of the railroad tracks, has a capacity of 80,000 barrels. Apples are trucked to New York City and shipped all over the world. The production of cider and vinegar is an important industry.

Opposite the Methodist Church on W. Market St. is a VILLAGE BLACKSMITH SHOP, now a rarity. The low, one-room building is cluttered with discarded horseshoes and iron work. The smith in charge remembers coach-and-four days and will talk of them.

At traffic light, *21.6 m.,* the route turns R. on State 199. *(See Section b.)*
For continuation of US 9 to county line see Tour No. 1C.

Section b. Red Hook—Junction State 199 and US 44. State 199. 23.5 m.

This section, across northern Dutchess, leads through a hilly region marked by self-contained hamlets, fruit orchards, and summer camps. The social life of the little agricultural communities centers in the grange hall and the church. Several high elevations along the route offer expansive views of the countryside.

From traffic light in Red Hook the route turns R. on State 199.

The RED HOOK COUNTRY CLUB, *3.3 m.* (R), is a private club with an excellent 18-hole golf course and boating facilities.

At *4 m.* is the junction with State 308 in ROCK CITY (360 alt., 75 pop.), a cross-roads hamlet named for the deep ravine on the edge of the village, through which a brook flows.

At *8.1 m.* is the entrance (L) to MARKS MEMORIAL CAMP OF THE TRIBUNE FRESH AIR FUND, sponsored by the New York *Herald-Tribune.* Throughout the summer, groups of under-privileged New York children enjoy two-week vacation periods here.

LA FAYETTEVILLE, *8.8 m.* (700 alt., 25 pop.), a one-street village with a few houses on each side and a country store, was named in honor of the Marquis de La Fayette. LA FAYETTEVILLE HOUSE (L), so named in 1824, is a weather-beaten clapboard structure with first- and second-story rickety white porches running across the front of the building. This house was a famous relay station and overnight stop for post riders before the railroad era.

At *11.6 m.* is the CHRISTIAN CHURCH (R), dedicated in 1859. This white frame building is one of the many churches which sprang up in the boom times of the railroad era following 1850, and remained standing in secluded spots long after the people who worshipped in them had moved to larger villages. The building is now used as a storehouse and garage.

At *14.5 m.* is junction with dirt road.

> Right, on the road, is STISSING LAKE, *.75 m.*, with Stissing Mt. (1,440 ft.) in the background. The road around the lake, which is bordered by wild flowers and mountain laurel, passes a large summer camp for Jewish people. The lake affords excellent small-mouthed bass and pickerel fishing. There are public beaches and boat liveries.

PINE PLAINS, *15.3 m.* (474 alt., 500 pop.).
Busses: Mid-County Bus Line.
Accommodations: Stissing House.
Motion Picture House: One.
Recreation: Small-mouthed bass and pickerel fishing in Mud and Miller lakes nearby.

Pine Plains is a peaceful country village built around a crossroads. Main St. (State 82) runs N. and S., crossing State 199 at traffic light. The homes, surrounded by wide, shady lawns, are set well back from the broad street.

The stone TOWER surmounted by the village clock, on Main St. just R. of intersection, is a memorial to Dr. Henry C. Wilber, a physician who practiced here from 1887 to 1919.

The COLE PHARMACY (L), on Main St., houses the FIRST PUBLIC LIBRARY in Dutchess County, which has been located in the same building since it was established in 1797.

The ENO LAW OFFICE, Main St. (L), a one-story, yellow clapboard structure, was erected in 1814 by Stephen Eno, celebrated Dutchess County jurist who is said to have worn knee breeches and his hair tied in a queue, after the manner of the 18th century gentleman, until his death in 1854 at the age of ninety.

> State 82 (Main St.), known as the Central Dutchess Highway, follows the E. bank of Wappinger Creek to a junction with US 44. *(See Tour No. 1 D.)*

Beyond Pine Plains, State 199 ascends gradually through a narrow, wooded, sparsely settled valley.

At *18.9 m.* is a rear view of the Dutchess hills backed by the glimmering Hudson and the bulk of the Catskill Mountains, 35 m. W.

At *23.5 m.* is junction with US 44. The main route turns R. on US 44.

Left on US 44 is MILLERTON, *1.3 m.* (600 alt., 919 pop.).
Railroad Station: New York Central R. R. (Harlem Valley Division), daily passenger and freight trains.

Accommodations: Brick Block Hotel.

Millerton derived its name from a contractor named Miller, who built the railroad through the village in 1845, and established his headquarters here. Millerton has a bustling business section and is a distribution center for a large dairy region, shipping the product by railroad and truck to New York City.

The village lies at the foot of the TACONIC TRI-STATE PARK, a recreation area 20 m. long, on the Massachusetts, Connecticut, and New York borders. Most of the New York section lies in Columbia County, immediately North.

North on Maple Ave. is RUDD POND CAMPSITE, *2 m.,* with foot trails, picnic grounds, and campsites along the shore of Rudd Pond, a 75-acre lake with canoe, boat, and fishing facilities, and hiking trails. Sites and tents may be rented nearby. Hills east of the lake have been planted with young pines; imported sand placed by CCC workers during 1935-36 has transformed the muddy lake shore into an ideal bathing beach.

South on Maple Ave. is INDIAN LAKE, *3 m.,* most of its 2-m. length in Connecticut; fishing and picnics.

Section c. Junction State 199 and US 44—Washington Hollow—Poughkeepsie. US 44. 32.2 m.

Unexpected curves and patched macadam on most of route. The New York Central R. R. (Harlem Valley Division) parallels the route to Amenia.

US 44 is a direct route from the Berkshires to the West. The Dutchess Turnpike, predecessor of US 44, was surveyed in 1802, and was completed from Litchfield, Conn., to Poughkeepsie in 1805. Since the days of the stagecoach, traffic over this route has increased in response to changing modes of transportation, until today the road is an important link between the East and the West. It has a gradual descending grade from 900 ft. to tidewater level. The highway at first winds through the beautiful Harlem valley, flanked on both sides by mountain ranges. Small farming communities on the floor of the valley present a contrast to the wild beauty of the wooded slopes.

From junction of State 199 and US 44, the route turns R. on US 44.

AMENIA, *6.8 m.* (573 alt., 1,560 pop.).
Railroad Station: New York Central (Harlem Valley Division).
Busses: Harlem Valley Bus Line.
Accommodations: Amenia Inn, De La Vergne Farms Hotel.

Dr. Thomas Young, a local poet, in 1762 named the village from the Latin word "Amoena," meaning "a pleasant place."

The growth and development of the village was largely determined by its location at a focal point for routes south and west. Here taverns and stables sprang up, and dwellings followed. Then came the discovery of iron in the mountains; and, with limestone for flux at hand, the community soon developed industrially. The Amenia Iron Co. mines, now abandoned, on the west bounds of the village, were an important factor in the growth. The present prosperity of Amenia is based on its excellent farm lands. Some of the most prosperous dairy farms of the county are within the township. The mountains afford little hunting but the small, rapid streams are well stocked with trout and attract many anglers in the fishing season.

The GRANGE HALL, Main St., is a popular social center.

AMENIA HIGH SCHOOL stands on the site of the Amenia Seminary, a Methodist school established in 1835. The Seminary existed for 53 years; students enrolled from every State in the Union.

At center of village is junction with State 200.

> Left on State 200 is TROUTBECK, *.75 m.*, the estate of J. E. Spingarn, nationally known critic, famous as the place where many authors have gathered and written. Here Luther Burbank spent much time and wrote the introduction to Charles Benton's book *Troutbeck.*
>
> At *3.5 m.* is the NEW YORK-CONNECTICUT STATE LINE. Before the boundary was definitely settled *(see* p.   ), the settlers in the doubtful territory quarreled. According to local tradition, "The Connecticut settlers were Yankees, and there were witches in Connecticut. They never came over the line into New York."

US 44 bears R. on West Main St.

At *7.7 m.* is LAKE AMENIA (L), one-half mile long, with swimming, boating, and fishing facilities and a bungalow colony.

Near the end of the lake the highway begins its S-curve ascent of De La Vergne Hill, 1.3 m. long. From a point at *8.8 m.*, near the top of the ascent, is a view (L) down the pasturelands of the Harlem valley, with a narrow rock pass far south, through which State 22 makes its way.

At the top of De La Vergne Hill (929 alt.), *9.3 m.*, is the junction (R) with State 82 A. *(See Tour 1D).*

For the next 9 m. the road gradually descends to an altitude of 565 ft. at Millbrook. This section is rocky and hilly, with few dwellings.

At *11.2 m.* is a dirt road (R), the entrance to MILLBROOK SCHOOL, a private preparatory school for boys, established in 1930.

At *12.6 m.* is the MILLBROOK THEATRE (L), one of the dozens of country playhouses developed by the little-theatre movement. Broadway try-outs are held here during July and August from Wednesday to Saturday (no matinees). The one-story building was originally a Quaker meeting house; the pews are still used and seat approximately 250 persons. The windows are of early design, with 6-in. square panes. Charles S. Howard and Edward Massey are directors.

At *15.2 m.* is an open-air SWIMMING POOL (L) *(admission 35c),* equipped with bathhouses and shower facilities.

MABBETTSVILLE, *15.4 m.* (692 alt., 40 pop.), a hamlet consisting of a store, a garage, and a cluster of houses, was early named Filkentown in honor of one of the Great Nine Partners. The present name was derived from James Mabbett, a commission auctioneer who settled here early in the 19th century.

Between Mabbettsville and Millbrook lies the large private estate DANHEIM (R), formerly the property of C. F. Dietrich. Its 2,500 acres are partly improved and partly in the natural wooded state.

At *16.9 m.,* opposite main gateway to Danheim (R), US 44 turns sharply L. and enters the village of MILLBROOK.

MILLBROOK, *17.2 m.* (565 alt., 1,296 pop.).
Railroad Station: New York, New Haven & Hartford R. R. (freight service only).
Accommodations: Millbrook Hotel and Millbrook Inn.

Millbrook grew with the building of the railroad and station in 1869. The name was given in compliment to George H. Brown, who was chiefly responsible for the completion of the road and who named his estate Millbrook Farms. The village, incorporated in 1895, is a landscaped expanse of modern homes with trim lawns and shade trees. The hamlets of Mabbettsville, South Millbrook, and Mechanics are suburbs. The surrounding countryside is particularly beautiful with hills, wooded slopes, and wide meadows. Much of this area is included in large estates, and several of the mansions are visible from the highway. A number of stables are maintained; riding and hunting are popular. Writers and artists have been attracted to Millbrook, and the summer theatre is enthusiastically supported.

Both the Hicksite and Orthodox Quakers have continued active here. The Hicksites meet occasionally in the Brick Meeting House in Mechanic, on State 343, E. of South Millbrook. In 1926 the Orthodox joined with the Dutch Reformed and Methodist congregations to build the Federated Church in Millbrook.

US 44 follows Franklin Ave. to North Ave. and turns L. on North Ave. At *17.8 m.* is junction with dirt road.

> Right, on this dirt road, is the HART HOMESTEAD, *.5 m.*, built in 1800 by Philip Hart, owner of a fulling mill. It is a Colonial frame house, with hand-carved paneling and elaborately decorated window cornices. A 6-ft. fireplace of simple hand-carved design is in the right wing. Antique furniture completes the picture of a pleasing old homestead. When the house was built the front was painted white and the rear red, in keeping with the general practice of the period.

At *18.4 m.* is the BENNETT SCHOOL and BENNETT SCHOOL JUNIOR COLLEGE (R). The Bennett School was founded by May Friend Bennett at Irvington-on-the-Hudson in 1891. In 1907 Miss Bennett purchased the former Halcyon Hall in Millbrook, a vacant hotel, and moved the school to the site it now occupies. The buildings are on a knoll, surrounded by a wide lawn. The tennis courts and archery range are visible from the highway. Three graduates of the school's drama department, Mildred Natwick, Helen Chandler, and Helen Trenholme, have appeared on Broadway. Betty Furness, featured film player, graduated from the high school department. Gail Bolger, another graduate, appeared with Helen Chandler in the 1936 production of *Pride and Prejudice.* Greek drama was first presented in 1920. In 1922 an outdoor Greek theatre was built, in which Greek Festivals are held each year.

In 1935 the school's department of liberal and applied arts was chartered as a junior college, covering the 4-year general or college preparatory course. It also offers a 2-year course in academic studies, dramatic art, music, fine and applied arts, household arts, and secretarial duties.

At *18.5 m.* is FOUR CORNERS MONUMENT, the junction of State 82, State 243, and US 44. A stone shaft at the center of the intersection gives directions. US 44 turns R.

SOUTH MILLBROOK, *18.5 m.,* was formerly known as the Four Corners and Washington Four Corners, and became Washington, N. Y., in 1869. The name confused postal clerks, who read the "D. C." (Dutchess County) as District of Columbia; and the name was therefore again changed to South Millbrook.

> Left on State 343 is the entrance (R) to the PHEASANT BREEDERS AND HUNTING ASSOCIATION, *.4 m.* A varying admission is charged for the privilege of hunting pheasants on the estate.
> At *.7 m.* is the MILLBROOK GOLF CLUB (L). Golfing, swimming, and tennis facilities are provided.
> The hamlet of MECHANIC, *1 m.,* so named because of the number of skilled workmen employed in the various blacksmith, carpentry, and wagon-making shops in the neighborhood, grew around the BRICK MEETING HOUSE (L), built in 1780 by the Nine Partners Meeting of Society of Friends. The two-story rectangular brick building, 40 by 75 ft., is in such excellent condition that a casual glance might give the impression that it is of recent construction. It is free from ornamentation. The interior was divided into two parts—one for men and one for women. A raised platform was provided for the speakers, and rough benches for the congregation. On both the women's and men's sides cast-iron woodburning stoves are still in position. No alterations have been made since the meeting house was erected. On the lawn in front of the building is a sun dial, donated by Jacob Willetts *(see below).* A horse block still remains on the driveway (R).
> Freed Negro slaves sought the protection of the Quakers a century ago and built a colony of huts near the church. The hovels were destroyed to make way for landscaping SANDANONA (Indian, *Sunshine*), the adjacent estate of John D. Wing.
> The site (R) of the NINE PARTNERS SCHOOL lies 500 ft. E. of the meeting house. This school was opened by the Society of Friends in 1796, especially for those of their faith who were in indigent circumstances. A thorough academic course was offered; attendance reached 100 students. It continued to prosper until the division of the Society of Friends in 1828 into Orthodox and Hicksite groups. *(See Tour No. 4.)* Upon this division the Hicksites withdrew from the Orthodox Nine Partners school and established a separate and similar school under the principalship of Jacob and Deborah Willets, who had been among the first pupils to attend the original school. Jacob Willetts was the author of popular arithmetic and geography textbooks: to his inspiration we owe the useful lyric beginning "Thirty days hath September." Deborah Rodgers Willetts was a noted grammarian and mathematician. The Nine Partners School continued under the management of the Orthodox branch until 1835. Later it was reopened and continued under other direction until 1864. The building was then removed, and part of it was incorporated in the construction of John D. Wing's private residence.

THORNDALE, *19.2 m.* (R), occupied by Oakleigh Thorne, is the old homestead made famous by the horses and cattle bred under the direction of Edwin and Samuel Thorne. In 1860, Samuel Thorne's herd of 70 short-horn Durhams, valued at $70,000, was regarded by authorities as the best herd in the United States. The low stone house built in 1725 by Isaac and Hannah Thorne still stands on the grounds. The extensive flower gardens are open to inspection during the spring.

At *20.8 m.* is view (R) across the Dutchess woods to the bulging blue line of the Catskills.

WASHINGTON HOLLOW, *23.8 m.* (321 alt., 80 pop.), is today a residential village for Poughkeepsie commuters. The small white frame houses on the one street are shaded by large maples. Settled before the end of the Revolution, it was in 1813 the camp ground for artillery trains bound for Sacketts Harbor. For a number of years it was the site of the Dutchess County Fair. The lonely bandstand, racetrack, and rambling hotel are still intact (R) at the edge of the village, adjoining the N. junction with State 82 (R).

At *23.9 m.*, about 200 ft. from the road, with the grounds enclosed by a fieldstone wall, is the ZACHEUS NEWCOMB HOUSE (L), one of the earliest examples of the Dutch brick house in Dutchess County, built in 1777 by Sarah Tobias Newcomb, while her husband, Zacheus, was away at war. Mrs. Newcomb not only superintended the construction of the house but also directed the manufacture of the bricks which were used in it. The pond visible from the highway, was formed by flooding the pit from which the brick clay was dug.

The house is Georgian, 2 stories high, with a gambrel roof. The floor plan is that of the usual 18th century house, with a central hall bisecting the structure. The bricks are laid in Flemish bond. The south porch is an exact reproduction of the original, and the front door is the one built with the house, as are the mantels, window seats, corner cupboards, wood trim, and blue tile.

At *24.5 m.* is a view (L) of the Hudson Highlands.

At *25.8 m.* is junction with dirt road.

> Left on this road is the JOHN NEWCOMB HOUSE *.7 m.* (L). In 1802 John Newcomb, a son of Zacheus Newcomb, built a fulling mill on the stream that crosses this tract. In 1808 he built the two-story frame structure. There is a leaded design over the Dutch door and small panes of glass on either side. The angles of the outside walls are bound with quoins of wood, and a rope design is employed under the eaves. The walls of the hall are plastered to resemble purple and white marble. In the southwest bedroom is a hand-carved mantel. The kitchen wing has a large stone fireplace, wide floor planks, and handhewn ceiling beams. A slave bench was once fastened to the wall beside the fireplace. This was a rough 6-ft. plank, an inch thick and a foot wide. When the slaves misbehaved they were forced to sit on the bench close to a huge dog tied at one end of the bench. The bench is in the possession of Mrs. Floyd Laird of Pleasant Valley. The property was purchased by Mrs. Alson Laird in 1867, and is now occupied by a tenant farmer. A few minor changes have been made, but in the main the house is in its original condition.

PLEASANT VALLEY, *26 m.* (200 alt., 300 pop.).

Railroad Station: The New York, New Haven & Hartford R. R. (Pine Plains Branch) (freight only).

Accommodations: **Barths Hotel.**

Settled in 1740 by Quakers and Presbyterians while still a part of the Crum Elbow Precinct, Pleasant Valley soon became a center for grist and cotton mills operated by the waters of Wappinger Creek. The largest cotton plant was built in 1815, which in 1860 operated 80 looms and employed 75 men, women, and children. Industry died at the end of the 19th century. The village today is a bustling Poughkeepsie suburb, its wide streets shaded by elms.

At *26.7 m.,* just beyond the village, is the new power station of the NIAGARA HUDSON POWER & LIGHT CORPORATION (R).

East of the plant stands a curious old stone barn, an interesting juxtaposition of the old and the modern. It is of interest primarily because its masonry is typical of the 18th century and because of openings formed in the walls, narrow on the outside, flaring within, similar to the loopholes in early blockhouses. Records of its origin are lost, but it is believed to have been erected in the 1750's as a defense post against possible French-Indian raids. There are four other such buildings in the Hudson Valley, at Harmon, New Paltz, Rensselaer, and Kerhonkson, Ulster County.

From this point to Poughkeepsie many tourist cabins line the highway and cottages extend down the slope on the S. to Wappinger Creek.

At *27.9 m.* is junction with a dirt road.

> Left on this road is ROCHDALE, *.5 m.,* a settlement of summer cottages. The hamlet is on Wappinger Creek, which provides boating and bathing. The excellent fishing in the creek includes bass, trout, eels, catfish, and suckers. Pheasants, rabbits, and squirrels are found in all parts of the township. The section is heavily wooded.

At *30.2 m.* is junction with a macadam road.

> Left on this road is the ZEPHANIAH PLATT HOUSE, *.4 m.* (L). The house was built in two parts. The older portion, erected about 1735 by Gilbert Palen, consisted of two rooms and a basement kitchen. Zephaniah Platt acquired the place in 1762, and before 1775 built the addition at the right which doubled the size of the house. The enlargement was doubtless made to accommodate the large family, for here twelve children were born to him and his wife, Mary, daughter of Theodorus Van Wyck, of Wiccopee. Platt was prominent in the political history of the State, serving in the Revolution as a colonel of militia and a member of the New York Provincial Congress; and later as a State senator and member of the Constitutional Convention at Poughkeepsie where he voted in favor of ratification. In 1798 he moved to the northern part of the State; with his three brothers, and others from Poughkeepsie, he founded the city of Plattsburgh.
>
> The house stands today practically unaltered. It is built of native fieldstone, with a second story in brick and a gambrel roof. The front door is of the Dutch double type and has a brass knocker of Revolutionary design. Two rooms are graced by deep fireplaces with carved mantels. The original cellar door is still in use. The hinges are of wood and the long bar that locks the door rests in crude wooden sockets.
>
> Left at the Platt House. At *.5 m.* across the White Bridge over Wappinger Creek. Proceed up the hill, where at *.8 m.* is the junction of three roads. Take L. fork and proceed straight ahead.

At *1.2 m.* is the SLEIGHT HOUSE (L), one of the few remaining examples of the early Dutch stone houses in Dutchess County. Of select native fieldstone, the building is 2 stories high, with a main hall bisecting it in the 18th century style. It was erected in 1798 by Jacobus Sleight, who married Elsie De Riemer, a descendant of Isaac De Riemer, one of the early mayors of New York City. The house was raised on the site of a smaller one built by Abram Sleight, father of Jacobus, in the second quarter of the 18th century. The old frame barn, E. of the house, in excellent condition, was put up in 1831. The present owner is a descendant of the builder.

Across the highway from the junction is a farmers' cooperative market, where fruit and vegetables are sold in season.

From the top of the hill at *31 m.* is a view of the suburb of Arlington.

At *31.4 m.* are the modern office structures (L) of the NEW YORK STATE HIGHWAY DEPARTMENT and the COUNTY HIGHWAY DEPARTMENT.

US 44 passes through the business section of Arlington, on the outskirts of Poughkeepsie.

At *32.2 m.* is the Poughkeepsie city line. *(See Poughkeepsie.)*

TOUR 1 A

Junction US 9 and Old Post Road—Staatsburg. Old Post Road. 1. 7 m.
Left from US 9 on Old Post Road.
STAATSBURG, *.5 m.* (90 alt., 530 pop.).
Railroad Station: New York Central, center of village.
Busses: Twilight Bus Line, flag stop.

In 1693, Captain Henry Pawling, an English officer, bought 4,000 acres of land in Dutchess County from the Indians. In 1698, his widow and children obtained a Crown patent, but in 1701 sold their rights to Dr. Samuel Staats and Dirck Van Der Burgh, both of New York City, for 130 pounds. The village name is a union of the names of the two owners.

In earlier years, ice cutting on the Hudson River was an important industry, directly west of the village of Staatsburg was one of the largest plants. In 1858, J. H. Bodenstein established a shop for the manufacture of ice-cutting implements. The business expanded, and today the Staatsburg Ice Tool Works sells its products throughout the United States and abroad.

Beneath Staatsburg is an underlying stratum of quicksand. Buildings in the village located above this stratum quiver when the New York Central trains pass over the section of the railroad tracks which crosses the quicksand.

At the south end of the village, opposite the high school, stands the OLD STONE HOUSE (R), built early in the 18th century. It is a substantial square building with four chimneys, the porch and wood trim painted red. Tradition says that it was an inn in the stage coach days.

About one-half mile L. from center of village on a narrow, macadam road is the LEWIS GORDON NORRIE PARK, on the banks of the Hudson. The entrance is marked by a monument. The park was donated to the people of Staatsburg by Geraldine Morgan Thompson in memory of a favorite nephew, who spent the summers of his childhood in Staatsburg. He died in 1923, before attaining his twenty-second birthday. The park has facilities for swimming, boating, and fishing, and fireplaces and tables for picnics.

One block east of Main St. is the TELEPHONE BUILDING, (L), a reproduction of a Colonial one-story stone house 25 ft. square. The wrought iron ornamentations are copies of 18th century handwork. The interior houses the village automatic dialing system.

ST. MARGARET'S CHURCH (R), in the center of the village was built in the Civil War period in an adaptation of the Gothic style. It has in its south wall two three-panel windows brought from Chartres, France, by Ogden Mills, Sr., as a memorial to his wife, Ruth Livingston Mills.

A NINE-HOLE GOLF COURSE (R) at the north end of the village is owned by R. P. Huntington.

At *1 m.* are the elaborate gates (L) of the ESTATE OF OGDEN LIVINGSTON MILLS.

MORGAN LEWIS, son of one of the signers of the Declaration of Independence, acquired this property in 1792. Judge Lewis was at the battle of Stillwater, and led the van of attack against Johnson and Brant at Klock's Field. At the bar and bench his appointments ranged from Attorney General of the State to Chief Justice of the Supreme Court of New York, and in politics from member of Assembly to Governor (1804-06). He served as president of the Society of the Cincinnati and is credited with being the founder of the common school system. He married Gertrude Livingston, sister of the Chancellor, and about 1795 built a brick house known as Staatsburg House. In his day the estate was noted for its hospitality; among the many distinguished visitors were Joseph Bonaparte, who was entertained here in 1816, and the Marquis de LaFayette, who stopped here while en route to Clermont. The brick house was destroyed by fire in 1832. The massive walls survived and became the nucleus of the second house, which was remodeled by Mr. and Mrs. Mills in 1895.

The property has remained in the possession of the descendants of Morgan Lewis; Ruth Livingston Mills, wife of Ogden Mills, Sr., was his great-granddaughter.

The two main entrances lead through high, ornamented, ivyclad iron gates bearing the initials "R.L.M.," in honor of Ruth Livingston Mills. The lands of the estate bordering the highway have been left in a natural wooded state. The property is divided into two sections, the farms with their extensive orchards and prize stock lie R. The residence estate is west of the New York Central R. R. on the river bank. The formal mansion, visible from the Hudson, is a large white house with Ionic columns, standing on the crest of a hill, its wide lawn sloping riverward.

At *1.6 m.,* adjoining the Mills estate, is THE LOCUSTS (L) the home of the late William B. Dinsmore. The large frame country house, surrounded by maples and evergreens and wide acres of farmlands, is a river estate typical of this region.

The Whitefield Oak
at Smithfield

A Family Burial
Ground north of
Rhinebeck

*Churchyard at St. James'
Church, Hyde Park*

*St. James' Church,
Hyde Park*

At *1.9 m.* is the entrance (L) to HOPELAND, the country estate of R. P. Huntington. "No Admittance" signs flank the gravel drive here and at other entrances (L). Only landscaped grounds and the peaks of modern barns are visible.

Beyond Hopeland, rifts among the trees offer glimpses of the Hudson above Esopus Island. Beyond the hills in blue masses to the N. W. tower the Catskill Mountains.

TOUR 1 B

Rhinebeck—Barrytown—Annandale—Tivoli. Barrytown Road. State 9G.

Macadam and 2-strip concrete road.

The route winds through the wooded countryside of the river-shore past huge estates and picturesque villages surrounded by fruit orchards. The road offers vista after vista of the wide river and the Catskills.

The route begins at junction of US 9 and Barrytown Road in Rhinebeck. L. on Barrytown Road. At .7 *m.*, L. on macadam road.

At *2 m.*, deep in the Astor woods and 50 ft. above the road, is the site (L) of SUCKLEY CHAPEL, built in 1883, as a home for aged clergymen. The project wa ssoon abandoned and the land was sold to the Astor family. The chapel was torn down during the winter of 1936.

At *3.5 m.* is the entrance (L) to ROKEBY. The house, not visible from the road, was originally a two-story, rectangular brick structure built during the war of 1812 by Gen. John Armstrong, then Secretary of War. The library wing and mansard roof were added by Mrs. William B. Astor, Armstrong's only daughter, who lived here until 1872. The estate is now owned and occupied by Margaret Aldrich, a descendant.

An officer in the Continental Army, Armstrong moved from Pennsylvania to Dutchess after the Revolution. Before becoming Secretary of War, he served successively as United States Senator from New York and Minister to France.

At *5.2 m.* is junction with State 199.

>Left on State 199 is BARRYTOWN, *1 m.* (100 alt., 469 pop.), known in the 18th century as Red Hook Landing. Granted a post office in 1828 by Postmaster-General W. T. Barry, the village was renamed in his honor. Besides the postoffice, it consists of the New York Central R. R. station and a few scattered houses.
>
>In 1777 the British fleet burned local storehouses filled with grain for the Continental Army.
>
>ST. JOSEPH'S NOVITIATE, across field at top of hill (R), is a Roman Catholic normal school dedicated in 1930 by Patrick Cardinal Hayes, Archbishop of New York.

At *5.6 m.* is the QUINN HOUSE (L), a one-and-one-half-story gray stone house of the early 18th century. The N. end has wide clapboards secured with handwrought nails. The floors are of broad, thick planks, and some of the original hardware remains. In the cellar is a huge Dutch fireplace. The stone slave house, 10 by 12 ft., still stands, unaltered externally, at the N. end of the building.

After burning the stores at Red Hook Landing, the British raiders seized and looted the Quinn House, then occupied by a family named Moore.

Just beyond the Quinn House is the entrance (L) to the old MONTGOMERY ESTATE, which, without a sale, has descended through six wills to the present owner, Gen. John Ross Delafield. The house, built in 1804 by the widow of Gen. Richard Montgomery, is of stone, with walls 2 ft. thick and great windows and high ceilings, after the fashion of the time. The portico, terrace, and roof balustrade were added in 1862.

Born in Ireland, Montgomery came to America in 1772 and settled in Rhinebeck, marrying Janet Livingston the following year. Until the outbreak of war, they were engaged in building Grasmere, 7 m. S. *(See p. 91.)* Montgomery was second in command under General Schuyler in the Canadian expedition of 1775. He captured Chambly, St. John's, and Montreal, only to be among the first to fall in the disastrous joint attack with Benedict Arnold on the fortress of Quebec, Dec. 31, 1775.

Mrs. Montgomery completed Grasmere, but moved to this new "Chateau de Montgomery" in 1804, where she lived until her death in 1828. In the summer of 1818 a steamer bearing Montgomery's remains from Quebec to St. Paul's Church, New York, paused before the house to fire a salute. Among various eminent men entertained here were LaFayette and Martin Van Buren.

The next owner of the estate was Edward Livingston, Mrs. Montgomery's youngest brother, counsel to the Lafitte Brothers, Louisiana pirates, and author of the *Louisiana Code*. He is generally believed to have been the author of President Andrew Jackson's *Nullification Proclamation* of December 10, 1832. His wife, Louise d'Avezac de Castera, a creole from Santo Domingo, lived on the estate for 25 years after his death. During her husband's term as United States Minister to France, she is said to have been regarded as the most gifted and most beautiful woman at the French Court.

At *6.1 m.* is ANNANDALE P. O. (180 alt., 182 pop.), and just beyond is a triangular road junction centered by an antique village pump. The route takes the left fork and proceeds straight ahead through the village.

The site of Annandale was part of the Schuyler Patent of 1688, and was first settled by Barent Van Benthuysen, who purchased the river-front from Schuyler in 1725.

At *6.8 m.* is the entrance (L) to BLITHEWOOD. In 1801 the estate was named Annandale by Mrs. John Allen (nee Johnstone), after a Scotch earldom in the Johnstone family. John Cox Stevens, one of the first prominent sportsmen in the United States and a founder of the New York Yacht Club, purchased the estate in 1810 and lived here until 1833. His ownership was followed by that of Robert Donaldson, under whom the estate became noted as an example of landscape gardening. The turf laid by Donaldson is still in place.

John Bard, founder of Bard College, bought the property in 1853 and revived the name Annandale, abandoned during the two previous occupancies, because of a connection between the Bard and Johnstone families. The name subsequently came to be used for the vicinage as well as the estate, and now designates only the former.

BARD COLLEGE, 6.9 m. (R) (formerly St. Stephen's), has 26 buildings, most of which are of English Collegiate Gothic architecture. The 34-acre campus overlooks the Hudson River Valley. There are 300 students.

Opposite the main entrance is a simple Gothic church (L), the CHAPEL OF THE HOLY INNOCENTS, built and named by Mr. John Bard, about 1858, as a memorial to his only son, and in 1860 designated as the college chapel.

The college was founded by John Bard in 1860 to provide a classical education leading to the A. B. degree for sons of the Episcopal clergy. For many years thereafter a large percentage of the graduates entered the Episcopal ministry directly or entered seminaries to prepare for the ministry, a fact which was probably responsible for the legend that St. Stephen's College was a theological seminary. Bard was a grandson of Dr. Samuel Bard, founder of St. James' Church in Hyde Park.

In 1828 the college became an integral but self-governing part of Columbia University, and in 1934 the name was changed to Bard College, in honor of the founder.

At the angle of the road turning east is WARD MANOR, 7.2 m. (L), a 2,000-acre property owned by the New York Association for Improving the Condition of the Poor and designed primarily as a home for the aged. The main building houses 50 persons and the secondary building 35, there being, in addition to these, 18 fully equipped bungalows, a convalescent unit, and summer camps for boys and girls.

A part of the Schuyler Patent, this neighborhood was owned by Barent Van Benthuysen from 1725 to 1790, the part that is now Ward Manor passing in the latter year to Gen. John Armstrong. The house built by Armstrong was destroyed by fire, and for many years the place lay idle. The gray stone Tudor edifice, main building of the present group, was built in 1915 by L. G. Hammersley of New York, who, however, never occupied it. In 1926 Robert Boyd Ward, a prominent bread manufacturer, purchased the estate and gave it to the present owners, together with an endowment of $1,000,000.

At Ward Manor is the junction with a one-way dirt road, requiring cautious driving.

> Left on this road is CRUGER'S ISLAND .75 m. Off the N. end of Cruger's Island, Henry Hudson is said to have anchored for a night on his voyage up the river. Local, too, is the legend of an extraordinary Indian trial-at-arms held here a century later following the admission of the Tuscaroras to the Iroquois Confederation. A controversy arose as to which of the tribes should be dominant. To settle the question it was agreed that fifty warriors should be chosen from each tribe to battle for supremacy. Cruger's Island, then known as Magdalen Island, was chosen as the site of the conflict. After a long and desperate struggle, only

Mohawks and Tuscaroras remained, with the latter holding a numerical advantage. The Mohawks fled in their canoes and took refuge on Goat Island (then alled Schlipsteen Island), a mile north. Lighting camp fires, they arranged logs and stones, covered them with blankets to simulate sleeping men, then hid in the underbrush. As anticipated, the Tuscaroras stole in during the night and fell upon the apparent group of sleepers. The Mohawks sprang from covert, surrounded and overwhelmed the Tuscaroras, and by this stratagem became the dominant tribe of the Confederacy.

John G. Cruger, once mayor of New York City, bought the island in 1835 and built a house upon it, the remains of which are still visible. A small chapel, standing on a rock at the S. end of the island, was constructed by Cruger in imitation of ruins discovered by John Lloyd Stevens, an American explorer, in Chiapis and Yucatan.

At *7.5 m.* is the junction with State 9G, a concrete road. The route turns L. on State 9G.

This route is known locally as the Apple Blossom Trail because of the many apple orchards which line it on both sides.

At *9.7 m.* is the junction with a concrete road. The route turns L. on this road.

TIVOLI-MADALIN, *9.8 m.* (152 alt., 1603 pop.), derives its name from one of those grandiose but impracticable schemes that caught the imagination of so many Europeans in the early days of the republic. After the Revolution a Frenchman named Delabegarre purchased the property now known as the Elmsdorf Place, and built on it a reproduction of a French chateau, surrounded by moats and high walls. He named his creation the Chateau de Tivoli and planned to build a city within the walls. The dream remained unrealized and all but a high octagonal tower was removed. The property then passed into the hands of the DePeysters, who built a house in which the tower was incorporated. This stood until 1930, when house and tower were torn down. Parts remain of the original wall that enclosed the estate. Madalin (once known as Myersville) and Tivoli were united and incorporated in 1872.

At *10.6 m.* is the junction with a dirt road.

> Right, on this road, is ST. PAUL'S EPISCOPAL CHURCH and VAULTS *0.2 m.* (L). The first wooden church building was erected in 1818. The present structure was begun in 1868, and stands on an esplanade facing E. Slate-roofed, and constructed of rough stone in the Norman Gothic style, it is almost entirely overgrown with ivy. The windows between the buttresses are of ground glass. In the semi-hexagonal transept on the S. are pews once used by the Livingstons and the DePeysters. In the immediate rear of the chancel, and abutting against the foundation wall of the church, is a vault of Hudson River bluestone containing the remains of Gen. John Watts DePeyster. On either side of the wrought-iron door are 10-pound Parrott guns. Northward, in a semicircle at the rear of the church ,are eight other mausoleums of somewhat similar design, four of which are owned by the Livingston family.

At *10.7 m.* is the entrance (L) to the CALLENDAR HOUSE, a large frame structure with thick brick-filled walls, built by Henry Gilbert Livingston in 1794. The interior remains unaltered. The Greek Revival veranda dates from the 1830's.

Before the Revolution the land was occupied by Indians, two of whose graves, containing skeletons, arrowheads, and carved stones, were discovered when the lawns were being graded in 1888. A part of the Schuyler Patent, the estate was acquired in 1781 by Joseph Ketcham, who built a dock on the riverfront, where the next owners, Jacob Bogardus and John Reade, conducted a store for a number of years. Chancellor Livingston, experimenting at that time with steamboats, constructed a 30-ton vessel in the North Bay cove of the property. The craft, however, failed to perform satisfactorily on its trial trip.

Henry Gilbert Livingston bought the estate in 1794 and built the house, selling it the following year to Philip H. Livingston. The latter named the place Sunning Hill and lived here until 1828. Among later owners, all of whom have been members of the Livingston family, have been Robert Tillotson; James Boorman, first president of the Hudson River R. R.; Henry De Koven, a rector of St. Paul's Church, Tivoli, and father of Reginald De Koven, the composer; and Johnstone Livingston, who renamed the property Callendar House. The present owner is Mrs. Katherine Johnstone Livingston Redmond.

At *10.8 m.* is the entrance (L) to THE PYNES, an estate owned by Mrs. Redmond of Callendar House, with which it is almost as closely linked in history as in location. The Empire vases on the gateposts were brought here from the old Chateau de Tivoli.

The main part of the house is believed to have been built in 1780 by John Reade, who, with Jacob Bogardus, operated a store on the riverfront. The interior, in the familiar 18th century design bisected by a central hall, has been renovated.

Henry Gilbert Livingston, a spy for Washington's army and builder of Callendar House, bought the property in 1794 from John Reade, his brother-in-law. The estate has never passed out of the possession of the Livingston family.

At *11.1 m.* is the New York Central R. R. station and the dock of the Sunrise Ferry Co., operating auto ferries between Tivoli-Madalin and Saugerties.

TOUR 1 C

Red Hook—Dutchess-Columbia County Line, US 9. 5.1 m.

The section through which this route passes is sparsely settled. Apple and cherry orchards border the highway.

The route begins in Red Hook at junction of US 9 and State 199, and follows US 9 N.

At *.4 m.* is the MARTIN HOMESTEAD (L), built in 1732 by Hendrick Martin. The stone walls were recently covered with white cement, but the interior remains in its original state. The walls enclose an airchamber, making the house cool in summer and warm in winter. Solid, hand-hewn beams, 12 x 14 inches, span the rooms. The flooring is composed of planks 14 to 28 inches wide. The two-piece doors, brass knobs, and wrought-iron hinges and knockers are original.

At *2.7 m.* is junction with macadam road.

> Right on this road *.3 m.* is Upper Red Hook. In the center of the hamlet is the THOMAS HOUSE, (R), a brick tavern used by Gen. Israel Putnam as a headquarters in 1777, and a station for stage coaches in the halcyon days before the railroad. Directly beyond the Thomas house take right fork to SPRING LAKE, *2 m.*, a private summer resort with facilities for tennis playing, swimming, boating, bathing, and fishing.

At *4.1 m.* is a junction with a macadam road.

> Left on this road is the REDDER HOMESTEAD, *.75 m.* (R), built about 1720. It is a one-floor and attic house of stone, painted white, with green shutters and a very steep roof.
> The original two-piece door has hinges, latches, and a door-knocker imported from Holland. The flooring-boards, 12 x 14 inches, are fastened by wooden pegs. Spanning the rooms are 14 x 18-inch hand-hewn beams with the draw-plane and adze marks visible. The molding and fireplace mantel are hand carved. While digging in the cellar, the owner uncovered coins dating back to 1722. These are still in his possession.

At *5.1 m.* is the DUTCHESS-COLUMBIA COUNTY LINE.

TOUR 1 D

Pine Plains—Washington Hollow. State 82. 17 m.

Leaving Pine Plains, the road leads into the Mid-Dutchess County valley. This is a dairy and fruit region; cultivated fields and orchards line the highway.

At *.5 m.* is the junction with State 82A, a macadam road (sharp curves).

> Left, State 82A traverses a wooded countryside. Wild strawberries and blackberries abound along the roadside. Coarse bunch grass and brush line the road and extend back as far as the eye can see. Fallow fields and dilapidated houses tell the story of a once busy farming section.
> At *5.5 m.* is the village of SHEKOMEKO *(665 alt., 45 pop.)*, named for the Indian village which was located about 3 m. NE. Christian Henry Rauch of the Moravian Missionary Society established a mission here in 1740. Upon his arrival Rauch found the tribal remnants that had gravitated to the ancient Indian village reduced to almost hopeless dissolution by the neighboring white settlers as the easiest way to intimidation and exploitation.
> In 1741 Bishop David Nitschman, associate of Count Zinzendorf, the founder of the Missionary movement, visited Shekomeko; and soon afterward Gottlob Buettner, a missionary from Bethlehem, Pa., came to stay. Count Zinzendorf himself visited Shekomeko with his daughter in the summer of 1742. Six Indians were baptised during Zinzendorf's visit, and a regular congregation was formed. The next year a bark-covered chapel was erected by the little group and the congregation grew to 63 members. Although German Protestant and quite without political or national bias, the missionaries were bitterly denounced as Jesuits, in league with the French.
> The Brothers of the Mission were brought to trial a number of times, each trial resulting in a clear acquittal. Finally on Dec. 17, 1744, they

were summoned to Poughkeepsie on an arbitrary charge of aiding the French, and were definitely ordered to leave the country.

The Indian congregation subsisted until its members were driven by force from Shekomeko on the pretense that they did not own the land. In February, 1745, Buettner, who had been unable to leave because of illness, died at the age of 29, and was buried by his Indian converts shortly before they scattered. A monument replacing the defaced original was erected over his grave in 1869 by the Moravian Historical Society.
SMITHFIELD, *9 m. (800 alt., 40 pop.)*, is a village with a cluster of attractive houses under fine old trees. Settled about 1712, the village stood at the center of an age-old hunting ground of the Pequot Indians. At a bend of the road, overlooking the cluster of houses, is the PRESBYTERIAN CHURCH (L), a square, low Greek Revival structure with Ionic porch columns, imposing in its simplicity. The dilapidated old horse-sheds still stand at the E. side. The burying ground across the road contains headstones bearing dates as early as 1757. At the entrance to the burying ground is a LARGE OAK TREE under which the great Methodist divine, George Whitefield, preached on June 19, 1770, a few months before his death. His sermons drew settlers from a 50-mile area; the crowd filled the graveyard and overflowed to surrounding fields.

Leaving Smithfield, the road winds through woods to a junction with US 44, W. of Amenia.

Retrace route to State 82.

On State 82 BRIARCLIFF FARMS, *1.4 m.* (R), a center for prize Aberdeen-Angus cattle, are owned by Oakleigh Thorne of Millbrook. Milk Lake, on the farm at *2 m.* (R), is so called because of the unusual white strip through its center. In stormy weather the streak widens and covers three-quarters of the lake surface.

At *.7 m.* is junction with dirt road.

> Left on this road is HUNNS LAKE, *2 m.* (80 acres), a private summer resort.

At *7.7 m.* is junction with dirt road.

> Left on this road is BANGALL, *.4 m. (400 alt., 60 pop.)*, a small village which owed its growth to the New York, New Haven & Hartford R. R. (formerly the Newburgh, Dutchess & Connecticut).

STANFORDVILLE, *8.5 m.* (327 alt., 111 pop.).

Railroad Station: New York, New Haven & Hartford R. R. (freight service only).
Busses: Mid-county busses stop on signal.

This is a one-street village on the hillside with church, school, and general store. The history of Stanfordville is that of the decadence of a small inland manufacturing center. Neither Bangall nor Stanfordville has shared in the suburban trend swelling the larger towns of the county. Both are agricultural communities, with social activities, centered in the school, churches, and grange.

At *10.5 m.* is junction with dirt road.

> Right on this road is UPTON LAKE, *3 m.* (L), (70 acres), a summer resort for camping, boating, bathing, and fishing.

South, the road is flanked by rich pasture lands and well cultivated farms.

At *14.5 m.* is an old MILL (L), once part of a large cotton manufacturing plant.

At *15.9 m.*, beside the old County Fair grounds of Washington Hollow (L), is the junction with US 44.

TOUR 2

Poughkeepsie—New Hackensack—Hopewell Junction—Pawling—Dover Plains—Amenia. State 376, 52, 216, 55, 22.
Poughkeepsie—Amenia, 53.3 m.
Road is 2-lane, chiefly macadam. Local bus lines.

This route makes a triangle covering a large part of Dutchess County. The entire route lies in a region of valley farms and foothills, rich in historic interest. The road curves and dips constantly, with few level stretches.
Section a. *Poughkeepsie—Gayhead. State 376, 15.4 m.*

This section of the route between Poughkeepsie and Pawling is the direct way between Poughkeepsie and southeastern points. The section on State 22, between Pawling and Amenia, follows the historic Harlem Valley connecting New York and the north.

The route starts at the Court House, Poughkeepsie.

R. on Main St. to intersection with Raymond Ave. R. on Raymond Ave. to State 376.

At *1.9 m.* is Vassar College (L).

At *2.7 m.* the route bears L. on State 376.

At *4 m.* is GRAY'S RIDING ACADEMY (L), the headquarters of the Rombout Riding and Hunt Club. The Vassar Horse Show is held here annually early in May; hunter trials are held in October.

At the entrance to the academy a lane (L) leads to the DuBOIS HOUSE, built in 1774 by Lewis DuBois. The front and gable-end walls are of yellow-painted brick, the thick rear wall of stone. The mansard roof, the porch, windows and shutters are alterations. The center hall and two adjacent rooms belong to the original design. Fine woodwork, a panelled dado, and staircase are the chief remnants of the 1774 interior.

The land was part of the Rombout Patent of 1685. The builder was a captain of the Continental Army in the Battle of Quebec, later promoted to the rank of major, and still later to general of the New York Militia. Subsequent owners include members of the Livingston, Greenleaf, Ingraham, Adriance and Varick families.

Just beyond the academy is the entrance (R) to GREENVALE PARK, where Wappinger Creek provides excellent swimming facilities. The stream at this point is approximately 75 ft. wide, with a depth varying from 2 to 15 ft. A large shallow area affords ideal wading for children. There are parking fields, picnic grounds, horseshoe pitching courts, and bath houses for men and women.

At *5 m.* is the POUGHKEEPSIE AIRPORT (R), a private enterprise. The route bears left on State 376.

From this point the curves of Wappinger Creek are followed through woods and pasture.

At *5.1 m.* a concrete bridge crosses Wappinger Creek. The old dam is the site of a vanished grist mill; and immediately S. is RED OAK MILLS (R), a picnic and bathing spot.

Many bungalows, recently built between Red Oak Mills and New Hackensack, are the homes of people who work in Poughkeepsie. They represent the same suburban trend found E. of the city in the villages of Washington Hollow and Pleasant Valley.

At *6.8 m.* is the STEPHEN THORN HOME (L), a brick residence painted white. The inscription on the cornerstone of the modern stone chimney reads: "Stephen Thorn—1772." The dormers, the rear frame addition, and the Greek Revival porch are of a later period.

The site is part of land deeded by the Indians in 1700 to Stephen Van Cortlandt, one of the original Rombout patentees. He held this land until 1733, when it passed to his sister, Mrs. John Schuyler, who sold it in 1734 to Tunis Van Benschoten. Samuel Thorn of Westchester subsequently acquired 210 acres, which were inherited by his son, Dr. Stephen Thorn, who built the house.

A ghost story is told about a maid of the Thorns who was said to have been bewitched by a peddler because she refused to kiss him. Strange rappings followed her through the house and the furniture moved mysteriously. The peddler was finally traced and confessed to causing the disturbance. He declared it would cease when a large stone in the attic was rolled down stairs. Such a thing came to pass and the trouble ended.

At *6.9 m.* is the entrance (R) to the NEW HACKENSACK AIRPORT, owned by the Federal Government, opened in 1932 as an emergency landing field. It lies in the direct airline between New York, Albany, and Montreal; measures 2,760 ft. by 2,110 ft.; is lighted and marked according to regulations; and is open 24 hours a day. The apparatus includes a wall map charting air beacons throughout the United States; a sending and receiving radio to check the course of planes; a teletype, which constantly reports weather conditions.

The REFORMED DUTCH CHURCH, *6.9 m.* (L), built in 1834, is a brick structure painted white. It is a curious combination of Greek and Gothic details. Buttresses to support the outer walls were a later addition. Windows and buttresses are pointed; portico and cornice are Greek Doric.

The congregation was formed in 1765. In 1766 Joris Brinckerhoff gave land for a church and burying ground. A wooden edifice was completed in 1766 and remained in use until 1834, when the present structure replaced it.

On the north side of the church the site of the original building is marked by the grave of the first resident pastor, Dominie Isaac Rysdyck, who in 1765 came to America from Holland to serve the Reformed Dutch churches of Poughkeepsie, Fishkill, New Hackensack, and Hopewell. He served the latter two churches until his death. A student of Greek, Latin, and Hebrew, he was, during part of his ministry, in charge of the Dutchess County

Academy at Fishkill. He died in 1790, leaving behind him a reputation as "the most learned man in the Dutch Church of America."

The cemetery adjoining the church contains many early graves. The tomb of Johannes Schurrie (d. 1784) is inscribed:

> "Behold and see as you pass by
> As you are now so once was I
> As I am now so you must be
> Prepare for death and follow me."

The WORONOCK INN, *7.1 m.* (R), a long white frame building with a two-storied porch, is said to date from 1750, although the visible details are of a later period.

NEW HACKENSACK, *7.4 m.* (110 alt., 130 pop.).
Busses: Local lines.
Accommodations: Woronock Inn.

State 376 cuts through the village down an arch of great elms and locusts.

The first settlers came here about 1750 from Hackensack, N. J., and named the hamlet New Hackensack. The region is still a highly productive farming country.

In the center of the village is junction (R) with a country road.

> Right, on this road, is the JACOB VAN BENSCHOTEN TELLER HOUSE, *.5 m.* (R), erected about 1830. The land on which it stands was part of the estate left by Jacob Van Benschoten (d. 1830) to his four nephews, each of whom was named for him. Jacob V. B. Teller, one of these nephews, built the present house. It is a two and one-half story white frame structure in the Greek Revival style; the portico has four fluted Doric columns 2 stories in height.

OLD HUNDRED, *7.5 m.* (L), a white farmhouse, was built in 1754 by Joseph Horton. The roof is a characteristic Dutch gambrel, more common in New Jersey than New York. The front is of brick painted white; side and east additions are frame. The stairs and the panelled fireplace walls of the living room and kitchen are Colonial.

The doors have some of their original wrought-iron hardware; the front door has exceptionally broad boards and handwrought nails.

Behind Old Hundred is the JANE RESIDENCE, an imposing mansion of brick painted white, of the Greek Revival style, set in a grove of aged hickory and locust trees.

At *10.2 m.,* beyond Sprout Creek bridge, is CRYSTAL SPRING MANOR (L), a red brick gambrel mansion of 19 rooms, 1½ stories high, erected in 1768 by Philip Verplanck, Jr. The date is built in the southwest wall in black brick figures 2 ft. high. Col. Richard Van Wyck, an officer of the Dutchess County militia and sheriff in 1819, purchased the home in 1827. The front and end walls are of brick, the rear of stone. The front facade has three dormers and delicate Corinthian fluting. The Dutch door with its two glass bulls-eyes, handwrought hinges, and brass knocker, is original. The broad hall which cuts through the whole depth has carved wainscoting 3¾ ft. high.

FISHKILL PLAINS, *10.5 m.* (300 alt., 60 pop.), is a one-street country hamlet with general store, blacksmith shop, and garages.

South, the road ascends a mile-long hill. From the top of the grade is a view (R) to the Fishkill Mountains.

Here the road makes a U turn and descends to the village of HOPEWELL JUNCTION, *12.5 m.* (220 alt., 305 pop.), once an important freight junction of the Central New England and Newburgh, Dutchess & Connecticut R. Rs. Both lines have been absorbed by the New York, New Haven & Hartford R. R. The junction gave origin to the village in 1869 and was once on a direct railroad route from Boston to Washington. Passenger service was discontinued several years ago.

At *13.2 m.* beyond the railroad tracks, is junction with State 82, the Mid-County Highway.

> Left on State 82 is the OLD BEEKMAN ROAD, *.4 m.* Straight ahead on broken macadam of the Old Beekman Road is OLD HOPEWELL, *.9 m. (300 alt., 65 pop.)*, settled in 1750 by Aaron Stockholm of Long Island, farmer and grist mill operator. Captain Thomas Storm was another early settler.
>
> The REFORMED DUTCH CHURCH, *1 m.* (L), is a yellow-painted brick building with four white columns, built in 1833 on the site of a church dating from 1764. The adjacent cemetery contains graves of the first settlers. Among them is that of Garret, son of Capt. Thomas Storm, who died in 1776, aged 2 years. It is inscribed, "I was born, look't round and died."
>
> At *2.5 m.* is junction with the EASTERN STATE PARKWAY (not open in spring of 1937).
>
> At *2.7 m.* is the STORM-ADRIANCE-BRINCKERHOFF HOUSE (L), a white frame residence with a red roof, surrounded by a white picket fence. On the lawn is a concrete marker recording Washington's sojourn here in 1778 when the army was marching from Fishkill to Connecticut. On that occasion, the commander-in-chief mildly rebuked the assembled residents for what he considered uncalled for obeisance. A rude stone bowl set on the marker is an Indian handmill found on the premises.
>
> The western or left end of the house is the oldest part. Porches and dormers are modern. In parts of the interior the old hand-hewn beams are still visible. A Dutch oven projects from the wall at the end of the oldest part. Some of the doors have original HL hinges. A trap-door in the old sitting room leads to a cellar where Capt. Thomas Storm is said to have kept his prisoners during the Revolution.

Left, a dirt road north of the Storm-Adriance-Brinckerhoff House leads to Sylvan Lake *(see p. 134.)*

At junction, State 52 turns R. into State 82, and 200 ft. W. turns L.

At *14.3 m.* is the entrance (L) to EMMADINE FARMS, model dairy and stock farms owned by J. C. Penny, chain store magnate. The enterprise includes 1,000 acres of land, and supports a herd of 500 Guernsey cattle. The milk product is distributed directly from the farms to consumers.

At *16.1 m.* is the once thriving village of GAYHEAD (officially known as EAST FISHKILL) (300 alt., 40 pop.), now merely a junction for State 376 and State 54.

A mill pond (L) and an old dam (R) are remnants of a 19th century grist mill. A local tradition asserts that the town came by its name because of an early inhabitant who wore bright feathers in his cap. The first settler was Aaron Van Vlack, a Hollander, who bought 500 acres from Madam Brett when the countryside was yet a wilderness. His son, Tunis, built the first grist mill by the pond.

Section b. Gayhead—Pawling. State 52, 216, 55. 14.8 m.

In Gayhead the route bears L. from State 376 on State 52.

At *.9 m.* is underpass beneath the EASTERN STATE PARKWAY. This was the northern terminus of the parkway in the spring of 1937.

At *2.9 m.* is road (L) down which Sibyl Ludington, daughter of a colonel of Continental militia, galloped on the night of April 26, 1777, to rouse the men of her father's regiment for a sally against British forces at Danbury, Conn.

At *3 m.* is junction with State 216 (L). The route turns L. on State 216.

> Straight ahead on State 52 is STORMVILLE, *.3 m. (340 alt., 157 pop.)*, settled in 1730 by Garret George, and Isaac Storm. The village had 20 houses in 1860 and has changed little since then. Villagers still tell the story of Polly Tidd, who was kidnapped with a brother and sister by Indians from the family home 7 m. east. The brother was killed in nearby woods. Polly and her sister were carried across the Hudson and adopted by a tribe of Delaware Indians.
>
> One of the braves demanded Polly's sister in marriage. She refused and was slain. Later Polly received a similar demand. Warned by a friendly squaw to remember her sister's fate, she accepted. Two boys were born from the marriage. The young mother several years later escaped with her children to her old home, and found that her parents had died. After difficulty she established her identity, and recovered her father's property. The two sons died in early manhood. Polly lived alone until her death at an advanced age.
>
> Beyond the village, the road crosses wooded hills which offer panoramic views across the Hudson Valley, with the slopes of the Highlands S. and the blue lines of the Catskills N.
>
> At *3.7 m.* is the entrance (R) to the LINCOLN DUDE RANCH, with recreational facilities simulating those of a western ranch. A small lake provides bathing, boating, and fishing; bridle paths radiate from the main building.
>
> PECKSVILLE, *5.3 m. (600 alt., 30 pop.)*, is an unmarked crossroads with a one-room general store and a half dozen houses. An unusually large grave in the old burying ground (R) near the crossroads is said to be the last resting place of one of Polly Tidd's sons. In the orchard at the top of the hill is the rock on which the Indians are said to have tomahawked her brother.

On State 216 at *4.1 m.* is the STORMVILLE SPEEDWAY (R), an oval dirt track, one-half mile long, the scene of auto races every other Sunday afternoon from Memorial Day until late November.

BROAD ACRES, *4.8 m.* (L), close to the highway, is a large farm operated by the Hudson River State Hospital.

GREEN HAVEN, *5.2 m.* (380 alt., 112 pop.), is the home of the Hudson Valley Nurseries (L), operated by the State Conservation Department.

At *5.9 m.* is the entrance (L) to LIME RIDGE FARM, a private estate of 1,200 acres with large fruit orchards, owned by A. H. Fortington. Lime Ridge apples have an exclusive New York City market and many are exported to Europe. The owner maintains a kennel for pedigreed dogs and a stable of thoroughbred horses. At the center of the farm is a private airport, well lighted and marked, with an expert mechanic always on duty.

POUGHQUAG, *7.9 m.* (400 alt., 180 pop.), (Indian for *round lake*), a little hamlet with an old-time atmosphere. The village store is the traditional rendezvous of local yarn-spinners.

For the next 2 miles the road follows a narrow, wooded valley, paralleling the course of a clear mountain brook with numerous rapids and waterfalls.

At *10 m.* is junction with State 55. The route turns L. on State 55. STONEHOUSE (L) now vacant is a landmark, recorded on old county maps, and once served as a post office for about 15 families.

> Right on State 52 to WHALEY LAKE (L), *1.7 m.* (690 alt.), 2½ m. long x ½ m. wide, the largest lake and most popular lake resort in Dutchess County. The road skirts the shore which is bordered by summer cottages. Set in the midst of wooded hills, the lake offers bathing, boating and fishing facilities.
> At *6.4 m.* is the Dutchess-Putnam County line.

State 55 climbs Pawling Mountain. The steepest grade of ascent is reached at *10.9 m.;* the crest of the hill is at *11.3 m.* The steep, twisting road descends for nearly a mile.

The steep, twisting road descends for nearly a mile.

PAWLING, *13.7 m.* (420 alt., 1,204 pop.).
Railroad Stations: New York Central R. R. (Harlem Valley Division).
Busses: Two bus lines.
Accommodations: Dutcher House, Hayes Hotel, Pawling Inn.
Motion Picture Theatre: One.

The village, lying in the Pawling-Dover valley, was settled about 1740 by English Quakers. The first hamlet was known as Gorsetown; the present name derives from the Paulding or Pawling family, Colonial landholders.

The business section is confined to Main and Railroad Sts. with residential streets radiating from this center. The railroad bisects the village. Farming is locally on the decline and the land is being bought up by New Yorkers as summer estates.

The village has been an important dairying center since 1850 and once shipped 200,000 quarts of milk a day to New York City. Upstate and western competition has closed several of the shipping stations.

State 55 follows West Main St. and Main St. (R) through the village.

At *14.5 m.* is the Pawling nine-hole GOLF COURSE (R), once the farm of William Prendergrast, leader of the Anti-Rent Rebellion of 1766. *(See p. 12.)*

At *14.6 m.* is the JOHN KANE HOUSE (L), a white frame residence. The original building was occupied by Washington from Sept. to Nov. 1778, and a copper tablet commemorating the fact is affixed to a large sycamore tree on the lawn. The tree was used as a whipping post by Continental officers during the war. The present house was built in the 1830's, except for the kitchen wing, with small-paned windows and a Dutch oven (bricked up), which may have formed part of the original house.

At *14.8 m.* is the junction with State 22. The main route turns L. on State 22. Here also is junction with Quaker Hill Road. *(See Tour No. 2 A.)*

> Right on State 22, just S. of the intersection, is a sign (L) indicating PURGATORY HILL, so named because "it is halfway between Quaker Hill and everywhere else." Continental troops camped here from 1778 to 1779.
>
> At *1.4 m.* is the entrance (L) to MANUMIT SCHOOL, a co-educational elementary school for children from 5 to 12 years of age, the curriculum extending through the eighth grade and preparing students for high school. It is a non-profit-sharing corporation, founded in 1924 by the late William Mann Fincke, and directed by William Mann Fincke, Jr., with a staff of 22 instructors and counselors. The school is housed in five frame buildings, with 175 acres of wood and farm land attached. It is an experimental institution designed as a correlating link between city and farm life; the students are employed upon the farm in duties suitable to their age. Adequate recreational facilities are provided.

Section c. *Junction of State 55 and State 22—Amenia. State 22. 23.1 m.*

This is the Harlem Valley route along the east border of Dutchess County, paralleling the Harlem Valley Division of the New York Central R. R. Underpasses are all old and narrow. The pavement is for the most part macadam with sharp curves. The plain is cut by the Ten Mile River, formed by the confluence of Webatuck and Wassaic Creeks. The scenery is attractive.

At *.9 m.* is the GRAVE OF ADMIRAL JOHN LORIMER WORDEN (L), marked by a large gray granite tombstone with an anchor in bas-relief. Born in 1816, Admiral Worden was commander of the ironclad *Monitor* in the battle with the Merrimac in 1862, and in 1863 commanded the *Montauk* in the operation against Fort Sumter. From 1870 to 1874 he was superintendent of the Naval Academy at Annapolis, and from 1875 to 1877 commanded the European squadron.

At *1.1 m.* is the PAWLING SCHOOL FOR BOYS (R), a college preparatory school accommodating 250 boys, founded in 1907 by Dr. Frederick L. Gamage. The brick buildings stand on a hillside commanding a view of the Harlem Valley.

At *3.1 m.* is the entrance (L) to the SHEFFIELD-PAWLING FARMS, with model wood and stone buildings. Most of the milk supply from this section of the Harlem Valley is handled here.

North of this point the road is hilly and winding, and there are few houses. On both sides of the highway are wild growths of young trees and underbrush.

At *5.9 m.* is the entrance (R) to the HARLEM VALLEY STATE

HOSPITAL for the mentally defective. A small city in itself, it occupies 1,200 acres and is planned to accommodate over 4,000 patients and a personnel of 900. Originally designed as a prison, three buildings were started in 1912. They stood vacant until 1924, when the New York State Department of Mental Hygiene took them over. Other groups of buildings have since been added, the latest in 1932.

At *6.8 m.* on a slight elevation at the north end of the grounds, stands the ALFRED WING HOMESTEAD (R), a white frame residence in a grove of old trees, built about 1849. Greek Revival in style, it was considerably altered when the hospital buildings were erected. It is now occupied by the steward of the hospital. The portico has square wooden columns, and the exterior and interior molding is Greek in design.

At *7 m.* is the JACKSON WING INN (L), a two-story red brick building with a hipped gambrel roof resembling the later French mansard. The 24 windows have flat brick arches. The south end and west wings are clapboarded. The gable on the west wing is the only one on the building.

The numerous Wing family and their kinsmen, the Prestons, were prominent in the early settlement of the region. Jackson Wing is said to have built the house in 1806, and it soon became a favorite drovers' hostelry on the Harlem Valley road. Known as the Moosehead Tavern, it was used at one time for local elections. There were many such taverns in the late Colonial period, but this and the Old Drovers Inn 3.8 m. N. *(See below),* are the only two remaining today. The road was already well traveled by 1775, and by 1800 an increasing number of Vermont and New Hampshire farmers used it to drive their livestock to market in New York City. A map dated 1814, now in the office of the clerk of Dutchess County, shows both these hostelries, and describes the highway as "The Great road from New York to Albany and Vermont, much traveled by Drovers and others."

At *7.5 m.* junction with State 55 (R). Route continues straight ahead.

SOUTH DOVER, *7.8 m.* (390 alt., 35 pop.), was once noted for the quarry of the South Dover Marble Co.

At *9.1 m.* (R) across an old bridge is the abandoned quarry. The large pit, the remains of three brick and cement buildings, and the piles of huge marble blocks suggest the scale on which the quarry was operated. The half dozen village buildings along the highway face the stream. The stone is chiefly dolomite, a composition of the carbonates of lime and magnesia in varying proportions. The Dover formation is coarse grained. Erosion has so softened some of the stone that it crumbles as readily as lump sugar.

At *10.8 m.* is the OLD DROVERS INN (L). The site was part of a large area owned by Ebenezer Preston, who settled here in 1727. It was he who named the Preston Mountains to the NE. The building was erected about 1750. John Preston, an heir, opened the inn about 1810. It soon became a favorite with the drovers.

John Preston was an eccentric landlord and a spinner of yarns. An anecdote relates his alleged method of fattening cattle: "My plan," he said, "is to plow a furrow or two around the grove of trees and plant gourd seeds; the vines run up among the branches and the cows climb the trees and fatten on the gourds."

The low-ceilinged, rambling structure is still open to guests. The Georgian paneling of the interior and the shell cupboard are perfectly preserved, as is much of the old handmade glass, the hardware, and the hand-hewn beams. At the end of the center passage are three broad planks forming a partition rising from cellar to upper floor. The old tinder box in which flint and steel were kept dry, and the pig-scalding boiler may still be seen. The present floor in the former kitchen covers a cooling well, with shelves for food.

Across the road (R) is the former coach house; on its gable end is a fresco (restored) of drovers and their cattle, inscribed, "Free Conscience; Void of Offence 1840." The sign salved the scruples of a landlord whose clientele compelled him to sell liquor against his principles.

Cross creek and at *12.6 m.* (L) is the junction with a dirt road.

> Left on dirt road is DOVER FURNACE, across a pasture at *2.1 m.*
> Beyond grass-covered heaps of slag, is the abandoned iron furnace. Behind the furnace a winding stream has cut a ravine through the hill; an old dam forms picturesque falls. The iron mines lie farther back in the hills.
> At *2.7 m.* is the entrance (R) to SHARPAROON POND, a large summer camp operated by the New York Mission Society as a memorial to Russell Sage.
> The village of DOVER FURNACE is at *3.2 m.*

DOVER PLAINS, *14.3 m.* (400 alt., 800 pop.).
Railroad Stations: N. Y. Central R. R. (Harlem Valley Division).
Busses: Two bus lines.
Accommodations: Herbert's Hotel and Harlem Valley Inn.
Motion Picture House: One.

The highway crosses the western end of the village, passing for about 4 blocks under arching trees. The business section huddles about the railroad station.

The names of Benson, Dutcher, and Van Dusen appear among the first settlers of Dover Plains. They came as early as 1750. Until 1807 the village was known as Pawlingtown. The name Dover Plains was given by Jackson Wing. The town is bounded on the west by hills extending southward to the Fishkill Mountains. These hills contain iron ore and marble, which were the basis of important quarrying and mining industries 30 years ago. Deep pits and abandoned iron furnaces remain. Since then the principal occupation of the community has been dairy farming. The Harlem Valley State Hospital has revived economic life.

A former Dover citizen, Theodore R. Timby (b. 1822), was the originator of what is known as the "Revolving Turret System of Offensive and Defensive Warfare to be used on Land and Water." Ericsson is popularly known as the originator of the plans, but when he, with John Flack Winslow, filed a caveat, he found that Timby had an earlier patent. Timby was paid $5,000 for a release of patent rights; and Winslow, J. A. Griswold, Ericsson, and Bushnell received for their plans $275,000 which they divided evenly.

Left from the center of Dover Plains on road marked "The Stone

Doorway of the Oblong Meeting House at Quaker Hill

Sycamore Tree, with embedded plaque, used as a whipping post during the Revolution, John Kane House, Pawling

Oblong Meeting House, Quaker Hill

Church," is a deep ravine *1.5 m.*, in which the process of erosion has carved a chamber with a Gothic type door locally known as *The Stone Church*. It may be reached by a lane and footpath, but a wire fence must be climbed and the stream crossed on stepping stones. Formerly the mountain brook plunged over the top of a 75-ft. precipice in a waterfall. Eventually the stream worked through a fault in the rock, and now flows into the upper end of the chamber and out the open door an arch 70 ft. high and 14 ft. wide. Pine trees grow in the soil lodged in the ledge that forms the roof of the chamber.

According to local legend, Sacassas, sachem of the Pequot Indians, was once compelled to come here for safety after a disastrous battle. He took refuge in the cave, where he subsisted on berries for some days, and finally made his way through the territory of his enemies, the Mohicans, to the land of the Mohawks.

At *14.9* is junction with dirt road (L).

Left on this road is CHESTNUT RIDGE, *3 m.*, formerly the home of Benson J. Lossing (d. 1891), historian and newspaperman. His best known works are *Field Book of the Revolution*, and *Our Country*. His former residence stands at an elevation of 1,100 ft., and commands a view 60 miles wide, between the Shawangunk and Catskill Mts.

At *16.2 m.* is junction with State 343. Route turns R. on State 22.

At *18.3 m.* is the entrance (R) to the WASSAIC STATE SCHOOL, administered by the Department of Mental Hygiene. Those admitted must be capable of some degree of training. The school attempts social readjustment. There are facilities for housing and training 3,400 patients.

WASSAIC *20 m.* (458 alt., 260 pop.), is a small village of frame cottages. Most of the residents were formerly employes of the Borden Co. The mountains overshadow the village, which lies in the narrow valley cut by Wassaic Creek.

The BORDEN MILK CO. PLANT, across tracks from railroad, was the first in the United States to produce condensed milk. Later it was developed as a pasteurizing and bottling plant, the milk being distributed by the Borden Co. in the metropolitan area. In 1935 pasteurizing and bottling were discontinued, but the plant continued as a milk station. A part of the plant is now utilized by the Wassaic Fire Co. to house their apparatus.

The first of the Borden milk companies was formed in 1857 by Gail Borden (b. Norwich, N. Y., 1801), who developed the vacuum process for condensing fluid milk. His experiments with milk condensation began about 1851. Mr. Borden's first application for a patent, made in 1853, was rejected. At that time he had established a factory at Wassaic. It is said he peddled the limited output of his first factory from a basket. Patent No. 15,553 for "producing concentrated sweet milk by evaporating in vacuo, substantially set forth,—the same having no sugar or other foreign matter mixed with it," was granted on Aug. 19, 1856.

Just N. of the village the road reaches the northern end of the Harlem valley. On the valley floor are scattered morainic hills.

AMENIA, *23.1 m.* is the junction with US 44. *(See Tour No. 1.)*

TOUR 2 A

Junction State 55 and 22—Quaker Hill. Quaker Hill Road. 5.4 m.
Opposite junction State 55 and State 22, in Pawling, is macadam road leading E. and uphill. The route follows this road.

QUAKER HILL, *4.2 m.*, is part of the vast acreage known since Colonial times as the Oblong Patent, one of the most historical regions in Dutchess County. It is really a plateau 800 to 1,000 ft. high with hills rising as high as 1,600 ft. It is ideally suited to dairy farming, but is taken up for the most part by large estates, the country homes of wealthy New Yorkers.

The territory was early settled by Quakers from New England and Long Island, who purchased it from Wappinger Indians. First to come was Nathan Birdsall, in 1728, and after him the Quaker preacher, Benjamin Ferris. In 1732 the century-old dispute over the boundary line between Connecticut and New York was settled *(see p. 9)*, and the disputed territory of the Oblong was thrown open to colonizers. Fifty years later, by the time of the Revolution, Quaker Hill was fully as settled as it is today. Many of the estates were in the hands of the same families until 1930, when the ingress of New Yorkers began.

The important role the Quakers played in the early history of the United States is richly illustrated in this region. In Colonial times, 100 years before the emancipation of the negroes, the Quakers declared their opposition to slavery, and it was the Oblong Meeting which first prepared a "Querie" to this effect in 1767. By 1775 slave holding was completely eradicated among Quakers.

As pacifists, the Quakers were in a difficult position throughout the Revolution, and the question of their allegiance was the cause of much deliberation among them. As a result of efforts to remain uninvolved, they were accused more than once of espionage by the opposing sides, while on the other hand both Whigs and Tories struggled to obtain their active cooperation. The records of Quaker Hill contain many confessions of "error" and penance by Quakers who were forced to some kind of compromise between their religion and their necessities, such as the purchase of their release from military service. It is probable that the majority of Quakers were Loyalists because of their belief in non-resistance, a belief which undoubtedly cost them much moral and physical hardship, especially during the period of Washington's encampment here in 1778.

CLOVER BROOK FARM, *2 m.* (R), home of Lowell Thomas, author, traveler, and radio commentator, lies at the foot of a steep ascent and includes nearly all of the long ridge known as Purgatory Hill, as well as a part of Quaker Hill and the valley between the two. The house is early American Colonial, built by the Quakers more than a century ago. Nearby are gardens and a swimming pool. The farm has been occupied for approximately 215 years.

The New York-Connecticut line once ran through it, and near the house stands a MONUMENT erected by the New York State Historical Association, giving the date when the two states settled their dispute and shifted the line several miles farther east.

A half-mile from the main house are the home of the superintendent and the fur ranch, with pens for some 500 silver fox, mink, and fitch, which are raised both for their pelts and for breeding purposes. One building, erected as a combination theatre and gymnasium, contains a radio studio fully equipped with special lines to New York, so that the owner may deliver his nightly broadcast here at will.

At *3.2 m.* is MIZZENTOP MOUNTAIN (1,000 alt.), from the summit of which a magnificent view includes the Harlem Valley and surrounding mountains.

The elaborate grounds and buildings of the AKIN HALL ASSOCIATION (R), founded by Albert J. Akin on Aug. 10, 1882, with the object of promoting benevolence and mutual improvement in religion and knowledge, and providing and maintaining a place of education, moral training, and worship.

The society was later re-incorporated to consist of a membership of 16 or more and a board of 5 trustees. An endowment of $100,000 was left by Mr. Akin when he died in January, 1903, for the upkeep of the Association, and $50,000 for completing and furnishing the library.

At *4.1 m.* is junction with dirt road.

> Right, on the road at *.4 m.* is the AKIN FREE LIBRARY (L), erected in 1898. The library consists of approximately 4,000 volumes selected by a committee. The historical room contains complete collection of local antique household articles, old deeds, letters, Indian reiics, and Quaker wearing apparel. The most noted item in the collection is the key to George Washington's bed from the Reed Ferris house, where he stayed about one week
>
> Just ahead at *.5 m.* is a splendid view (R) of the valley. The white frame CHURCH nearby, stipulated as non-denominational in the Akin will, maintains a summer pastorate. The inn and cottages are also maintained by the Association.

At *5.3 m.* is junction (R) with macadam road. The route bears R. on this road.

The old OBLONG MEETING HOUSE, *5.4 m.,* erected in 1764, is the most interesting landmark on Quaker hill. The exterior is unpainted shingle, with 24-light windows, for the most part still glazed with the wavy glass of long ago. On the south side facing the road are two batten doors close together, one on the men's side of the church, the other on the women's. The interior is divided by a partition separating the sexes by means of vertically sliding panels. The door on the east side has eight panels and is surmounted by a simple pediment. These three doors still have their original iron drop handles. The balcony is supported by turned columns. The entire inner arrangement is very similar to that of the better-preserved Nine Partners' Meeting House near Millbrook. Across the road is a CEMETERY containing the graves of soldiers of the Revolutionary Army.

For 150 years this little building was the center of community activity.

Here the famous anti-slavery "Querie" was adopted by the Oblong Meeting. During the Revolution the building was used as a hospital by both patriots and loyalists.

After the Quaker schism in 1828 *(see pp. 148-149)*, the Hicksites took over the Oblong Meeting House. For the next 75 years Orthodox and Hicksite went each his own way, but the disunion ultimately led to the disappearance of both sects from Quaker Hill.

TOUR 3

Poughkeepsie—Wappingers Falls—Beacon — Fishkill — Brinckerhoff — Hopewell Junction—Billings—Poughkeepsie to US 9. State 9D, 52, 82, 55. Poughkeepsie—Poughkeepsie *40.4 m.* Roads concrete with short stretches of macadam; US 9 is three lane. Between Poughkeepsie and Beacon US 9 and State 9D are paralleled by the main line of the New York Central. In other sections the roads parallel freight lines of the New York, New Haven & Hartford. Pizzùto Bus Lines, Poughkeepsie to Beacon. Beacon City Bus Line, Beacon to Fishkill.

This route provides a circular tour of the southwestern corner of Dutchess, predominantly a rolling dairy country. The first section, following the Hudson south, offers sweeping vistas of the Highlands; the second section traverses historic ground associated with the military and political events of the Revolution in New York State; the third section passes through a typical Dutchess countryside.

Section a. Poughkeepsie—Beacon. US 9 State 9D. 14.9 m. South from Court House on Market St. (US 9.)

At *1.7 m.* about 100 ft. up a slight hill is a spring (L), called by the Indians UPPUQUI-IPIS-ING, "reed-covered lodge by the little water place." This is claimed by reliable authorities to have been the origin of the name Poughkeepsie. *(See p. 30.)*

At *2.2 m.* is the entrance (R) to LOCUST GROVE *(inspection by appointment)*, a 100-acre estate which was the home of Samuel F. B. Morse (1791-1872) during the last 25 years of his life. Numerous locust trees, ferns, and wild flowers provide the grounds with a setting of natural beauty. The broad view surveys the Fishkill Mountains rising in the south and the Catskills across the Hudson to the west. The famed "Long Reach" of Henry Hudson's first mate, Robert Juet, who kept the chronicle of the voyage of the *Half-Moon,* extends straight and true to the northward, and is the setting of many a varied scene in the saga of sail and stream. Of the estate as a whole, Mr. Morse, in a letter to his brother, dated July 30, 1847, wrote: "I am almost afraid to tell you of its beauties."

The estate was first called "Locust Grove" by Henry Livingston, Jr., whose father, Dutchess County clerk (1737-1789) and representative in the Provincial Assembly (1759-1768), gave him the property on the occasion of his marriage. Mr. Morse bought the place in 1847 from John B. Montgomery, who had purchased it from the Livingston heirs. Mr. Montgomery removed the old house and built a new residence, which is the nucleus of the present building—a two-story, rambling frame building painted a pale green. A wide veranda extends along the south side; and a *porte cochére* extends over the entrance driveway. Doorways in the old section are finished with carved-leaf decorations, a novelty in this section in 1830. Mr. Morse added the *porte cochére* and the cupola, a reproduction of one in Italy which he admired.

Mr. Morse was a man of unusually versatile ability. He studied art abroad, became a painter, organized the association which became the present National Academy of Design, and taught painting and sculpture in the University of the City of New York (now New York University). With scientific and financial aid from others, he invented the telegraph, and in 1842 laid the first submarine telegraph line. In 1836 he ran for mayor. His interest in photography led him into an association with John W. Draper, with whom he set up the first daguerreotype apparatus in America. He took part in the founding of Vassar College in 1861.

The JOHN FREAR HOUSE, *2.3 m.* (L), at the entrance to the Poughkeepsie Nursery, was built of stone about 1755. A section of the original structure was torn down and rebuilt with part wood construction as it appears today. John Frear was colonel of the Poughkeepsie regiment of militia in the Revolutionary War.

At *2.4 m.* is the entrance (L) to the DUTCHESS GOLF AND COUNTRY CLUB, an 18-hole private course.

The SILVER SWAN INN, *3.1 m.* (R), an old residence now converted into an inn, was built in 1751 in Dutch Colonial style. The house has been enlarged to meet the needs of its successive occupants, but the pleasing lines and proportions of the original structure have been preserved. The old brick fireplace, opposite the inn lounge, was uncovered in 1930 after having been hidden by plaster and wall paper for perhaps a century. In the dining room are the remains of a great Dutch oven, with the hooks that supported the crane.

In the late 17th century, an Indian popularly known as "Speck" had his lodge near the site of this house. Speck and two other Indians put their marks on a deed conveying land hereabout as a free-will offering to their Dutch benefactors. This was the Arnant Comelise Viele deed, the earliest recorded in this section. The transfer included the present site of the Silver Swan Inn. Thus the early associations of the inn can be definitely traced as far back as 1680.

Two springs, near the summit of the hill across the Albany Post Road from the inn, supply the water which flows unfailingly, winter and summer, through the channel of the Spackenkill. In the old deeds this water source is called by the Dutch word *fonteyn*. The water from these springs has long been famous, and people drive from miles around to fill bottles and jugs from the tap by the roadside a few rods to the south. The Indian, the Dutch colonist, the English settler, and the modern motor tourist have, each in his turn, been refreshed by this pure spring water. It is likely that these springs helped to determine the course of the highway.

The brook or *kill* that runs by the Silver Swan was dammed to form a pond that supplied water for the Indians, and it came to be known as "Speck's Brook," or, in Dutch, *Speck Zyn Kil.* In the course of two centuries the name has been corrupted to Spackenkill. This brook lends its name to the road that forms a junction with US 9 opposite the inn.

OAKWOOD SCHOOL, *3.2 m.* (L), is a co-educational, college preparatory boarding school conducted by the New York Yearly Meeting of Friends (Quakers). First established in 1796 at Mechanic, in the northern outskirts of Millbrook, it was subsequently moved to Union Springs and incorporated, in 1860, under the name of Friends' Academy. In 1876 it became Oakwood Seminary. In 1920 it was moved to the present location, and the name was changed to Oakwood School.

The campus of 30 acres, with the main entrance on the Spackenkill Road, is situated on a hill overlooking the Hudson River valley. The plant includes dormitories, dining hall, gymnasium, library, and administration building, as well as barns and other farm structures.

The TREASURE CHEST TAVERN, *3.6 m.* (R), built about 1741 by Kasparus Westervelt, is one of many buildings in the county expressive of Dutch influence. The original exterior walls have been clapboarded and part of the cellar has been converted into a spacious dining room. The north wall of the adjoining basement room is 6 or 7 ft. thick and includes the original huge fireplace and Dutch oven. A few years ago an iron chimney head-piece of Flemish origin, dated 1620, was unearthed several feet from the house. This has been affixed to the north outer wall. The present owner possesses the original land grant from King George II for this site.

The ABRAHAM FORT HOMESTEAD, *4.4 m.* (L), an attractive Colonial residence 1½ stories high, was built by Johannes A. Fort about 1759. It is of stone, though the front wall and the gable ends above the lower story have been faced with brick and stone painted white. The house has lost its original lines by the addition of dormers, a porch, and a south wing. Portions of the original woodwork and hardware have been preserved.

One of the panes in a window on the western side of the house has been the subject of considerable interest to local historians. The pane is marked "Jane Fort 1778—Henry Dawkin—Engraver." Maj. Abraham Fort, a member of the Poughkeepsie militia, resided here in that year, and Jane Fort was his wife. She is buried across the road in a private cemetery.

At *4.8 m.* (R), at the base of a steep incline, is junction with macadam road. *(See Tour No. 3A.)*

At *6.1 m.* (traffic light) is junction with concrete road, State 9D. The route turns R. on State 9D.

WAPPINGERS FALLS, *6.8 m.* (115 alt., 3,235 pop.). In the center of the village the highway crosses a concrete bridge over Wappinger Creek. Just below is the FALLS, which give the village its name. The water here drops a sheer 75 ft., the highest falls in the county.

The word Wappinger comes from the Indian name *Wapani,* an Algonquin (Lenni-Lenape) tribe which roamed the eastern shore of the Hudson River until the middle of the 18th century.

The creek waters have long been the chief stimulus to the growth of the village. Prior to the Revolution numerous grist mills lined the bank of the creek. At the foot of McKinley St. is a SHIPYARD SITE where Matthew Mesier built several sloops to carry wheat to the New York market. In 1829 James Ingham, an Englishman, established here the first cotton print works in America. Its site is now occupied by the large plant of the DUTCHESS BLEACHERY, which normally employs two-thirds of the working inhabitants of the village.

The SWEET-ORR COMPANY, Mill St., founded by James Orr in California in 1849, has been known as the "pioneer overall business of America." In 1871 it was moved to Wappingers Falls and conducted by James Orr's nephews, Clayton E. and Clinton W. Sweet. The establishment grew and by 1876 had a force of 250 employees producing 1,000 pairs of overalls weekly. In 1880 the plant was enlarged, and factories were opened in Newburgh and in other cities, and the manufacture of coats, trousers, and shirts added.

Across East Main St. is the MESIER HOMESTEAD (L), now the property of the village. Nicholas Brewer, one of the first settlers, built the original house, now the rear wing, in 1741; the addition was put up in 1750. The building is a white frame structure with green roof and trim, little altered since its erection. Matthew Mesier, tea merchant and ship builder, acquired the property in 1777, and his heirs retained it until 1890, when the house and land became village property. Here in 1777 occurred the "Wappingers Tea Party," a rebellion of the housewives against Mesier's exorbitant charges for tea: they rose in revolt and compelled Matthew Mesier to reduce his price.

At *7.6 m.* the route turns R.

HUGHSONVILLE, *8.2 m.* (180 alt., 690 pop.), was settled as early as 1800. Small white houses line both sides of the main street. An old two-story frame building (L) with long porches across the front, was once an inn.

At *9 m.* is junction with a two-strip concrete road.

> Right on this road is the entrance to the W. W. REESE HOUSE, *.2 m.*, one of the four original Houghson houses. The building has been considerably altered; and, although a portion of it may have been built before 1800, the front door and leaded light, a parlor mantel, and the interior door frames are all of the style of the 1830's.

South of Hughsonville the highway runs through a tract formerly part of the original Verplanck estate, acquired by purchase from the Indians and by patent from the British Crown.

At *9.3 m.* appears a broad view of the entire Fishkill Range in the distance, and in the foreground rolling farm lands of the fertile valley.

At *10 m.* (R) is junction with dirt road. *(See Tour No. 3B.)*

At *11.5 m.* is junction with dirt road.

> Left on this road is BAXTERTOWN, *2 m.*, a settlement of whites and negroes, now dwindled to a thin sprinkling of humble dwellings and

the ruins of the M. E. Zion Church, the roof of which has caved in from the weight of snow. In the blood of these negroes flows also that of the Wappinger Indians. Old residents speak of a former Indian reservation in the nearby woods, and one ancient grandmother tells of the return of Red Men in search of relatives. As white settlers took possession of the best land, the Indians were relegated to the poorer acres. Negroes, originally slaves intermarried with them, and the two races merged. Some of the first negro settlers were slaves in Fishkill families; others had bought their freedom or had come north on the underground railroad. The land on which they settled is rocky or marshy, unfavorable to agriculture. Today 4 negro and 10 white families remain. In their community cemetery on the crest of Osborn Hill are markers dating back to 1832. Some are for Civil War volunteers; one is in memory of James Gomer, "for 42 years a servant in the family of Prof. Charles Davies."

At *12.1 m.* is the entrance (R) to STONY KILL, built in 1842, the residence of the Verplanck family, direct descendants of Gulian Verplanck, the original patentee. Title to the land has never passed out of the family. The house contains many valuable paintings and family heirlooms.

At *12.2 m.,* at the SE. corner of a by-road leading eastward to Glenham, is a little RED SCHOOL HOUSE (L), standing as it has stood for more than a hundred years, with school still in session. The Little Red School House Club maintains an active interest in its continued usefulness to local children.

At *12.4 m.,* at the foot of the hill S. of the school house, is the STONY-KILL DAIRY FARMHOUSE (R), an early stone dwelling believed to be over 200 years old, which gives an old world touch to the landscape. Nearby is another stone structure comparatively new, built to match the old house.

At *12.7 m.* is junction (R) with concrete road.

> Right on concrete road is the U. S. VETERANS' HOSPITAL, *1 m. (visitors admitted 11-12, 3-5, 7-8),* situated on a bluff commanding a broad sweep of the Hudson, the distant Shawangunk Range, and the near Fishkill Range. This hospital for disabled tubercular veterans is administered by the Veterans Administration Facility of the Federal Government.
>
> The buildings include the usual institutional structures. The grounds cover 323 acres. The hospital has 479 beds and facilities for out-patients. It was erected in 1924, and opened in September of that year. In the first 12 years 7,217 veterans were cared for. Patients are drawn from 16 counties lying chiefly in the Hudson valley region.
>
> The government provides recreational activities, including two movies a week, and various organizations provide band concerts and other entertainment.
>
> Castle Point, the old name of Chelsea, has been adopted by the hospital as its name and post office address.

At *12.8 m.* MOUNT BEACON, 1,520 ft. high, looms on the L. On its summit overlooking the river the Mount Beacon Casino, reached by an inclined railway, is visible.

At *12.9 m.* is MAGNOLIA FARMS (R). George Gale Foster maintains a summer camp here for the use of Beacon Girl Scouts and similar organizations.

Across the highway, opposite Magnolia Farms and upon the summit of a gently rising hill, may be seen the massive red brick buildings of the MATTEAWAN STATE HOSPITAL for the criminal insane. The extensive grounds of the hospital enclosed by a high wirefence, border the highway for some distance. *(See Beacon.)* Before the State acquired the property, it was the home and training ground of famous trotting horses. In a grove of trees far back from the highway is the house that was once the country home of John J. Scannell, a prominent horseman and an associate of Richard Croker in the nineties. (See Beacon Point of Interest No. 24).

At *13.9 m.* stone gate posts and a white oak tree 15 ft. in diameter mark the entrance (R) to MOUNT GULIAN, the Verplanck estate. The historic garden, one of the oldest in Dutchess County, may still be seen, but the house was destroyed by fire in 1931, leaving only the fire-blackened walls, a stark ruin softened by half-concealing vines. Much of the contents of the house was fortunately saved and given in part to the New York Historical Society. The old mansion, built in 1740, one of the first residences in the county, was a fine example of Dutch Colonial architecture, with unusual stone mantels.

Many historic events occurred at Mt. Gulian. It was the headquarters of Baron von Steuben toward the close of the Revolution. Washington and LaFayette and other prominent leaders visited it. In 1783 the Society of the Cincinatti was formed here, with Washington as its first president. (The formation of this exclusive military order gave rise to its rival group, the Tammany Society.) During the Revolution the first Catholic mass in this region was celebrated here by two visiting priests. Great quantities of flour were stored for the use of Washington's Army in Verplanck's grist mill at the mouth of Stony Kill nearby.

Since Colonial days the Verplanck family has been prominent in war and peace. Gulian Verplanck, grandson of the patentee, was one of the first to develop the Hudson valley region. His son Samuel held office under

Mount Gulian, the Verplanck House, Fishkill-on-the-Hudson

129

the British crown, and was a governor of King's College, now **Columbia University**, a founder of the New York Chamber of Commerce, and during the Revolution a member of the Committee of Safety. Daniel C. Verplanck was a member of Congress and a judge of Dutchess County in the early 19th century. Gulian C. Verplanck (1786-1870), member of Congress, State senator, and a prominent member of Tammany Hall, was also a publicist and edited Shakespeare. William E. Verplanck, author and historian, occupied the house in the early 20th century.

The GLAD TIDINGS HOME, *14.1 m.* (L), is a summer home for poor children, a subsidiary to the Glad Tidings Tabernacle in New York City. All creeds and colors are represented. During the first two weeks after school closes in the spring, 50 girls are accommodated here; and during the second two weeks, 50 boys. This rotation is continued to the end of summer.

At *14.2 m.* on the outskirts of Beacon, a lane (R) leads to SPOOK FIELD, the J. B. R. Verplanck home, a modern country residence. Numerous antiques have been incorporated in it, such as the mantels and fireplaces of older dismantled houses, many of them associated with the Verplanck family. Several ancient millstones have been utilized in the construction of terrace and gardens. The odd name of the estate originated from an old legend that the ghost of a murdered Hessian soldier buried here often walks at night.

Nearby on the river shore is the site of the traditional LANDING PLACE OF HENRY HUDSON. His famous ship, *The Half Moon*, anchored offshore here, and a number of the crew landed. The rock upon which they were said to have landed was removed in the course of railroad construction. The Indians received them cordially, and even offered them land. The scene has been painted by Robert W. Weir (1803-1889), for 42 years professor of drawing at West Point.

At Bank Square in Beacon, *14.9 m.,* is the junction of State 52 and 9D. Section b follows State 52; for continuation of State 9D see Tour 3C.

Section b. Beacon—Fishkill—Brinckerhoff. State 52. 6.8 m. L. on Main St. (State 52).

The road between Beacon and Fishkill is one of the historic highways of Dutchess County, dating from the early settlements. It follows the north bank of Fishkill Creek, with occasional glimpses of the little stream flowing in a deep cut to the right. Parallel with the road and a mile to the right, towers the majestic Fishkill Mountain range, dominating the scene by its natural grandeur. The road, though for the most part straight, is hilly: the immediate countryside is devoted to agriculture.

At *2.3 m.* is junction (R) with macadam road.

>Right on this road is GLENHAM, *2.5 m. (200 alt., 825 pop.).* The name comes from the gorge cut through a ridge by Fishkill Creek. A dam impounds the water to form a long mill pond. Trees and underbrush have overgrown the ruins of old mills. At a bend in the creek, a falls furnishes electric power to this little industrial village.

Until the panic of 1873, Glenham was a thriving manufacturing town. The mill period began about 1811, and in 1822 the Glenham Mill for the manufacture of woolen goods was organized by Peter H. Schenck, John Jacob Astor, Philip Hone, Dr. Bartow White, and others. Later came the Darts, who supplied indigo blue goods to clothe the army during the Civil War. A. T. Stewart, the Manhattan merchant prince, built a woolen factory at the upper end of the glen. Most of these mills closed in 1873. On the site of the old Stewart woolen mill the Texaco Co. now maintains a laboratory for research in motor fuels.

The HENDRICK KIP HOUSE, *3.6 m.* (R), a long, low stone house painted red, was built in 1753. About 1777 it served as the Fishkill headquarters of Baron von Steuben; Washington and Count Pulaski visited here. The interior consists of a hall with one room on one side and three on the other. The kitchen wing was added in 1860. A door in the rear is a perfect 18th century divided door with bullseyes in the upper half. In the north front wall, in line with the chimney, is a stone marked "1753;" and immediately to the east of the front porch is another stone marked "HK 1753."

The ZEBULON SOUTHARD HOUSE, *3.9 m.* (L), built in the middle 18th century, is a small, rectangular house; but its simple lines and proportions create an impression of generous and comfortable living. Zebulon Southard, the builder, was a captain in a Dutchess regiment in the Revolution.

The thick, hard walls are made of a lath framework filled with a mixture of clay, straw, and cornstalks, then clapboarded. The interior comprises two rooms on the main floor and a large half-story above. The basement contains a built-in oven at one side of a large fireplace, large hand-cut ceiling beams, and great 18th century doors with wrought-iron hinges. On the main floor, opening upon the long front porch, are two divided Dutch doors which are battened and carry the original iron hardware. A steep, enclosed stairway in the southwest corner leads to the half-story.

Near the road, at *4 m.* (L) is the site of a FORGE, where in Revolutionary times John Bailey, a cutler who left New York when the British took possession, found temporary shelter and plied his trade. The forge existed as late as 1820, but Bailey returned to New York at the close of the Revolution. In this forge he made a sword for General Washington, and stamped it "J. Bailey, Fishkill." This sword, carried by Washington during the war, is now in the Smithsonian Institution in Washington, D. C. It is said to be the sword that is shown in Leutze's celebrated painting *Washington Crossing the Delaware.*

At *4.2 m.* on the hillside (R), is the NORWAY SKI CLUB JUMP. Sponsored by the Norway Ski Club, a private organization, many experts compete here during the winter months.

FISHKILL VILLAGE, *4.3 m. (See Fishkill Village.)*

At *5.1 m.* is junction with US 9. *(See Tour No. 3D.)*

At *6 m.* (L), 100 ft. N. on the old course of the highway, is the site of the FIRST ACADEMY in Dutchess County, which stood on the hill, now the Rowestone Farm. The date of its erection is not known, but prior to 1765 it was conducted as a grammar school, and after that date as an academy. From 1765 to 1790 Rev. Isaac Rysdyck, theologian and scholar, was in charge and many distinguished men received their early education here. *(See Tour No. 2.)* During the Revolution the building was used as a hospital, and several young physicians were quartered in a house nearby. For a time the Rev. Chauncey Graham supervised the academy. It was taken down shortly after the Revolution and rebuilt in Poughkeepsie. *(See Poughkeepsie.)*

At this point there is a splendid long-range view of the Fishkill valley. Fishkill Creek, with trees and shrubbery lining its banks, flows through the center of the flat, undeveloped lands, with bare, open spaces stretching away for miles.

BRINCKERHOFF, *6.4 m.,* called also Brinckerhoffville, once an important community with grist mill, church, academy, and general store, has lost all but the store. The village took its name from the Brinckerhoff family, the first to settle in this region. Derick Brinckerhoff came from Long Island and purchased 2,000 acres of land from Madam Brett in 1718. During the Revolution Abram Brinckerhoff kept a store: the building, though remodeled and greatly changed, is still standing. When tea became scarce during the war, Brinckerhoff was well supplied and took advantage of the scarcity to profiteer. An army of 100 indignant housewives of Fishkill and Beekman, commanded by Vrouw Catharine Schutt and marching in military order, drew up before the store, and demanded tea at the lawful price of six shillings per pound. Threatened with the destruction of his stock, Brinckerhoff quickly met the demands of the housewives.

The MIDDLE CHURCH (Presbyterian), *6.6 m.* (L), built in 1747, rebuilt in 1830, and burned in 1866, stood on a knoll west of the highway upon the present cemetery grounds. It was used as a military hospital during the Revolution.

DERICK BRINCKERHOFF HOUSE, *6.7 m.* (L), at the junction of State 52 and State 82, is a fine old Colonial mansion built about 1719. In this house LaFayette was ill many weeks during the Revolution and was attended by Dr. Cochran. A monument at the roadside was presented by LaFayette Post, D. A. R., in honor of LaFayette. The house has been remodeled several times, but has never passed from the possession of the Brinckerhoff family.

Site of the OLD STAR MILL (R), is beside the creek. It was built by Abram Brinckerhoff in 1735, razed by fire about 1777, and rebuilt by order of General Washington by troops encamped near Fishkill. This mill was used to grind grist for the Revolutionary army. When it was demolished of late years and a small electric transmission station erected, cannon balls were found beneath the floor.

At *6.8 m.* is junction with State 82.

Section c follows State 82; for continuation of State 52 *(See Tour No. 3E.)*

Section c. Brinckerhoff—Hopewell Junction—Billings. State 82. *11.2 m.*

At *1.3 m.* square stone gate posts mark the entrance (R) to a lane, bordered by old locust trees, leading to the COL. JOHN BRINCKERHOFF HOUSE, erected in 1738. General Washington, a frequent guest, made the house his headquarters while the Army was in Fishkill. He occupied the bedroom back of the parlor. Another distinguished guest was General LaFayette.

Architecturally the house represents an early type of stone construction, with brick gable ends and dormer windows. On the wall facing the road are the figures "1738" worked in black bricks against the red brick background. The house has two stories, the lower of stone and the upper of brick. The three dormers are later additions. The front is faced in stucco.

The house and surrounding land are now included in CAMP LAMOLA *(Finnish, vacation place),* established in 1926 by the Finnish Co-operative Society of New York and Brooklyn. A little removed from the cottages stands a simple frame building—the steam bath. Constructed according to Finnish models, it has three rooms, chief of which is the steam room, with benches tiered along the sides, and in one corner a huge Slavic stove. Large cobblestones on top of the stove are heated by wood fire inside, and when water is poured over them clouds of steam arise. The hour for the steam bath is struck—one bell for the men, and two for the women. The hardy devotees of the bath follow the steaming with a dip in the cold stream nearby.

At *1.7 m.* is junction (L) with dirt road (red schoolhouse on left).

> Left on this road stand (R) the ruins *.2 m.* of the first house of JACOBUS SWARTWOUT (1734-1827), who had a long and varied public career. He was a captain at Ticonderoga and Crown Point in 1759, saw active service during the Revolution, and was successively a member of the New York Assembly and Senate. As delegate to the State Constitutional Convention in Poughkeepsie in 1788, he voted against the ratification of the Federal Constitution.
>
> At *.4 m.* (R) is the later home of Jacobus Swartwout, which dates from about 1789. This excellently preserved frame building, painted white with green trim, retains the charm and dignity of 18th century houses. The porch, although of a later period, harmonizes with the original plan of the building. In 1824, at the age of 90, Swartwout journeyed from this house to Poughkeepsie to be present at a reception in honor of LaFayette.

GRIFFIN'S TAVERN, *1.9 m.* (L), enclosed by a wood picket fence, was known in Revolutionary times as Griffin's Tavern or the RENDEVOUS. In Rombout Precinct, which included the towns of Fishkill and East Fishkill, the Committee of Observation held three meetings in this tavern at the beginning of the war. The original record of the first meeting is still in the possession of a descendant of Colonel Griffin. Among the guests entertained here were Washington, LaFayette, Putnam, Von Steuben, and a number of French soldiers.

AARON STOCKHOLM HOUSE, *2.4 m.* (L), at a dirt lane, is a large, white clap-board house with fanlights in the gable ends. It is more than 100 years old.

At *3 m.* State 82 passes the site of the former village of SWARTW-OUTVILLE, now marked only by the foundation of former homes and stores. Swampy lands bordering the highway furnished peat for a wide neighborhood, and peat-mining and brick-manufacturing helped develop this section. At present dairying and farming are the major pursuits.

At *4 m.* is the CORNELIUS R. VAN WYCK HOUSE (L), built about 1785, a story and a half in height, with a gambrel roof and original panel shutters. On the first floor are four rooms and a central hall. The staircase is enclosed in mid-18th century manner. Behind the house are original frame buildings and a stone smoke-house. To the north and east is the family burial ground, enclosed by a stone wall.

Cornelius R. Van Wyck (1753-1820), a captain in the Revolution, was a member of one of the numerous Van Wyck families prominent in the early history of the county.

At *4.1 m.* is the junction with State 376 in the village of HOPEWELL JUNCTION. *(See Tour No. 2.)*

On State 82, at *4.4 m.*, the highway crosses the main line of the New York, New Haven & Hartford R. R. tracks over a new concrete bridge. North of this point the main section of the Mid-Dutchess County valley is followed through fertile, well-developed farm lands. Parallel to the highway are the New Haven tracks, formerly the Newburgh, Dutchess & Connecticut line.

At *4.9 m.* is junction with macadam road.

> Right on this road is SYLVAN LAKE, *4.5 m.*, an oval-shaped body of water *1 m.* long, its wooded shores marked by scattered summer camps. An iron mine formerly operating here was abandoned when a cave-in of a passageway beneath the lake flooded the mine.

At *7.8 m.* the new EASTERN PARKWAY will cross State 82. Grading operations of the lead-in roads are visible (R).

ARTHURSBURG, *7.9 m.*, a dairy-farming and fruit-raising hamlet, was named for Chester A. Arthur, twenty-first president of the United States, who when a boy was employed here during one summer in a relative's grocery store.

BILLINGS, *11.2 m.* (440 alt., 198 pop.), a station on the N. Y., N. H. & H. R. R., is a shipping point for the surrounding farming and dairy section. The Sheffield Milk Co. maintains a pasturizing plant here (open to the public).

In the village center is junction of State 55 and 82.

> Section d proceeds L. on State 55; for continuation of State 82, see Tour No. 3F.
>
> Section d. *Billings—Freedom Plains—Manchester—Poughkeepsie.*
> State 55. *7.5 m.*

This short section of the route has a fine concrete road, comparatively free of travel since it passes through sparsely settled farm lands. The road is winding and hilly, the high points offering extensive views which have made this a popular short drive out of Poughkeepsie.

FREEDOM PLAINS, *2 m.* (325 alt., 104 pop.). The name Freedom was given to the township in 1821 by Enoch Dorland, a Quaker preacher. In 1829 it was changed by the Board of Supervisors to LaGrange, after the ancestral estate of the Marquis de LaFayette in France. Later the name of the village was changed to that of the township in which it lies.

Freedom Plains is typical of the early 18th century American rural community. The FREEDOM PLAINS PRESBYTERIAN CHURCH, built in 1828, is constructed of wood in Colonial church style. It serves as the principal social center of the community. In and about Freedom Plains are many houses built early in the 19th century. Diversified farming is the principal occupation.

At *3 m.* is the top of a hill, from which a backward glance will reveal a panaramic view of the Mid-Dutchess County valley. The Berkshires in the far distance lie in a hazy blue cloak, and the nearer Fishkill Mountains rise on the right.

At the top of the hill, at *4.5 m.*, is another view. To the west lies the city of Poughkeepsie, the Hudson River, and the Catskills in the distance; on the southwest are the Fishkill and Shawangunk ranges. Many people drive for miles to view the sunset and the twinkling lights of Poughkeepsie from this vantage point.

At *5.7 m.* the highway leads under a bridge of the N. Y., N. H. & H. R. R. *(The driver should proceed carefully as the roadway is narrow.)* Immediately the road bears, (R) and crosses a bridge over Wappinger Creek.

MANCHESTER, *5.7 m.* The row of red brick houses (R) were formerly occupied by workers in a large brickyard recently abandoned. Limestone was quarried nearby, and there are clay pits in the vicinity. The site of the brickyards is now occupied by the office building of the Dutchess County Highway Department.

Intersection of State 55 and US 44, *7.5 m.* Straight ahead on Main St. to Poughkeepsie.

TOUR 3 A

Junction US 9 and New Hamburg Road—New Hamburg. New Hamburg Road. 3.8 m.

This route over a macadam and concrete road to New Hamburg closely parallels US 9. It has the quiet surroundings of a country road, with pleasant vales and undulating hills at frequent intervals.

At *.4 m.* is junction with two roads. The route continues straight ahead. The GALLAUDET HOME FOR DEAF MUTES, *1.1 m.* (R) *(visitors welcome),* is situated on a high knoll occupying over 100 well-cultivated acres; the front lawn affords a view of the Hudson River. The institution was founded in 1872 by Dr. Thomas Gallaudet, who introduced deaf mute sign language in the United States.

At *1.3 m.* is junction with dirt road.

Right on dirt road is STONECO, *1 m.*, occupied entirely by the New

York Trap Rock Company, owner of the largest dolomite quarry in the world. Its product, calcium magnesium carbonate (Ca Mg (Co$_3$)$_2$), used in road and building construction, is shipped all over the United States. The average daily output under normal conditions is nearly 5,000 tons of stone. The ridge from which the stone is quarried is from 80 to 100 ft. high and is known to extend more than 180 ft. below the river level. The product is 94 to 97 per cent dolomite with very thin layers of quartz. The surface stratum is calcareous sand. The houses in Stoneco are occupied by employes of the quarry and are owned by the company.

Within the firm's acreage is the site of the former homestead of DeWitt Clinton.

At *3.3 m.* is junction with 2-strip concrete road. The route turns R. on this road.

NEW HAMBURG, *3.8 m.* (20 alt., 500 pop.) is located on a point of land extending out into the Hudson River above the mouth of Wappinger Creek. Its station on the New York Central R. R. is the shipping point for the village of Wappingers Falls, *1.5 m.* NE. Fishing, the chief industry, is particularly active during the latter part of April when shad are running. A yacht club is maintained privately.

Early 19th century river commerce aided in the development of the community, but the village grew slowly until the opening of Hudson River R. R. in 1850. Then several prominent families from the metropolitan district built summer homes here, many of which have been vacated in the past twenty years.

A FERRY HOUSE, now used as a storehouse, built in 1813 to serve the ferry previously inaugurated between the New Hamburg and Marlborough, still remains. In the outer wall of the building are several fine specimen of ripple limestone.

TOUR 3 B

Junction of State 9D and Chelsea Rd.—Chelsea Rd. 1.9 m.
The route turns R. from State 9D on Chelsea Rd.

At *.4 m.* is intersection with another dirt road. The route turns R. and continues toward the river.

At *.9 m.*, on a high bluff with a magnificent view of the Hudson and the distant Catskills, stands the DERICK BRINCKERHOFF HOUSE (R), a white frame structure one and one-half stories high, consisting of a main unit and a west wing. The design in lead over the door is of the style of the 1820's. In the east gable are two quarter-circle windows, a design common in houses of this period. A north-south hall with a center arch divides the main portion of the house with two rooms on each side. One of the two rooms in the wing has a built-in oven at the side of the fireplace.

In Colonial times the site was the farm of Jacobus Ter Bosch. The house was erected before 1810, and in 1820 was sold to Derick Brinckerhoff of New York City, who made the place a summer home; the title remained in the family until 1873.

Pasture Lands   near Dover Furnace

De La Vergne Hill   near Amenia

Old Mill and Falls Dover Furnace

The road descends nearly to the river shore, and turns aburptly L.

CHELSEA, *1.9 m.* (.10 alt., 150 pop.), served by the New York Central R. R., is a quiet hamlet shielded on the E. by the hilly bulk of the Van Wyck Ridge rising nearly 400 ft., and still retains the riverside atmosphere of its former shipping days. Picturesque frame houses stand close together in narrow streets which border the shore. Small river craft, sail and motor-powered, line the waterfront.

The broad promontory upon which the village lies was by the shore-dwelling Indians called Low Point to distinguish it from the higher promontory at New Hamburg, up the river. Taking its name finally from the Chelsea Paper Mill, a short-lived enterprise, the settlement had earlier been known as Castle Point, Carthage, and Carthage Landing.

Chelsea has always been a riverman's village. Several captains well known in river history have made it their last anchorage, among them Capt. Moses W. Collyer, a one-time sailing master and co-author with Wm. E. Verplanck of *Sloops of the Hudson*. Chelsea was really a seaport, avers the captain, recalling the halcyon days when nine captains and their ships, besides fishermen with their smaller craft, sailed from here. The Chelsea Yacht Club, instituted by Captain Collyer about 1870, was originally an ice-yacht club. Many of the fastest of winter craft skimmed over the frozen river out of Low Point.

A shipyard was formerly operated here by a man named Carman, who is locally claimed to have been the inventor of the center-board. The sloop Matteawan, built by him, was the first boat in which his invention was installed. He also originated other devices, and even constructed a steamboat in the face of sailing masters' skepticism.

Other industries came and went, among them Knox's stream flour mill, the Chelsea Paper Mill, and a Portland cement experiment. It is said that the first Portland cement in America was produced here.

Route continues straight ahead through the village making sharp right turn toward the river, and parallels the waterfront.

At *12.7 m.* (L) behind a lilac hedge, stands the four-columned yellow LE FEVRE HOUSE, overlooking the river.

TOUR 3 C

Beacon to Dutchess-Putnam County Line. State 9D. 6.7 m.
From Bank Square, Beacon, S. on State 9D. L. at .6 m. on Wolcott Ave. R. at 1.8 m. on Howland Ave.

9D enters the SW. corner of Dutchess County, bounded by mountains on the E. and the Hudson River on the W. The present Dutchess-Putnam County Line was fixed in 1812.

As the highway leaves Beacon it runs along a high bench at the base of Breakneck Ridge (L), known as GRAND VIEW. This elevation offers one of the most attractive motor road vistas along the course of the river. To the R., in the area of the 9-hole golf course of Craig House, a promontory vaguely known as Little Plum Point is seen about due E. of the tip of Dennings Point. Plum Point, another larger promontory, is almost opposite across the river.

JOHANNES VAN WORMER VAN VLIET HOUSE, *3.1 m.* (R), is a typical 18th century stone dwelling, now falling to ruin. It was located on the old Phillipse patent and was at one time owned by Judith Cromwell, a widow, who sold the farm to J. V. W. Van Vliet.

CAMP NITGEDAIGET, *3.4 m.* (R), a workers' camp on the river-facing slope of Breakneck Ridge, is operated by the Beacon Camp Corporation as a rest and recreation resort. Accommodations are provided in cabins, tents, and a year-round hotel. The camp draws its patronage chiefly from New York City and from a social group known as "The Workers' Institution."

At *3.7 m.* the highway crosses **MELZINGAH RAVINE**, a place of sylvan beauty where a small stream falls precipitously from its sources in springs among rocky ledges high in Breakneck Ridge. A disastrous flood occurred here in 1897, after an unprecedented rainfall. Two dams gave way, flooding a brickyard settlement on the river bank. Seven lives were lost, and much property was damaged.

An old **LEGEND of MELZINGAH** tells of the spirit of the glen held in sacred reverence by the Indian hunter who cast food into the water as a sacrifice to gain the good will of the spirits and be blessed with success in the chase.

At *4.4 m.* the highway begins the descent of the long Breakneck grade toward the river. This is one of the most scenic stretches of the whole Hudson valley highway system. Close to the road, at *4.8 m.*, stands a deserted vine-clad **STONE HOUSE** (R) of the 18th century, picturesque in its dilapidation.

At this point **POLOPEL'S ISLAND (BANNERMAN'S ISLAND)** (R) can be seen just off the shore. Solitary and rocky, it rises from the river surmounted by an imitation medieval castle. The island is generally known as Bannerman's, named for the man who owned it, erected the buildings, and stored here a strange collection of arms and war material discarded and sold by the Federal Government after the Civil and Spanish American wars. Some of this material was utilized by the U. S. Army during the World War. The group of massive buildings, constructed chiefly of "Belgian" stone paving blocks from New York City, is intended to represent the fortressed retreat of a medieval baron, with moats and locked harbor, towers and lookouts. "Legend hangs thick about this rock," says Wilstach, "and on its adjacent shores are supposed to dwell the goblins which ride the storms in the Highlands. In sailing days it was the custom of the older sailors to toss apprentices overboard here, ostensibly in the belief that the ducking made them immune from the sorcery of storm goblins."

During the Revolution, in 1779, the Americans under the supervision of Gen. George Clinton obstructed the river at this point in an attempt to prevent the passage of British ships. They stretched a line of iron-pointed pikes and cribs in the form of *chevaux de frise* from Polopel's Island to a point near Murderer's Creek opposite. The isle was used also as a military prison during that war. Before the advent of Bannerman's arsenal, the island was the solitary home of a fisherman and the kingdom of his erratic wife, who imagined herself Queen of England and her husband the Prince Consort.

Not far above river level the highway approaches the rugged bulk of BREAKNECK MOUNTAIN (1,220 ft.) (L), the north portal of the Highlands. Here the road parallels the Storm King Highway across the river, and yields nothing to its better-known rival in scenic splendor. The view at *6. m.* of the natural gateway through the mountains extends nearly to West Point. This opening through which the Hudson enters the straits as through a tunnel, was once known as the *Wey Gat* or Wind Gate. Two peaks guard the passage, Breakneck on one side and Storm King on the other. In the early days of white settlement the former was known as Broken Neck Hill from its jagged cliffs; the Dutch called the other peak *Beutter* or Bailiff, which was translated into English as "Butter Hill." It was re-christened Storm King by N. P. Willis, the poet, though to the older generation it still remains "Butter Hill." Here the Fisher's Reach begins and Vorsen Reach ends its hazardous course through the Highlands.

At *6.7 m.* the highway enters the 600 ft. TUNNEL, bored in 1932, which pierces Breakneck Mountain and passes from one county to the other. The excavation of about 20,000 cu. yds. of rock—solid gneiss and gray granite—was completed in 27 working days, a world's record.

Through the tip of Breakneck Point, just W. of the highway and at the riverside, run two railroad tunnels. One, which has existed since the railroad was built, has been enlarged and lined with concrete to accommodate the two west bound tracks; the other was bored in 1928 for the two east bound tracks.

The New York Aqueduct, bringing water from Ashokan, passes under all three tunnels, highway, and railroad, at a depth of from 250 to 280 ft. below these bores. This mammoth engineering and construction feat was completed in 1917. From the north slope of Storm King, at Cornwall across the river, a syphon leads under the river at a depth of 1,100 ft. below sea level at its deepest point, off Storm King Mountain. On the east side of the river, the aqueduct climbs the north slope of Breakneck, then continues by tunnels through the mountains southward.

TOUR 3 D

Fishkill to Dutchess-Putnam County line US 9.
3.7 m. R. on US 9 from State 52.

Just outside Fishkill, at *.3 m.,* the highway crosses FISHKILL CREEK, called by the Dutch *Vis Kil.*

West of the creek stretches several miles of tranquil plain, the scene of military activity during the Revolution. Of late years the West Point cadets have camped on this ground during their summer tour. Columbia University has experimented in agriculture on this fertile soil, where horses of the Continental Army were once corralled.

At *.5 m.,* beside the creek, surrounded by spacious grounds is the **BLODGETT MANSION** (L), built by Richard Rapalje about 1800. It has two full stories and gambrel roof. The house contains several mantels and an arch, evidently imported, although the rest of the trim is of local origin. The exterior is marked by a double Dutch entrance doorway. A cornice with a dentil course, panels displaying rope design, brass mantels, doorways, stairways, and arched recesses in the dining room, decorated in plaster and typical of the Adam period: all give distinction to the house.

The **CORNELIUS C. VAN WYCK HOUSE** *.9 m.* (L), was built about 1790. Lumber salvaged from the Revolutionary barracks, tradition says, was used in its construction. The house is a story and a half high; the 18th century simplicity of the kitchen wing is unspoiled. A broad hall runs through the center of the house. An open staircase and a dado in raised bevelled panels around the hall belong to the post-Revolutionary era. At the rear of the hall a Dutch door, pre-Revolutionary in style, is hung on the original iron-hinged hardware of 18th century pattern.

South on US 9 is the so-called **WHARTON HOUSE**, *1 m.* (L) *(open only on application),* built by Cornelius Van Wyck about 1735 and the scene of stirring events related in James Fenimore Cooper's novel *The Spy.* Officers in command of troops stationed at the head of the Highland pass during the Revolution used it as their headquarters. It also served as General Putnam's headquarters, and records show that John Jay, Alexander Hamilton, Washington, LaFayette, and Von Steuben were among its guests. In this house the Committee of Safety conducted the mock trial of Enoch Crosby, the original of Cooper's Harvey Birch.

The clapboard sides, the primitive east wing, and the interior finish of the house show work done before and soon after the Revolution. The mantels, staircase, and leaded light over the front door are typical of the late 18th and early 19th centuries.

Close to the highway, 1,000 ft. S. of the Wharton House, is the **SITE** (R) of Revolutionary army barracks, workshops, magazines, and stockade within which Tories were imprisoned. This was the chief depot and winter quarters of the American forces. On the open plain and in the woods at the foot of the mountain there were at least 10 large barracks; after the war, many a house and barn was built in the neighborhood from wood "salvaged" from these barracks.

At *1.3 m.,* near the base of the mountain, a gray granite marker by the roadside (L) commemorates a **SOLDIERS' BURIAL GROUND.** Many of the unrecorded dead were State militiamen. Few cemeteries in the State have as many graves of Revolutionary soldiers as are found in this long unnoticed spot. The Indian heroes, Daniel Ninham, chief sachem of the Wappinger tribe in 1740, and his son, David, a Christian tribesman, who fought in the Colonial cause and was injured in battle with the British at Cortlandt Ridge, are said to be buried here.

An old-time **POST ROAD MILESTONE**, *1.4 m.* (R), of red sandstone and well-preserved, reads: "66 Miles to N. York." Directly opposite is junction with dirt road.

> Left on this road, the Van Wyck Lake road, along the N. slope of the mountains, is the country estate of WILLOWLAKE, *6 m.* (R), the home of MARGARET SANGER (Mrs. J. Noah H. Slee), leader of the birth control movement. The residence stands on the brink of a mountain lake 7 acres in area. It is built of native field stone, variegated and laid in line, with a steep Gothic type of roof, heavily slated. In the terraced gardens are valuable horticultural specimens—a rare yew, and a hedge unusual in this country. The elevation commands a wide view of the Hudson valley and the distant Shawangunk and Catskill ranges.

The Post Road enters WICCOPEE PASS at *3.1 m.* This is a region of exceptional interest historically, topographically, and geologically. The pass was named for the Wiccopee Indians, a branch of the Waranoaks, who dwelt in these Highlands. On the heights overlooking this pass, Harvey Birch, hero of Cooper's *The Spy,* had his mysterious interview with Washington after his escape from threatened execution at Fishkill.

The highway makes its tortuous way along Clove Creek, through groups of rounded hillocks, 50 to 100 ft. high, which close in at the south portal of the pass. In the background, the towering, heavily wooded mountains dwarf these valley "knobs," which appear like over-sized haystacks in comparison. These mound formations in the bottom of the mountain defile, some barren, some green with scattered cedars, are mainly made up of glacial till, a deposit of gravel and small boulders.

Countless years ago this region was the legendary home of a giant race, hunters of great water rats, fierce fighters that dwelt in the lake covering all the country north of the Highlands. To exterminate these racial enemies, the giants drained the valley until only the stream and the little conical hills, playhouses of the baby rats, remained. The bodies of the giants, their bathing place vanished, began to harden, and where they finally fell, springs of water bubbled forth. The high Fishkill range (R), the "long house" of the watery tribe, gradually solidified through the ages into the hardest of rock.

At *3.3 m.* is the southern defile of WICCOPEE PASS, a strategic point vigilantly guarded by three batteries from 1776 to 1783 to prevent the British from seizing the military stores at Fishkill. On the hills (R) rae the REDOUBTS, marked at the roadside by a tablet affixed to a large field stone The lines of the earthworks, located several hundred feet apart in the form of a triangle, are still traceable on the hilltops. A substantial American force was stationed in this neighborhood' during the campaign of 1777. Stockades and fortifications, erected on commanding positions to guard the approach, were regularly manned by detachments from the main camp. Two cannon were mounted in each fort to cover the important military road (Post Road) laid out by Lord Louden about 1755, during the French and Indian War. Toward the SW. may be seen a LOOKOUT POINT, used in relaying messages from Washington's headquarters at Newburgh. There were skirmishes in the vicinity of the redoubts but no pitched battle. Thirteen interments were made in a cemetery on the N. side of the main hill.

Directly under the N. slope is the much remodeled FORT HILL FARM, now an inn, once home of Stephen, son of Capt. John Haight, the Revolutionary officer who directed the building of the forts which he commanded. The Captain's old homestead still stands (R) about 1 m. S. on the Post Road, at the border of the "Neutral Ground," the "No Man's Land" of the Revolution.

TOUR 3 E

At *3.7 m.* is the Dutchess-Putnam county line.

> Brinckerhoff—Wiccopee—Dutchess—Putnam County line. State 52 and county roads. *6.1 m.*

Right from junction of State 52 and 82, on State 52.

At *.2 m.* the highway crosses a bridge over Fishkill Creek and bears L. over the foothills of Honness Mountain.

At *1.1 m.* is junction with gravel road. The main route turns R. on gravel road.

> Left on this road is the JOHNSVILLE METHODIST EPISCOPAL CHURCH, *.2 m.*, erected in 1825. A little white church with a graceful conical spire, it stands solitary, with old locust trees and a small burying ground beside it. It has exceptionally large windows, four on each side and two in front. The entire interior is of paneled woodwork in a simple design.
>
> Straight ahead on State 52 is the JOHN JAY HOUSE, .7 m. (R). Built in 1740, it is a large Colonial residence situated 300 yds. from the highway. This house was used by John Jay as a refuge when the British advance into Westchester County forced him to flee from his home. In a tavern nearby he presided over a local court. Jay (1745-1829) was one of the leaders of the Revolutionary period in state and nation: member of the First and econd Continental Congresses, President of the Provincial Congress, Chief Justice of the tate, Minister to Spain, Secretary of Foreign Aairs, and first Chief Justice of the United States Supreme Court.
>
> During the unsettled war times, bands of outlaws, the "cowboys" from the neighboring mountains, frequently invaded the settlements, and a party of them robbed the Jay family of a large amount of silver. John Jay's mother died here in 1777, and he frequently came here to rest from his many duties.
>
> The house is on the original Theodorus Van Wyck farm, purchased from Madam Brett in 1736. The Wappinger (or Wiccopee) Indians cultivated a part of this land until shortly before the Revolution. Van Wyck, son of the first settler of that name, first physician in the vicinity and member of the Committee of Safety, built the house.
>
> About one-half mile to the rear of the Jay House once stood a gristmill. The mill and the homestead near it (still standing) were built about 1760 by William Van Wyck.

Right on gravel road is WICCOPEE, *1.4 m.* (220 alt., 100 pop.). The Indian name Wiccopee, attached to settlement, stream, and region, was borrowed from the sub-tribe that occupied a site in the Hook. *(See following.)*

At one time the hamlet was called Johnsville, after the first Dutch settler, Johannes (or John) Swartwout, who leased a farm from Madam Brett for "three fat fowls a year." The original name has been revived in recent years.

The first mechanic in Wiccopee was William Cushman, a blacksmith who bought 6 acres in 1783 and built his house and shop of timbers from the barracks of the Revolutionary army camp near Fishkill. When first settled, Wiccopee was in the midst of dense forest, streams, and marsh pools. Settlers were obliged to keep their stock penned at night as a protection from wolves and panthers which infested the nearby mountains. Near Wiccopee there once stood a large pine tree on which, during the Revolution, "cow boys" banditti of the "neutral ground," were hanged without benefit of judge or jury. The site of Connor's Tavern of Revolutionary fame is said to have been on the Brinckerhoff Road (State 52) near the highway bridge. John Jay, first Chief Justice, is reputed to have held important sessions there. Meetings for arranging election matters took place in it, and tradition says that the inn was at the time known as The Dog's Nest, from the fact that each visitor when on public business was accompanied by one or more dogs to act as bodyguard to their masters.

In the center of Wiccopee at *1.4 m.* is junction with dirt road. The route turns R. on the road. *(Caution, sharp curves.)*

FISHKILL DAIRY FARMS, *2.3 m.* (R), is part of the Morgenthau estate, operated on a lease.

At this point *(2.7 m.)* is a forked intersection. The main route takes the L. fork.

> The right fork leads into the FISHKILL HOOK, *2 m.*, as this region is called. "The Hook" retains many memories of the pioneers and Indians who lingered here later than elsewhere in eastern New York. A few of the apple trees planted by the Indians remained standing on the Waldo Farm until recent years.
>
> FORT HILL, a ridge north of the Hook, is the site of an Indian fort of Sachem Ninham's tribe, a powerful tribe which as late as 1700 numbered more than 1,000 warriors. Their village was located in a pocket on the hillside.

Storm—Adriance—Brinckerhoff House, Old Hopewell

On the L. fork is The ESTATE OF HENRY MORGENTHAU, Jr., *3 m.* (R), Secretary of the U. S. Treasury (1934....). The senior Morgenthau, once Ambassador to Turkey, came to Dutchess County when Henry Morgenthau, Jr., was a boy. They then occupied the Hupfel place near Hopewell.

The home is a large two-and-one-half-story Colonial structure. The north side was the original front, but alterations have placed wings to the front and rear, with the main entrance on the west side. French dormer windows and leaded-light doorway enhance the beauty of the house.

Beyond the estate is SEKUNA HILLS, *6.1 m.,* a 1,000-acre bungalow resort colony.

Just beyond Sekuna Hills is the Dutchess-Putnam County line.

TOUR 3 F

Junction State 55 and 82—Moores Mills—Verbank—Clove Valley. State 82 and Clove Valley Road. 13.3 m.

From the junction of State 55 and 82 the route follows State 82.

MOORES MILLS, *2.5 m.* (460 alt., 99 pop.), was named for a mill operated by Alfred Moore on a tributary of Sprout Creek.

At the crossroad, the center of the village, is the ROBERT WATCHORN HOMESTEAD (R), situated on a picturesque knoll. A small creek flows through the landscaped grounds. Little falls are spanned by bridges, and summer houses and benches stand under the fine shade trees. Robert Watchorn was commissioner of immigration during the administration of President Theodore Roosevelt.

Adjacent to the Watchorn homestead is a gravel road.

> Right on gravel road is OSWEGO, *1 m.,* a small hamlet settled in 1761, by Quakers who established a meetinghouse of the Society of Friends. The original structure gave way in 1828 to the meetinghouse now standing. This simple frame building of usual Quaker meetinghouse design stands high on a hillside and overlooks the cemetery in which headstones date from 1766. At present the hamlet consists of scattered farm homes. Many of the original settlers established themselves in Moores Mills. Some of the dwellings, built by the first settlers, still stand near the present meetinghouse.

North of the homestead the road ascends gradually for a distance of *4 m.*

VERBANK, *5.3 m.* (560 alt., 147 pop.), was settled by the Dutch in the latter part of the 17th century. The settlement is said to have derived its name from the verdant hillsides. The surrounding hills are well wooded with ash and hemlock. For years the village was the center of a tanning and charcoal industry. Hemlock trees were felled and stripped of their bark for the tanyard, while in the pits the logs were burned into charcoal. These pits still remain with traces of charcoal.

Directly north of the pits is an area thickly strewn with chips of flint stone, from which arrowheads were made by the Indians. A great number

144

of arrowheads have been found here. The site is locally known as the "Indian Workshop."

A mill pond in the eastern end of t' village affords good trout fishing in season.

At *5.5 m.* (R) is the junction with a gravel road. (M. E. Church at corners). The route turns R. and leads through CLOVE VALLEY, a picturesque farming country.

At *10.1 m.* is the junction with an improved macadam road. The route turns R. on this road.

Clove Valley, extending N. and S., derives its name from the cleft or clove in the mountains at its northern end. It is a pastoral valley, long and narrow, hemmed in on both sides by low-lying ridges.

At *10.8 m.* is the driveway entrance (L) to the FLORAL GARDENS and 1,100-acre estate of the Hon. John E. Mack *(visitors welcome on weekdays during June).* These gardens, occupying the western slope of Chestnut Ridge (L), rise on a series of long terraces from the base to the summit, and contain 1,500 varieties of flowers, shrubs, and trees, including many rare and unusual specimens introduced from Europe and the Orient and from the Southern States. During June 400,000 peonies of rare colorings and varieties are in bloom. Here, too, are 32,000 rhododendrons in three varieties. Long rows of decorative shrubs and junipers, including the lacy Irish juniper, first acclimated by Mr. Mack, set off the flower gardens. In uncultured areas, mountain laurel, trailing arbutus, and a great variety of native wild flowers bloom in profusion. Upon the summit of the ridge a reforested tract of 300,000 white and red pine trees provide cover for wild deer, and wheat and other forage is grown for them. Since hunting upon the estate is prohibited, deer are numerous. Pheasants are raised on the property and released each year.

A winding road extends to the crest of the ridge. From this vantage point, the whole valley may be seen, 6 m. long and 1 m. wide, pocketed cozily between the flanking ridges, which rise to an altitude of 1,000 ft. A panoramic view extending to a distance of 50 miles, spreads away to the NW. with the rugged peaks of the Catskills standing in silhouette against the sky. To the SW. Mt. Beacon and Storm King stand like grim sentinels, guarding the Hudson Highlands, through which the river flows oceanward.

JOHN E. MACK, lawyer and jurist, was born at Arlington, Dutchess County, June 10, 1874. He has attained state-wide prominence as a member of the bar and has served on the New York Supreme Court bench. He placed Franklin D. Roosevelt in nomination for President before the Democratic National conventions in 1932 and 1936.

The CLOVE VALLEY METHODIST CHURCH, 300 ft. S. of the Mack homestead, was built in 1832, but alterations with the passing years have changed it greatly. It is included in the land of and is maintained by the Mack estate.

At *10.9 m.* is the EMIGH HOUSE (R) in a field 200 ft. back from the road, and reached by a little-used driveway *(open to visitors)*. Nicholas Emigh, credited with having been the first white settler in Dutchess County *(see Beacon)*, is also credited with having been the first settler in Clove Valley. The date of his coming is not known, but it is known that he first built and occupied a log cabin and in the year 1740 built this commodious house. The date 1740 appears on the south chimney. It is a story-and-a-half stone structure, well preserved and outwardly little changed, though there is a clapboard addition on its south end. The doors and much of the interior trim and hardware are, however, of later date. Lath and plaster walls cover the massive 9 x 12 inch beams, which in Emigh's day were exposed. The fireplaces have been closed with brick and mortar. The floors, trod by early pioneers and primitive Indians, are the original 18-inch oak planks hewn and trimmed from primeval trees and fastened to the beams with hand-wrought nails. Emigh built this house with enduring Dutch thoroughness.

The foundation of the windowless slave quarters, an 8 x 10 ft. building, can still be traced 8 ft. from the main house and opposite the east door. The Coe family, whose descendants now occupy the white frame farm house (R) next beyond the Emigh house and own the farm upon which it stands, was associated with Emigh in building the house and in clearing and developing the land.

Some 600 ft. W. of the old Emigh house, is CLOVE SPRING, discharging several hundred gallons of water a minute. The spring was a factor in influencing the early settlement of Clove Valley.

At *12 m.* is the junction with a macadam road.

> Right on macadam road is the entrance of the CLOVE VALLEY ROD AND GUN CLUB, *.25 m.* (private). It is located on the W. side of the valley and controls an area of 5,000 acres of woodland and meadow. In its aviaries 5,000 ducks and 7,000 pheasants are annually reared and liberated. A pond upon this property is restocked each year with 9,000 trout. The club membership is limited to 55.

The CHRISTIE HOMESTEAD, *12.5 m.* (R), a stone house built in 1747, is typical of the period. The house has been modernized and shingled; the hand-hewn ceiling beams and the fireplaces remain unchanged.

At *13.1 m.* is junction with a dirt road.

> Right on dirt road, the second house, *.6 m.* (R), is the home of the late JEAN WEBSTER, author of DADDY LONG LEGS, and the PATTY BOOKS. She was born in Binghamton, N. Y. in 1876, graduated from Vassar College in 1901, and died in 1916, shortly after her marriage. The house, locally known as the Skidmore homestead, is an outstanding example of early 19th century Colonial. It is painted white, and is surrounded by spacious lawns and formal flower gardens. A red brick wall separates the lawns and gardens from the highway.

At *14.9 m.* is the furnace (R) of the abandoned Sterling Mines, its high stack a monument to past prosperity. In 1831 Elisha Sterling built a charcoal furnace here for the smelting of hematite ore, which he mined in the nearby hills. The furnace prospered for several years, but was finally abandoned and only its ruins remain. In 1873, the Clove Valley Iron Company was organized and an anthracite furnace was built. Barges brought black ore from Port Henry on Lake Champlain, through the Champlain Canal, and down the Hudson River. This was transported in ox-drawn wagons to the Clove Valley furnace, and when mixed with the local ore produced an excellent grade of steel. In 1877 the Clove Valley Branch R. R. was extended four miles from Sylvan Lake to the mines. In 1883 the furnace closed, and one year later the railroad was abandoned. Thus ended the last attempt at industrial development in Clove Valley.

From this point, the route returns to the village of Verbank, State 82, and turns L. to junction of State 82 and 55.

TOUR 4

Poughkeepsie—East Park—Pleasant Plains—Wurtemburg—Schultzville—Clinton Hollow—Salt Point—Poughkeepsie. State 9 F and county roads.
Poughkeepsie to Poughkeepsie, *38.2 m.*
Country roads; no R. R's. bus connections, or hotels.

This route through a sparsely settled region over town roads should be taken only in summer. The reward is an intimate view of the mid-Hudson countryside. The character of the area changes under the influence of the variety of soils, which ranges from a rich productive loam to sand and gravel. Miles of stone walls paralleling the highway in the beginning of the route suggest the arduous labor expended in clearing the land.

The comparative isolation and the numerous lakes make the region ideal for camping. Several camps have already been established, and there are indications that the recreational possibilities of the region will soon be more widely enjoyed.

The route starts at the Courthouse, Main and Market Sts.

E. on Main St. to North Hamilton St., L. on North Hamilton St. R. on Parker Ave. across bridge over N. Y., N. H. & H. R. R. tracks on Vilet Ave. (State 9F).

At *1.7 m.* (R) is entrance to Bowne Memorial Hospital. Route bears L.
At *2.9 m.* (L) and (R), are the entrances to the Hudson River State Hospital *(see Tour No. 1.)*

CHAPEL CORNERS, *3.5 m.*, is a small but growing community of modest homes occupied by the Hudson River State Hospital employees.

North of this point and for the next mile the Catskill Mts. are outlined against the horizon (L).

VAL KIL HANDICRAFT CENTER, 4.8 m. (R), a small modern building adjacent to a clump of pine trees, contains equipment for the production of hand-woven cloth from homespun and machine-spun yarn; the former is in greater demand. The center was established by Mrs. Franklin D. Roosevelt as one of the Val Kil projects to encourage handcrafts and provide employment for the townspeople. It is under the direction of Mrs. Nellie Johanneson, who has utilized family patterns brought from Sweden.

147

At *4.9 m.* (R) is the entrance to the first VAL KIL FURNITURE AND CRAFT CENTER, established in 1927 by Mrs. Roosevelt for the reproduction of antique furniture, metal work, and other handcrafts. Reproductions of many fine museum pieces, constructed in the furniture department under the direction of Mr. Otto Berge, are on display at the Metropolitan Museum of Art and the Brooklyn Museum of Art, New York City. The metal crafts department, under Mr. Arnold Berge, specializes in reproductions of pewter pieces of Colonial days. In May, 1936, the enterprise was turned over to the department managers, who continue to work along the established lines. Mr. Arnold Berge continues the metal and forge work at the original Val Kil shops, and Mrs. Johanneson the weaving in the handcraft center nearby. The furniture and cabinet department was moved to the rear of Otto Berge's home, the William Stoutenburgh house in East Park. The Berges were trained in their father's shop in Norway.

At *6.6 m.* (L) is the WILLIAM STOUTENBURGH HOUSE, the present home of Otto Berge. The original section is a rectangular stone building overshadowed by a frame wing of later date. At the right of the front door the figures "1750" are marked in the stone, and at the left "1765." It is not certain which is the date of erection. William Stoutenburgh was the son of Jacobus Stoutenburgh, an early settler.

EAST PARK, *6.7 m.* (233 alt., 204 pop.) Junction with a macadam road (R). *(See Tour No. 4A.)* Main route straight ahead on dirt road.

At *7.3 m.* (R), stands a weather-beaten RED BARN. Knowledge of its age, origin, and early history has faded with the past. The miniature six-sided cupola, or belfry, and the half-round window tops similar to the windows in the old Dutch Reformed Church at Fishkill, suggest that it may once have been a church.

Beyond the red barn a brook (L) parallels the road. Lanes leading to farmhouses on the other side cross the brook on picturesque rural bridges of fieldstone and rough timber.

At *8.3 m.*, and continuing for several thousand feet E. of the brook, extensive outcrops of limestone are visible on either side of the road. The strata are nearly vertical and trend southeastward. These outcrops are mainly in low ridges with a few ranging from 30 to 40 ft. in elevation.

At *9.5 m.* is junction with dirt road. Main route L.

> Right on this road at *1.4 m.*, is junction with macadam road, known locally as Quaker Lane. Right on Quaker Lane is the CRUM ELBOW QUAKER MEETING HOUSE (L), at *1.5 m.* in a valley of prosperous farms. This simple, white, two-story building, erected about 1780, has been carefully restored, so that its stark rectangular lines still bespeak the honest simplicity of the early Quaker faith. The cemetery in the rear contains many old graves, some of the mounds unidentified, others marked by rough, moss-grown slabs with crudely lettered, now undecipherable legends.
>
> Elias Hicks, founder of the Hicksite branch of Friends, frequently preached here. In this church he and the English Friends who opposed him engaged in the controversy which eventually resulted in the division of the Quakers into the Hicksite and Orthodox branches.

The controversy arose out of a difference of emphasis as between faith and theology on the one hand, and reason and morality on the other. During the 18th century the intuitive faith in the mystical communion with God which characterized the Quaker religion had developed to a high degree of self-righteous anti-intellectualism. By the early 19th century, however, the currents of rationalism had reached these farmers and appealed to them on behalf of freedom of thought. New philosophies and a nascent industrialism called for a greater emphasis on logic and conduct and the practical issues of this world. Hicks was a product of these new forces. While his views did not depart radically from those of the orthodox church, they showed the way, and his followers gradually took the side of the intellectuals.

Approaching Pleasant Plains, at *11.9 m.* (R) before crossing the bridge, is a lovely waterfall.

PLEASANT PLAINS, *12 m.* (300 alt., 600 pop.), was once called Le Roys Corners after John Le Roy, one of the owners of the DeWitt house. Today the name applies not only to the few buildings at the corners, but also to the surrounding area of level, fertile land and scattered farmhouses. General and dairy farming are the principal sources of income.

The DeWITT HOUSE (L), at the four corners, a white, frame dwelling, green trimmed, resting upon a high field-stone foundation was built by John DeWitt in 1773. Four years later the construction of an addition relocated the entrance, and in 1855 a later owner added the west wing.

DeWitt served as an officer in the American Army during the Revolution, as sheriff of Dutchess County, and as member of the New York State Assembly. As delegate to the Constitutional Convention of 1788 in Poughkeepsie he voted in favor of the ratification of the Constitution of the United States.

Directly opposite the DeWitt house is an old red GRISTMILL, built by John DeWitt in 1775 and operated by him for 27 years. The three-and-one-half-story building is in an excellent state of preservation. The original hand-forged iron hinges are on all doors. The rigging of the water wheel can still be seen on the south side.

At the corners main route straight ahead.

> Road right from the corners up a hill, leads to the PLEASANT PLAINS WESTMINSTER PRESBYTERIAN CHURCH, *.9 m.* (R), a white frame building with Doric columns along the front. The original building, erected in 1837, was enlarged to its present proportions in 1859. The church was organized on March 28, 1837, by Rev. Alonzo Welton of Poughkeepsie.

At *15.2 m.* is the white WURTEMBURG LUTHERAN CHURCH (R), the third oldest church in the township of Rhinebeck. This frame building with gable roof and steeple was built by the Palatines in 1760 and enlarged in 1861. The original windows have been replaced by modern ones. The sides are clapboarded; the entrances have leaded lights. The site offers a commanding view of the rolling hills of *Whitaberger Land* (a variable spelling of Wurtemburg), the name locally applied to this region.

At *16.2 m.* is junction with gravel road. The route turns R. on this road.

This section of the county is sparsely settled and heavily wooded.

At *17.3 m.* bear R. at *18 m.* bear L.

The topography of this region is of glacial origin; the scattered hills, compased of boulders and gravel, are technically known as morainic hills.

At *19.2 m.* is a SLATE QUARRY (R), extending back into the hills. It was once extensively worked. In 1798 it provided the slate that roofed the house of Mrs. Richard Montgomery of Rhinebeck. (See Tour No. 1B.) After 25 years of operation quarrying was discontinued. In 1866 the quarry was reopened and continued in operation until 1896. Since that date it has remained idle.

At *20.2 m.* is junction with narrow dirt road. The main route turns R. on road, across a small stream and up a hill.

> Road straight ahead to JOHN TELLER HOUSE, bears L. at .4 m. and .9 m. The house *1.1 m.* (R) was built in 1764 by John Teller, great-grandson of William Teller, founder of the Teller family in the Hudson Valley. It is a stuccoed stone house, 1½ stories high, with a central hall and two rooms on the first floor. A so-called "witch-beam," with power to keep the witches away, was built against the wall on a stairway landing in the rear of the hall.

At *20.7 m.* is junction with three roads. The route turns L.

This crossroads affords a view (R) of LONG POND, the largest of the three lakes on this tour. It is well stocked with sunfish, pickerel, bass, and perch. CAMP BOIBERIK, a large camp for Jewish people, is on the western shore.

The road winds N. of Long Pond, then turns S. and follows the E. bank of Salt Point Creek.

Left at *21.9 m.* over creek.

SCHULTZVILLE, *22.1 m.* (375 alt., 46 pop.), is named for the Schultz family, early settlers.

WARREN LODGE No. 32 (formerly No. 157) F. & A. M. (R), is housed in a small, white clapboarded two-story structure with an octagonal tower trimmed in green. The lodge is the oldest in the county and sixth oldest in the state. Warren Lodge No. 157 was instituted in 1807 and named for Gen. Joseph Warren, a general in the Continental Army who fell at the battle of Bunker Hill. In 1839 the name was changed to Warren Lodge No. 32 as part of the reorganization after the Morgan and anti-Masonic excitement which this lodge successfully withstood. In 1861 it was removed from Pine Plains to Lafayetteville, where it remained until 1864, its fifty-seventh anniversary. It was then moved to Schultzville, where it has since remained, meeting in a temple erected in 1865.

At the junction at Schultzville, the route turns R. and proceeds straight ahead. The road parallels a winding brook which at intervals cascades over miniature falls. Where it now and then widens into a more pretentious stream, shade trees on little islands provide inviting natural picnic grounds.

Approaching Clinton Hollow, the stream expands into a pond formed by an old mill dam in the center of the village.

CLINTON HOLLOW, *24.6 m.* (300 alt., 311 pop.), lies in a deep valley of Salt Point Creek. The surrounding hills, none of which exceeds 500 ft. in altitude, are densely wooded. The top soil, fertile, slaty loam, supports prosperous dairy farms. Resident families have lived here for many years; 95 percent of the population are native born.

At *24.6 m.* is junction with dirt road.

> Left on this road, up a steep hill, is the REGINALD GOODE THEATRE, *.3 m.* (R), a summer theatre in which legitimate plays are presented by Broadway actors. The theatre is an old barn painted white, about 25 by 35 ft. and 2 stories high. The elevation offers a commanding view of the valley.

At the junction in Clinton Hollow the main route turns L. and then immediately R. on the Clinton Hollow Road. This hilly, winding road, bordered by field-stone walls, passes through a narrow valley with restricted views and the road closely parallels Salt Point Creek, which widens here to 30 ft.

At *27.9 m.* is junction with macadam road.

> Left on this road is CLINTON CORNERS, *2.5 m. (288 alt., 330 pop.),* a small hamlet in which the N. Y., N. H. & H. R. R. maintains express and freight service.
>
> Little is known of the early history of the village, but it is believed to have been settled in 1760. Clinton Corners early became a Quaker settlement; before the meetinghouse was built services were held regularly in the house of Jonathan Hoag, an early settler and community leader.
>
> THE QUAKER MEETING HOUSE, *2.6 m.* (L), locally known as the Creek Meeting House, is a two-and-a-half story field-stone building, impressive in its solid simplicity. It was begun in 1772, but since construction was discontinued during the Revolutionary War, it was not completed until 1782. Outwardly it has undergone no change other than the laying of an asbestos shingle roof and the addition of a porch in 1874. The interior, however, has been remodeled to meet present needs, and the partition that separated men and women (the two entrances for the two sexes are still there) has been removed. The building is now occupied by Upton Lake Grange No. 802, though the Quakers still hold an annual meeting here.
>
> Adjacent to the meeting house is the BURIAL GROUND, one of the oldest in Dutchess County. The graves of many of the local pioneers are marked by simple slate headstones, the inscriptions almost obliterated.

SALT POINT, *28 m.* (240 alt., 250 pop.), is a pleasant country village, with the main street bordering the Salt Point Turnpike. The simple frame houses, set back from the road, are surrounded by aged shade trees. According to local tradition, the name came from the early settlers' custom of making salt licks to attract deer.

In the first third of the 19th century, the valley for which Salt Point is today the freight transportation center was one of the most important wheat-growing sections of New York State. Up to about 1835 more than 1/3 of the grain shipped from New York City was grown in Dutchess County, most of it in this valley. But the competition of western wheat after the opening of the Erie Canal and soil exhaustion through lack of crop rotation and fertilization, brought wheat-raising to an end. Today the rolling, sparsely wooded land is used principally for pasturage, and the large dairy farms in the vicinity serve a wide area centering in Poughkeepsie.

At 28 m., in the center of Salt Point, is junction with dirt road, called locally the Washington Hollow road.

> Left on Washington Hollow road .7 m. is junction with dirt road (R). R. on dirt road is CAMP NOOTEEMING, (L) .8 m., the Dutchess County Boy Scout camp conducted by the Dutchess County Council. Its 176 acres embrace an artificial lake called Pocket Lake by the scouts. With its facilities for fishing, swimming, boating, and nature study, the camp provides all-round summer camping under adult supervision.

At 28.9 m. is junction with Salt Point Turnpike, a macadam road. The main route turns R. and follows this macadam road past the many country roads that serve the widespread farms.

At 37.5 m. (L) is junction with CREEK ROAD which becomes Smith St. at this point.

R. from Smith St. on Main St.; Tour ends at Court House Square, 38.2 m.

TOUR 4 A

East Park—Netherwood—Spelmann Road. 6.1 m.

From junction with Tour No. 4 in East Park, the route turns R. on macadam road. The road crosses a wide plain dotted with small dairy farms and reaching to low rolling hills in the distance. This unfrequently traveled road makes an ideal short rural tour in the summer.

The GARRIGUE SCHOOL, *1.2 m.* (L), organized in 1933, is a modern private farm school for superior children from 4 to 8 years. It is a year-round boarding school with a capacity of 30 pupils. The two-story Colonial house is painted white, with green blinds. Standing on a knoll about .2 m. from the road, it commands a beautiful view of the valley.

At *1.3 m.* (L), at the top of a low hill, is a beacon marking the eastern line of the New York-Montreal airline.

At this point the contour of the land changes abruptly and becomes rugged and hilly.

The dairy and small truck farmers have dammed the little streams to make ponds, from which ice is cut in the winter months for household use and for cooling milk in summer.

At *1.6 m.* is junction with a secondary macadam road. The route turns L. on this road.

CAMP WINETKA, *2.3 m.* (L), a large camp for Jewish people, comprises a number of separate yellow cabins on a shaded tract overlooking a small pond. The main building is a mid-19th century white house. A large barn serves as camp theatre.

At *2.8 m.* is intersection of two roads. The route proceeds straight ahead, on middle road, over the hill.

At *3.4 m.,* at the fork of two roads, is the ISRAEL MARSHALL HOUSE (L), one of the most dignified and imposing buildings in the vicinity. It is a large, two-story Colonial structure painted white. Four Doric columns support the front porch; a large half-round window near the peak of the roof is an added ornament. The figures "IM 1844" are carved in the stone steps leading to the eastern entrance. Israel Marshall erected this building as a tavern in 1844; after serving as such for 12 years, it was remodeled to its present state. It has remained in the Marshall family to the present time.

Opposite the Marshall House at *3.4 m.* the route bears R.

The NETHERWOOD BAPTIST CHURCH, *6 m.* (L), was founded in 1791 and is "the original home of the Explorers' Club," founded in January 1931, for children of this section. The present structure, a simple white frame building with a square belfry and an octagonal, shuttered window above the door, was erected in 1863 on the old site of the first church, built in 1795. The adjoining cemetery contains many crudely cut field-stones; the oldest decipherable stone bears the date 1789.

At *6.1 m.* is junction with Salt Point Turnpike. *(See Tour No. 4.)*

Abraham Fort Homestead, near Poughkeepsie

BIBLIOGRAPHY

Account Book of a Country Store Keeper in the 18th Century.
Poughkeepsie, N. Y. Vassar Brothers Institute. 1911.

Account of the Exercises of the One Hundred Seventy-Fifth Anniversary of the First Reformed Dutch Church of Fishkill, 1891, An.
Fishkill, N. Y. *Fishkill Weekly Times.* 1891.

Alexander, De Alva Stanwood.
Political History of the State of New York, A.
New York. Henry Holt and Co. 1906.

American Archives. Fourth and Fifth Series. 9 vols.
Washington, D. C. M. St. Clair Clarke and Peter Force. 1837-53.

Americana, The.
Beach, Frederick Converse, Editor-in-Chief. 20 vols.
Supervised by the *Scientific American* Editorial Dept.
Scientific American Compiling Dept. New York. 1910.

Bacon, Edgar Mayhew.
The Hudson River from Ocean to Source.
New York and London. G. P. Putnam's Sons. The Knickerbocker Press. 1903.

Bailey, Henry DuBois.
Local Tales and Historical Sketches.
Fishkill Landing, N. Y. John W. Spaight. 1874.

Barnum, H. L.
The Spy Unmasked or, Memoirs of Enoch Crosby.
New York. J. and J. Harper. 1828.

Bayne, Martha Collins.
The Dutchess County Farmer. Vassar College Norrie Fellowship Report, 1935-6.
Poughkeepsie, N. Y. The Women's City and County Club and Vassar College. 1936.

Benton, Charles E.
Troutbeck, A Dutchess County Homestead.
Dutchess County Historical Society. 1916.

Blanchard, Frank D.
History of the Reformed Dutch Church of Rhinebeck Flatts, N. Y.
Albany, N. Y. J. B. Lyon Co. 1931.

Books of the Supervisors of Dutchess County. 3 vols.
Poughkeepsie, N. Y. Vassar Brothers Institute. 1907-11.

Brinkerhoff, Richard.
The Family of Joris Dircksen Brinckerhoff, 1638.
New York. Published by the author. 1887.

Calendar of Historical Manuscripts in the Office of the Secretary of State, Albany, N. Y. 2 vols.
Albany. Weed, Parsons & Co. 1865-66.

Calendar of Historical Manuscripts Relating to the War of the Revolution. 2 vols.
Albany. Weed, Parsons & Co. 1868.

Calendar of New York Colonial Manuscripts Endorsed Land Papers, 1643-1803.
Albany. Weed, Parsons & Co. 1883.

Centennial of the Reformed Church of Beacon, N. Y., 1813-1913.
Hammond, Benjamin; Verplanck, Mrs. Samuel; and MacCullum, Rev. E. A.; compilers.
Beacon, N. Y. Charles E. Spaight. 1913.

Century of Population Growth, 1790-1900.
Washington, D. C. Government Printing Office. 1909.

Civil List and Constitutional History of the Colony and State of New York.
Werner, Edgar A., editor.
Albany, Weed, Parsons & Co. 1883.

Cobb, Sanford, H.
The Story of the Palatines.
New York. G. P. Putnam's Sons. 1897.

Colonial Laws of New York from the Year 1664 to the Revolution. 5 vols.
Albany, N. Y. James B. Lyon. 1894.

Commemorative Biographical Record of Dutchess County, New York.
Chicago. J. H. Beers & Co. 1897.

Common Trees of New York.
Washington, D. C. American Tree Association.

Cook, Stephen Guernsey.
The Dutchess County Regiment, (150th Regiment of New York State Volunteer Infantry) in the Civil War.
Danbury, Conn. The Danbury Medical Printing Co., Inc. 1907.

Corning, A. Elwood.
Washington at Temple Hill.
Newburgh, N. Y. The Lanmere Publishing Co. 1932.

Corwine, W. R.
History of the Poughkeepsie Bridge.
Poughkeepsie, N. Y. Poughkeepsie Chamber of Commerce, 1925.

Deeds, documents and maps, County Clerk's Office, Poughkeepsie, N. Y.

Directories of cities and towns in Dutchess County.
Ditmars, Raymond Lee.

Reptile Book.
New York. Doubleday, Page & Co. 1907.

Documentary History of the State of New York.
O'Callaghan, E. B. editor.
Albany. Weed, Parsons & Co. 1850-51.

Documents Relative to the Colonial History of the State of New York.
O'Callaghan, E. B. editor.
Albany. Weed, Parsons & Co. 1856-1887.

Dyer, Edward O.
Gnadensee, The Lake of Grace. A Moravian Picture in a Connecticut Frame.
Boston, Chicago. The Pilgrim Press. 1903.

Emmot, James.
Letters About Hudson River and Vicinity.
New York. Freeman Hunt & Co. 1837.

Encyclopedia Britannica. 14th edition.
Encyclopedia Britannica, Inc. 1929.

Gazetteer of the State of New York.
Albany. J. Disturnell. 1842.

Gazetteer of the State of New York. 6th edition.
French, J. H., editor.
Syracuse, N. Y. R. Pearsall Smith. 1860.

Haswell, Charles H.
Reminiscences of an Octogenarian of the City of New York, 1816-60.
New York. Harper & Bros. 1897.

Haviland, John, and Birdsall, William M.
History of the Nine Partners, Quarterly Meeting and the Creek or Clinton Corners Meeting of Friends.
Publication unknown.

Hine, C. G.
The New York and Albany Post Road.
New York. Published by the author. 1905.

Historic New York. The Half-Moon Papers. Series 2.
Goodwin, Royce, Putnam and Brownell, editors.
New York and London. G. P. Putnam's Sons. 1899.

Historical Notes of Saint James Parish, Hyde Park-on-Hudson.
Newton, E. P., compiler.
Poughkeepsie, N. Y. A. V. Haight. 1913.

Historical Sketch and Directory of the Town of Fishkill, with an Appendix of Much Useful Information.
Fishkill Landing, N. Y. Standard Office. 1866.

History of Dutchess County, N. Y., The.
Hasbrouck, Frank, editor.
Poughkeepsie, N. Y. S. A. Matthieu. 1909.

History of New York State, 1523-1927. 10 vols.
Sullivan, James, editor-in-chief.
New York. Lewis Historical Publishing Co., Inc. 1927.

History of the Bench and Bar of New York. 2 vols.
New York. New York History Company. 1897.

Hodge, Frederick Witt.
Handbook of the American Indians North of Mexico.
Smithsonian Institution. Bureau of American Ethnology.
Washington, D. C. Government Printing Office. 1910.

Hunt, Thomas.
Historical Sketch of the Town of Clermont, A.
Hudson, N. Y. The Hudson Press. 1928.

Huntting, Isaac.
History of Little Nine Partners of North East Precinct, and Pine Plains, New York. Dutchess County. Vol. I.
Amenia, N. Y. Charles Walsh & Co. 1897.

156

Jenkins, Stephen.
The Greatest Street in the World.
New York and London. G. P. Putnam's Sons. 1911.

Johnston, Henry P.
The Storming of Stony Point on the Hudson.
New York. James T. White & Co. 1900.

Jones, Thomas.
History of New York During the Revolutionary War. 2 vols.
New York. New York Historical Society. 1879.

Jordan, David Starr, and Evermann, B. W.
American Food and Game Fishes.
New York. Doubleday, Page & Co. 1902.

Journal of the Legislative Council of the Colony of New York. 2 vols.
Albany. Weed, Parsons & Co. 1861.

Kip, Francis M.
Discourse Delivered on the 12th of September, 1866, at the Celebration of the 150th Anniversary of the First Reformed Church, Fishkill, N. Y., A.
New York. Wynkoop & Hallenbeck. 1866.

Ladd, Horatio O.
Founding of the Episcopal Church in Dutchess County, New York, The.
Fishkill, N. Y. Times Print. 1895.

Lamb, Martha J.
History of the City of New York. 2 vols.
New York and Chicago. A. S. Barnes & Co. 1877.

Lathrop, Elise.
Early American Inns and Taverns.
New York. R. McBride & Co. 1926.

Legislative Manual.
Albany, N.Y. J. B. Lyon Co. 1933.

Lewis, John N.
Reminiscences of Annandale, New York. Lecture delivered before officers and students of St. Stephen's College. (Reprint from the *American Historical Register*). Pamphlet.

Lossing, Benson J.
The Hudson, from the Wilderness to the Sea.
New York. Virtue and Yorston. 1866.

Lossing, Benson J.
The Pictorial Field Book of the Revolution. 2 vols.
New York. Harper & Bros. 1851-52.

Maher, Richard Francis.
Historic Dover.
Dover Plains, N. Y. 1908.

Matthews, F. Schuyler.
Field Book of American Trees and Shrubs.
New York. G. Putnam's Sons. The Knickerbocker Press. 1915.

Mershon, Stephen L.
Power of the Crown in the Valley of the Hudson, The.
Brattleboro, Vt. Vermont Printing Co. 1925.

Monell, J. J.
Historical Sketches. Washington's Headquarters, Newburgh, New York, and Adjacent Localities.
Newburgh, N. Y. E. M. Ruttenber. 1872.

Mooney, Charles N. and Belden, H. L.
Soil Survey of Dutchess County, N. Y.
U. S. Department of Agriculture.
Washington, D. C. Government Printing Office. 1909.

Morse, Howard H.
Historic Old Rhinebeck.
Rhinebeck, N. Y. Published by the author. 1908.

Muirhead, J. H. H.
Map of Dutchess County, N. Y.
New York. Dolph & Stewart. 1935.

National Cyclopedia of American Biography.
New York. James T. White Co. 1934.

Neilson, Charles.
An Original, Compiled and Corrected Account of Burgoyne's Campaign.
Albany, N. Y. J. Munsell. 1844.

New York in the Revolution as Colony and State. 2 vols.
Roberts, James A., compiler.
Albany, Brandow Printing Co. 1898 (1st vol.).
Albany, J. B. Lyon Co. 1904 (2d vol.).

Newspaper files and original documents.
Adriance Memorial Library. Poughkeepsie, N. Y.

Old Gravestones of Dutchess County, N. Y.
Poucher, J. Wilson and Reynolds, Helen Wilkinson, compilers.
Poughkeepsie, N. Y. Enterprize Publishing Co., and Hanson & Pralow. 1924.

Partition Map of Dutchess County Showing Patent Divisions.
Poughkeepsie, N. Y. County Clerk's Office.

Pelletreau, William S.
History of Putnam County, N. Y.
Philadelphia. W. W. Preston & Co. 1886.

Platt, Edmund.
The Eagle's History of Poughkeepsie from the Earliest Settlements, 1683 to 1905.
Poughkeepsie, N. Y. Platt & Platt. 1905.

Platt, Isaac.
Collection of Historical Documents and Maps. (Originals).

Poughkeepsie, Charter and Laws of the Corporation of the Village of.
Poughkeepsie, N. Y. Platt and Ranney. 1843.

Poughkeepsie, Charter, Ordinances and By-Laws.
1874-1881, 1898, 1901, 1907.

Poughkeepsie, Charter, Ordinances of the City of.
Poughkeepsie, N. Y. Platt & Son. 1865.

Poughkeepsie Eagle (Souvenir Edition)
Poughkeepsie, N. Y. Platt & Platt. 1889.

Powell, J. W.
Indian Linguistic Families of America, North of Mexico.
Washington, D. C. Government Printing Office. 1891.

Public Papers of George Clinton, 1st Governor of New York State. 10 vols.
Albany, N. Y. State of New York. 1899 to 1914.

Quaker Hill Local History Series. 16 vols.
Pawling, N. Y. Quaker Hill Conference Association. 1902-1908.

Records of Christ Church, Poughkeepsie, N. Y.
Reynolds, Helen Wilkinson, editor.
Poughkeepsie, N. Y. Frank B. Howard. 1911.

Records of the Reformed Dutch Church of New Hackensack, Dutchess County, N. Y.
Tower, Maria Bockee Carpenter, compiler.
Poughkeepsie, N. Y. 1932.

Records of the Town of Hyde Park, Dutchess County.
Roosevelt, Franklin Delano, editor.
Vol. III.
Hyde Park. Dutchess County Historical Society. 1928.

Reed, Newton.
Early History of Amenia.
Amenia, N. Y. DeLacey & Wiley. 1875.

Reichel, W. C.
Memorial of the Dedication of Monuments Erected by the Moravian Historical Society to Mark the Sites of Ancient Missionary Stations in New York and Connecticut, A.
Philadelphia. J. B. Lippincott. 1860.

Reynolds, Helen Wilkinson.
Annals of a Century Old Business.
Poughkeepsie, N. Y. Frank B. Howard. 1920.

Reynolds, Helen Wilkinson.
Dutch Houses in the Hudson Valley Before 1776.
New York. Payson & Clarke, Ltd. 1929.

Reynolds, Helen Wilkinson.
Dutchess County Doorways and Other Examples of Period-Work in Wood, 1730 to 1830.
New York. William Farquhar Payson. 1931.

Reynolds, Helen Wilkinson.
Poughkeepsie, the Origin and Meaning of the Word. Vol. I.
Poughkeepsie, N. Y. 1924.

Reynolds, James.
Diary. (From January, 1839 to December, 1843,—in manuscript).
Mr. Reynolds was a resident of Poughkeepsie.

Rothery, John and William.
John Rothery's Files, 1895.
New York. Dennison & Brown. 1895.

Ruttenber, Edward Manning.
Footprints of the Red Men.
Auspices of the New York State Historical Association.
Newburgh, N. Y. Newburgh Journal. 1906.

Ruttenber, Edward Manning.
History of the Indian Tribes of Hudson's River.
Albany, N. Y. J. Munsell. 1872.

Scott, Henry W.
Courts of the State of New York, The.
New York. Wilson Publishing Co. 1909.

Sidney, J. C.
Map of Dutchess County, New York. (1850).
Place of publication unknown. John E. Gillet. 1850.

Smith, Edward M.
Documentary History of Rhinebeck in Dutchess County, N. Y.
Rhinebeck. 1881.

Smith, James H. (assisted by Gale, Hume H. and Roscoe, William E.)
History of Duchess County, N. Y.
Syracuse, N. Y. D. Mason & Co. 1882.

Smith, Philip H.
General History of Duchess County from 1609 to 1876.
Pawling, N. Y. Published by the author. 1877.

Spaight, F. D.
Looking Backward.
Fishkill-on-Hudson, N. Y. Fishkill Standard Print. 1896.

Stone, W. and Cram, W. E.
American Animals.
New York. Doubleday, Page & Co. 1902.

Sutcliffe, Alice Crary.
The Homestead of a Colonial Dame: A Monograph.
Poughkeepsie, N. Y. A. V. Haight Co. 1909.

Sylvester, Nathaniel Bartlett.
History of Rensselaer County, N. Y.
Philadelphia. Everts & Peck. 1880.

Thompson, Helen D.
Report of a Housing Survey in the City of Poughkeepsie, A.
Poughkeepsie, N. Y. The Enterprize Pub. Co.

Tombstone Inscriptions from the Churchyard of the First Reformed Dutch Church, Fishkill Village, Dutchess County, N. Y.
Van Voorhis, compiler.
New York. G. P. Putnam's Sons.

Van Gieson, Rev. A. P.
Anniversary Discourse and History of the First Reformed Church of Poughkeepsie, N. Y.
Poughkeepsie, N. Y. A. V. Haight. 1893.

Van Gieson, Rev. A. P.
The Ratification of the Constitution by the State of New York.
Poughkeepsie, N. Y. Vassar Brothers Institute. 1895.

Van Rensselaer, Mrs. John King.
The Goede Vrouw of Mana-ha-ta, 1609-1760.
New York. Charles Scribner's Sons. 1898.

Van Wyck, Anne.
Descendants of Cornelius Barentse Van Wyck and Anna Polhemus.
New York. Tobias A. Wright. 1912.

Verplanck, Virginia E.
The Verplanck Garden at Mount Gulian, Fishkill-on-Hudson.
Privately printed. No date.

Verplanck, William E.
The Birthplace of the Order of the Cincinnati.
The New England Magazine. August, 1896.

Verplanck, William E.
Old Dutch Houses on the Hudson.
The New England Magazine. March, 1895.

Verplanck, William E. and Collyer, Moses W.
The Sloops of the Hudson.
New York and London. G. P. Putnam's Sons. The Knickerbocker Press. 1908.

Wheeler, Francis Brown.
John Flack Winslow and the Monitor.
Publication unknown. 1893.

Wilson, Warren H.
Quaker Hill, A Sociological Study.
New York. 1907.

Wilstach, Paul.
Hudson River Landings.
Indianapolis. The Bobbs-Merrill Co. 1933.

Wing, Conway P.
Historical and Genealogical Register of John Wing of Sandwich, Mass. and His Descendants, 1632.
New York. De Vinne Press. 1888.

Yearbooks of the Dutchess County Historical Society.
Rhinebeck, N. Y. *Rhinebeck Gazette.* 1914-1937. (none published in 1920).

Yearbooks of the New York Genealogical and Biographical Record. Vols. 1 to 68.
New York. 1870-1937.

Yearbooks of the New York Historical Society.
1868-1936.

Yearbooks of the New York State Historical Association. Vols. 1 to 34.
1901-1936.

INDEX

A

Adams, John, 32
Adriance Memorial Library, 38
Agriculture, 17
Akin Free Library, 123
Akin Hall Association, 123
Albany Post Road, 15, 74, 140
Amenia High School, 98; Lake 98; Village, 97, 121; Iron Co. Mines, 97
American Bridge Company, of Chicago 41; of New York 44
Annan House, 72
Annandale, 106
"Anti-Rent War", 12, 117
Apokeepsing, 30
Architecture, 21
Arlington, 34, 103
Armstrong, Gen. John, 105
Arnold Cotton Mill, 39; Homestead 43; Lumber Co., 43
Arthur, Chester A., 134
Arthursburg, 134
Astor Flats, 94; John Jacob, 65, 131; Vincent, 92, 94; Vincent, Convalescent School for Girls, 92
Avery Hall, 59

B

Bailey, Col. John, 31
Bacon, Georgeanna Woolsey, 71
Bald Hill, 73
Bangall, 111
Bannerman's Island, 138
Bard College, 19, 107
Bard, Dr. Samuel, 90
Bard, John, 107
Baxtertown, 127
Beacon, 62
Beardsley, Rev. John, 84
Beecher, Henry Ward (Home of), 72
Beekman Arms Hotel, 93
Beekman, Henry, 92, 93; William, 92.
Bennett School, 19, 99.
Billings, 134
Birch, Harvey, (See Enoch Crosby), 140
Birdsall, Nathan, 122
Bisselle, Alfred, 51
Blacksmith shops, 95
Blodgett, John Woods, 83; Mansion, 140
Blodgett Hall of Evthenics, 58
Bodenstein, J. H., 103
Bogardus, Jacob, 109; Peter, 77
Bogardus-DeWindt-VanHouten House, 77
Borden Milk Co., 121
Bowery House, 93
Browne, Memorial Hospital, 53, 147, Obadiah (house of), 84
Breakneck Mountain, 139
Brett, Madam (Catharyna), 63, 65, 70, 83, 84, 132; Robert, 75, 82, 84; Roger, 71, 75; Mill, 71; Francis, 75
Brett-Teller House (See Teller Homestead)
Briarcliff Farms, 111
Brick Meeting House, 99, 100
Brinckerhoff, Abram, 93, 132; Derick, 132, 136, (House of, at Brinckerhoffville, Col. John (House of), 133, Jovis, 113
Brinckerhoffville, 132
Broad Acres, 116
Burr, Aaron, 82, 93
"Butter Hill" (Storm King), 139
Byrnesville, cemetery, 70

C

Caldwell, Dr. Samuel, 54
Callendar House, 108, 109
Camp Lamola, 133
Camp Ramapo, 94
Camp Stover (See University Settlement)
Cory, Rev. Dr. Robert Fulton, 75
Casino, 78
Casperkill, 31
Caul Rock (See Kaal Rock)
Central Hudson Steamboat Co., 43
Chapel Corners, 147
Chapel of the Holy Innocents, 107
Chase, Rev. Philander, 84
Chateau de Tivoli, 108, 109
Chelsea, 137; Paper Mill, 137
Chestnut Ridge, 121
Christ Church, Poughkeepsie, 38, 84
Christian Church, 96
Church of the Messiah, 94
Cincinnati, Society of the, 129
Circle, The, 57
City Hall, Poughkeepsie, 36
City Home and Infirmary, 50
Civil War, 33, 34
Clarke, Hon. George, 67
Clay, Henry, 82
Clear Everitt House, 48
Clinton, DeWitt (Homestead site of), 49, 93
Clinton, Gov. George (General), 49, 138
Clinton Corners, 151
Clinton Hollow, 151
Clove Valley, 145; Iron Co., 147; Methodist Church, 145; Rod and Gun Club, 146; Spring, 146; Furnace, 147
Clover Brook Farm, 122
Cole, Timothy, 51
College Hill Park, 46
Collyer, Captain Moses W., 137
Committees of Safety, 130
Congdon's, (Mrs.) Seminary, 33
Connors Tavern, site of, 143
Continental, Army, 12
Coons, Ethan, greenhouses, 94
Cooper, James Fenimore, 140
County Government, 11
Creek Meeting House, 151
Creek Road, 152
Crooke, Charles. 88
Crosby, Enoch, 140
Cruger's Island, 107
Crum Elbow, 88
Crum Elbow Quaker Meeting House, 148
Crumwold, 89
Crystal Spring Manor, 114, 146
Cushing House, 58

D

Daheim, 98
Davies, Prof. Charles, 128
De Chastellux, 15, 79
DeKoven, Reginald, 109
Delabegarre, Pierre, 108
De La Vergne Hill, 98
DeLaval Separator Co., 45
Dennings Point, 62, 72, 77; Brick Works, 77
De Peyster, Abraham, 70
De Peyster-Newlin-Byrnes House, 70
De Windt, Peter John, 77
De Witt, grist mill, 149; Simeon, 78
Dickens, Charles, 69
Dietrich, C. F., estate of, 98

162

Dinsmore, William B., estate of, 104
Divisional Produce Market, 50
Donaldson, Robert, 106
Dover Furnace, 120; Plains, 120
Du Bois Lewis (House of), 112
Duer, W. A., 91
Dutch Reformed Churches (see Reformed Churches)
Dutchess In the Revolution, 12
Dutchess County Fair, (old), 101
Dutchess Avenue Dock, 40
Dutchess Bleachery, 127
Dutchess County, boundaries original, 9; boundaries present, 1; deriviation of name of, 9; geology of, 3
Dutchess County Academy, 39, 50, 114; Court House, 36
Dutchess Golf and Country Club, 125
Dutchess Turnpike, 97
Dutton Lumber Co., 40

E

Early Exploration and Indians, 5
East Main Street Bridge, Deacon, 74
East Park, 148.
Eastern State Parkway, 115, 134
Eastman, Business College, 33; Harvey G. 33; Park, 38
Education, 18
Edward VIII, 89
Ellerslie, 91
Emigh, Nicholas, 64; (House of), 145
Emmadine Farms, 115
Eno Law Office, 96
"Equivalent Tract," 9
Ericsson, John, 120
Eustatia, 76

F

Fairy Island, 71
Fauconier Patent, 9
Fenner, Thomas (House of), 48
Fenton, Clarence, 51
Ferris, Benjamin, 122
First Public Library in Dutchess County, 96
Fish, 5, 102
Fishkill, Creek, 131, 139; Dairy Farms, 143; grill, 83; Hook, 143; Landing, 64, 66; Plains, 115; Village, 64, 79, 139
Flanagan, Hallie, 59
Flora and Fauna, 3
Forge, Bailey's, 131
Fort, Abraham Homestead, 126
Fort Hill Farm, 142, 143
Four Corners Monument, Millbrook, 100
Fowler, Alice M., 50
Fox Hollow School, 19
Fox's Point, 13; Shipyard, 45
Frear, John (House of), 125
Freedom Plains, 135
Friends (see Quakers), 148
Frigates, 13
Fulton, Robert, 75

G

Gallaudet Home for Deaf Mutes, 135
Garrigue School, 152
Gayhead, 115
Geography and Geology, 1
"Ghost Train," 34
Gillet, Louis A., house of, 69
Given House, James, 82
Glad Tidings Home, 130
Glebe House, 48, 49
Glenham, 130
Governor Clinton House (see Clair Everitt House)
Graham, Rev. Chauncey, 132
Grand View, 137
Grasmere, 91, 106

Gray's Riding Academy, 112
Great Nine Partners Patent, 9
Green Haven, 117
Greenvale Park, 112
Gregory House, 45
Griffin's Tavern, 133
Groveville Flats Park, 74

H

Half-Moon, 6
Hamilton, Alexander, 14, 90, 93, 140
Hamilton, Lieut. Philip, 70
Hammersley, L. G., 107
Hammond, Benjamin, 67
Harlem Valley State Hospital, 118
Hell Hollow (Boulder Glen), 73
Hicks, Elias, 148; Hicksite-Orthodox Controversy, (See Quakers)
Hiddenbrooke, 74
Highlands (See Hudson Highlands)
Hiker's Trail, 73
History, 30
Hoffman House, 42
Hone, Philip, 65, 131
Honess Mountain, 142
Hopeland, 105
Hopewell Junction, 115, 134
Hospitals, Hudson River State, 116; Harlem Valley State, 118
Howland, General (House of), 71; Library, 77
Hudson, Henry, 6, 124, 130
Hudson Highlands, 2, 80
Hudson Valley Nurseries, 116
Hughsonville, 127
Huguenots, French, 31
Hyde, Edward, 89

I

Indian Lake, 97; Picture Rock, 92
Indians, Pequot, 121; Mohicans, 121, 126, 128
Inns (see taverns)
Intercollegiate Regatta, 28
Irving, Washington, 82

J

Jackson Wing Inn, 119
James Roosevelt Memorial Library, 90
Jane Residence, 114
Jay, John, 14, 140, 143; (House of), 142
Jewett, Milo P., 54; (House), 57
Johnsville, (see Wiccoppee); Methodist Episcopal Church, 142
"Josh Billings," 33
Juet, Robert, 6, 88, 124

K

Kaal Rock, 44
Kane, John Kane House, 117
Kent, Chancellor James, 32
Kimlin Cider Mill, 52
King's Highway, 10, 87, (See also Albany Post Road)
Kip, (Rombout patentee), 8; Hendrick and Jacobus, 8; Hendrick (House of), 131
Knevels-Stearns House, 77
Kosciuszko, 32
Krum Elbow (See Crum Elbow)

L

LaFayette, Marquis de, 104, 133, 135, 140
Lafayetteville, 96; House, 96
Lakes, Sepasco, 94; Indian, 97; Aerica, 98; Spring, 110; Hunns, 111; Whaley, 117

163

Landing Place of Henry Hudson, 130
Land Tenure, 11
Lane Brothers Hardware Co., 52
Lange Rak, (See Long Beach)
Lansing, John, 14
Lasinck, Peter, 31
Le Roys Corners (Pleasant Plains), 149
Le Fevre House, 137
Lewis, Morgan, 90
Lewis Gordon Norrie Park, 103
Lime Ridge Farm, 117
Lincoln, Abraham, 33; Center, 46; Dude . Ranch, 116
Little Nine Partners Patent, 9
Little Plum Point, 137
Livingston, Edward, 106; Gilbert, 15, 94; Col. Henry, 14; Henry, Jr., 124; Henry Gilbert, 109; Janet, 106, (see Mrs. Richard Montgomery); Robert (First Lord of the Manor), 64; Robert R. (Chancellor), 14, 109
Locust Grove, 124
Locusts, the, 104
Lomas, Alfred, 66
Long Pond, 150
Long Reach, 88, 124
Long Wharf, Beacon, 68
Lookout Point, 141
Lossing, Benson J., 82, 121
Loudon, Samuel, 84, 141
Lower Landing, Beacon, 67; Poughkeepsie, 45
Lown Memorial Rock Garden, 47
Lydia Booth's Seminary, 33

M

Mabbettsville, 98
MacCracken, Dr. Henry Noble, 54
Mack, John E., 145
Mackin, James, 76
Magnolia Farms, 128
Main Street Landing, Poughkeepsie, 43
Mechanic, 100
Manumit School, 19, 118
Margaret Lewis Norrie State Park, 91
Marks Memorial Camp of the Tribune Fresh Air Fund, 95
Marshall House, Israel, 153
Martin Homestead, 109
Matteawan, 63; Company, 65; State Hospital, 76, 129
Mechanic, 106
Melringah Ravine, 138
Mesier, Matthew (Homestead), 127
Mid-Hudson Bridge, 43
Middle Church, 132
Millbrook, 99; School, 19, 98; Theatre, 98
Millerton, 96
Mills, Ogden Livingston (Estate of), 104
Mitchell, Maria, 58
Mizzentop Mountain, 123
Modjeski, Ralph, 44
Moline Plow Company, 45
Monell, Judge John, 76
Monitor, The, 41, 118
Montgomery, estate, 106; Gen. Richard, 91, 106; Mrs. Richard Montgomery (Janet Livingston), 150
Moores Mills, 144
Moran, Daniel E., 44
Moravians, 8, 110, 111
Morgenthau, Henry, Jr. (Estate of), 144
Morse, Samuel F. B., 124
Morton, Helen, 91; Levi P., 91, 94; Mary, 92; Mount Beacon, 73, 78, 128; Inclined Railway, 72
Mount Gulian, 129
Mountain Chapel, 73

N

Nazarene, Camp Meeting Association, Church, Society, 74
Negroes, 75, 128
Nelson House, 37
Netherwood Baptist Church, 153
New Hackensack, 114; Airport 113
New Hamburg, 136;
New York-Connecticut Boundary Dispute, 98
New York Provincial Convention, 80
Newcomb, John (House of), 101; Zacheus (House of), 101
Nine Partners School, 100
Nine Partners Meeting House, 123
Ninham, Daniel and David, 140
Nitgedaiget, Camp, 138
Nitschman, Bishop David, 110
Northern Dutchess Health Center, 94
Norway Ski Jump, 131

O

Oakley, George P., 42, Mill, 42, House 43
Oakwood School, 19, 126
Oblong, the, 9
Oblong Meeting, 122
Oblong Meeting House, 123
Observatory, Vassar, 58
Old Beekman Road, 115
Old Drovers Inn, 119
Old Hopewell, 115
Old Hundred, 114
Old Ladies' Home, 50
Old Men's Home, 37
Old Star Mill, 132
Old Stone Church, 94
Old Stone House, 103
Orthodox (See Quakers)
Oswego, 144
Oswego Meeting House, 144

P

Palatines, 92
Parthenon, 91
Patents,
Paulding, James Kirke, 90, 91
Pawling, 117; Mountain, 117; Patent, 9; School for Boys, 19, 118
Pecksville, 116
Pheasant Breeders and Hunting Association, 100
Pine Plains, 96
Placentia, 91
Piatt, John I., 41; Zephaniah, 15; Zephaniah (House of), 102.
Pleasant Plains, 149; Westminster Presbyterian Church, 149
Pleasant Valley, 101
Political Organizations, 18
Polopels Island, 138,
Pooghkeepsingh, 30
Population, 18
Post Road, Old, (See Albany Post Road)
Poughkeepsie, 24
Poughquag, 117,
Prendergast, William, 117
Presbyterian Church, at Freedom Plains, 135
Preston, John, 119
Presqu'Ile, 77
Pringle Memorial Home, 51
Provincial Convention, 12, 80
Pulaski, Count, 131
Pultz Tavern, 93
Purgatory Hill, 118, 122
Putnam, General Israel, 110
Pynes, The, 109

Q

Quaker Hill, 122; Road, 118
Quaker Meeting House in Poughkeepsie, 51

164

Quaker Meeting House, 151
Quakers, 20; 126
Queen Anne, 71
Quinn House, 105

R

Railroad Bridge, Poughkeepsie, 41
Railroads, 16, 81, 115, 134
Ratification of Federal Constitution, 14
Rauch, Henry 110
Raymond, John H., 54
Reade, John, 109
Red Hook, 95; Cold Storage Company, 95; Country Club, 95
Red Oak Mills, 113
Redder Homestead, 110
Redoubts, the, 141
Reese, W. W. (House of), 127
Reformed Churches, Beacon 20, 68,; Fishkill, 82; Hyde Park, 90; New Hackensack, 113; Old Hopewell, 115; Poughkeepsie, 51; Rhinebeck, 92
Regatta, Intercollegiate, 28
Reginald Goode Theatre, 151
Religion, 20
Reynolds, Helen Wilkinson, 30
Revolution, 31, 93
Rhinebeck, 92; Cemetery, 92; Patent, 9
Rochdale, 102
Rock City, 94, 95
Rogers, Col. Archibald, 89; Herman, 89
Rokeby, 105
Rombout, Catharyna, (See Madam Brett); Patent, 6, 112
Roosevelt, Franklin Delano, 68; (See Crum Elbow); Mrs. Franklin Delano, 147; Mrs. James R. (Estate of), 88; Mrs. Sara Delano, 90; Theodore, 89, 93, 144, 145
Rothery, John, 66
Rudd Pond, 97
Rust Plaets, 30
Rysdyck, Rev. Isaac, 83, 113, 132

S

St. James' Church, 90, 94, 107
St. Joseph's Novitiate, 91, 105
St. Luke's Episcopal Church, Beacon, 72
St. Margaret's Church, Staatsburg, 104
St. Paul's Episcopal Church and Churchyard, Tivoli, 108
St. Peter's Church, Poughkeepsie, 40; School, 40
Salmagundi Papers, 91.
Salt Point, 151; Turnpike, 151
Sandanona, 100
Schenck, Major Henry, 75; Peter A., 65; Peter H., 131
Schultzville, 150
Schuyler, Patent, 106, 109
Seabury, Justice Samuel, 84
Seabury, Rev. Samuel, 83
Sekuna Hills, 144.
Sharparoon Pond, 120
Shaw, Henry Wheller, 33
Sheffield Pawling Farms, 118
Shekomeko, 8, 110
"Shillelagh", 82
Shipyards, site, 127
Silver Swan Inn, 125
Slate, 150
Sleight, Jacobus (House of), 103
Smith, Andrew, 50; Melancthon, 14; William W., 50
Smith Brothers, Inc., 50; Restaurant, 37.
Smithfield, Presbyterian Church 111; Burying Ground 111
Social Life, 21
Society of Friends (See Quakers)
Solarium, Guilford Dudley Memorial, 47
Soldiers' Burial Ground near Fishkill, 140

Soldiers' Monument, Poughkeepsie, 38
South Beacon Peak, 78
South Dover, 119
South Millbrook, 100
Southard, Zebulon, (House of), 131
Southern Dutchess Country Club, 76
Southwick House, 45
"Speck", 125
Spook Field, 130
Spottiswood, Countess Sally Britton, 76
Spy, The, 140
Spy Hill, Beacon, 68
Staats, Dr. Samuel, 103
Staatsburg, 103; Ice Tool Works, 103
Stanfordville, 111
Sterling Mines, 146
Stevens, John Cox, 106
Stewart, A. T., 66, 131
Stissing Lake, 96
Stockholm Aaron, 133
"Stone Church, The", 121
Stoneco, 135
Stonehouse, 117, 138
Stony Kill, 117, 138, 128, 129; Dairy Farmhouse 128
Storm-Adriance-Brinckerhoff House, 115
Storm King, 68, 139
Stormville, 116; Speedway, 116
Stoutenburgh, Judge Jacobus, 89, 148; William, (House of), 89, 148
Stover Camp, (See University Settlement)
Suckley Chapel, site of, 105
Surveyor's Office, Beacon, 78
Swartwout, Jacobus, 133
Swartwoutville, 134
Swartwout, Capt. Abraham, 34; Johannes, 34
Sweet-Orr Company, 127
Sylvan Lake, 134

T.

Taconic State Park, 97
Taylor, James M., 54
Telephone Building, Staatsburg, 104
Teller, Homestead, 74; Jacob, 114; John, (House of), 150
Ter Boss, Johannes, 72
Thomas House, the 110
Thomas, Lowell, 122
Thompson, Geraldine Morgan, 103; Memorial Library, 56; Thomas, 94
Thorn, Stephen, (House of), 113
Thorndale, 100
Thorne, Edwin and Samuel, 100; Oakleigh, 100-111
Tidd, Polly, 116
Timby, Theodore R., 120
Tivoli-Madalin, 108
Tories, 80
Traphagen, William, 92, 93
Treasure Chest Tavern, 126
Trinity Church, Fishkill, 83
Troutbeck, 98

U

Union Bridge Company, 42; Hotel, Fishkill, 82
University Settlement Summer Camp, 72
Upper Landing, Beacon, 67; Poughkeepsie, 42, 44
Upton Lake, 111
Ursuline Novitiate, 74

V

Val Kil (See Fallkill)
Val Kil Furniture and Craft Center, and Handicraft Center, 147
Van Benthuysen, Barent, 106
Van Buren, Martin, 82
Van Courtland, Stephen, 113; xviii-3
Van Der Burgh, Dirck, 103

165

Van Kleeck, Hugh, 48
Van Vliet, Van Wormer, House of, 138
Van Wyck, Cornelius; Cornelius C., (House of), 140; Cornelius R., (House of), 134; Hall, Fishkill; Col. Richard, 114; Theodorus, 102, 142
Vas, Rev. Petrus, 82
Vassar, College, 33; John Guy, 52; Matthew, 54; Matthew, Jr., 52
Vassar Brothers, Home for Aged Men, 37; Hospital, 52; Institute, 36; Laboratory, 60
Vassar College, 33, 54, 62, 112
Vassar College Buildings, See Tour of Campus, 56-62
Vaughn, General (Sir John), 89
Verbank, 144
Verplanck, Gulian (the patentee), 6, 75, 128, 129; Gulian (the younger), 84; William E., 137; Philipp, Jr., 114
Veterans' Hospital, 128
Vis Kil (See Kishkill)
Von Steuben, Baron, 131, 140

W

Wappinger, Creek, 2; Indians, 6
Wappingers Falls, Landing, 126; Tea Party, 127
Ward Joshua; Manor, 107; Robert Boyd, 107
Warfield, Mrs. Wallis, 89
Warren, Gen. Joseph, 150; Lodge, 150
Warner Jonathan A., 50
Washington George, 122, 131, 133, 140, 93; Hollow, 101, 113
Wassaic 121; State School, 121

Watchhorn, Robert (Homestead), 144
Webster, Jean, 146
Whaley Lake, 117
Wharton House, 140
White, Dr. Bartow (House of) 81, 131; Stanford, 94
White House Sanatorium, 69
White Plains, battle of, 13
Whitaberger Land, 149
Whitefield, George, 111
Wiccopee, 142; Pass, 80, 141
Wildercliff, 92
Willetts, Deborah and Jacob, 100
Willowlake, 141
Wilson, Benjamin Lee, 69
Wind Gate, 139
Winetka, Camp, 152
Wing, Alfred (Homestead), 119; Jackson (Inn), 119; John D. (Estate of), 100
Winslow, John Flack, 41, 120
Wodenethe, 70
Women's Christian Temperance Union, Poughkeepsie, 39
Woodcliff Recreation Park, 87
Worden, Admiral John Lorimer, 118
Woronock Inn, 114
Wurtemburg Lutheran Church, 149

Y

Yates, Robert, 14
Ye Olde Fishkill Inne, 82

Z

Zinzendorff, Count, 110

Doorway of the Brett-Teller House, Beacon

I. Belding
Mine Hole
V. Kleek
Van Bommel
Seabury
Everit
S. Freer
Boerum
Mills
H. A. Livingston
Fall Kill
Dutch Church
MAIN STREET
CANNON ST
CHURCH ST
Nelson
POST ROAD
Nelson
Reade
Slang Klip
Caül Rock
Pondakrien
ivingston's Store
Union Store
HUD

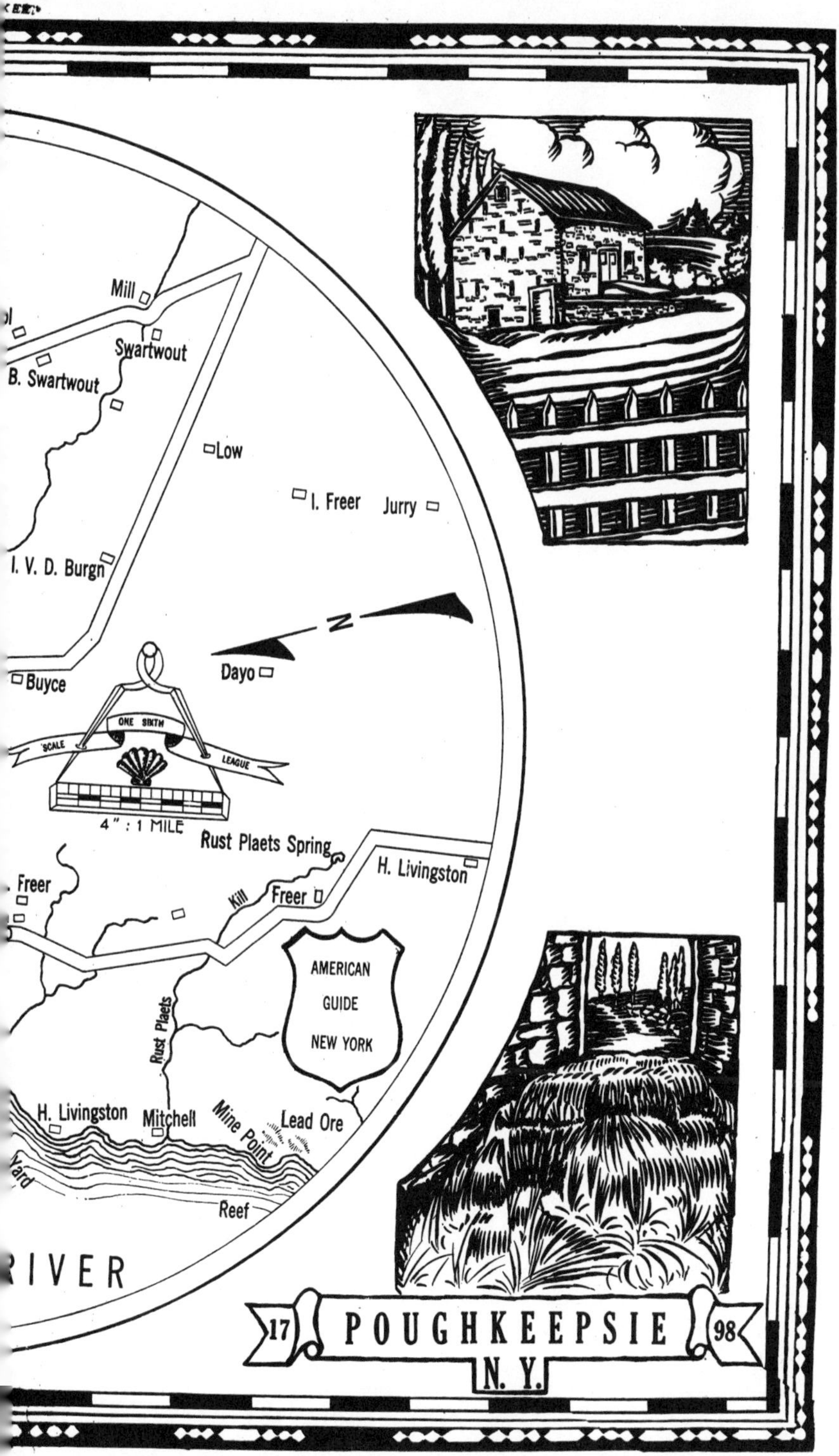
Mill
Swartwout
B. Swartwout
Low
I. Freer
Jurry
I. V. D. Burgn
N
Dayo
Buyce
ONE SIXTH
SCALE
LEAGUE
4" : 1 MILE
Rust Plaets Spring
H. Livingston
Freer
Kill
Freer
AMERICAN
GUIDE
NEW YORK
Rust Plaets
H. Livingston
Mitchell
Mine Point
Lead Ore
Reef
RIVER
17
POUGHKEEPSIE
98
N. Y.